PERU

CONTENTS

DISCOVER PERU 6

Welcome to Peru..................8	Peru Itineraries..................22
Reasons to Love Peru..........10	Peru Your Way..................36
Explore Peru......................14	A Year in Peru..................66
Getting to Know Peru..........16	A Brief History..................68

EXPERIENCE LIMA 76

3 Days in Lima..................80	Miraflores and San Isidro..........104
Lima Your Way..................82	Barranco..................116
Central Lima..................88	Beyond the Center..................126

EXPERIENCE PERU 134

The Southern Coast..................136	Cordillera Blanca..................206
Arequipa, Canyons, and Lake Titicaca..................150	The Northern Desert..................222
Cusco and the Sacred Valley.....170	The Northern Highlands..........236
Central Sierra..................196	The Amazon Basin..................248

NEED TO KNOW 266

Before You Go..................268	Index..................276
Getting Around..................270	Phrase Book..................284
Practical Information..................274	Acknowledgments..................287

Left: Hand-woven textiles in Pisac market
Previous page: Turquoise lake in the Andes
Front cover: Machu Picchu, the 15th-century Inca citadel

DISCOVER

Cusco with the Andes rising behind

Welcome to Peru	8
Reasons to Love Peru	10
Explore Peru	14
Getting to Know Peru	16
Peru Itineraries	22
Peru Your Way	36
A Year in Peru	66
A Brief History	68

WELCOME TO PERU

Peru overflows with riches: steaming Amazon jungle, scorched coastal desert, fascinating ancient cultures, a fabulous array of wildlife, and the legendary Inca ruins of Machu Picchu. Whatever your dream trip to Peru entails, this DK travel guide will prove the perfect companion.

1 Surfer riding a wave at Punta Hermosa, Lima.

2 Arequipa's Monasterio de Santa Catalina.

3 Dancers at a Candelaria folk parade in Lima.

4 Cobbled road at sunset in Ollantaytambo, Cusco.

Stretching from the western to the central part of South America, Peru is known worldwide for its extensive coastline and archaeological wonders. The capital city, Lima, presides over the coast with its Spanish colonial center and hip neighborhoods buzzing with pisco bars, live music, and some of the finest restaurants in the world. Heading north, a fun-loving surfing paradise beckons round Máncora, while to the south, the desert-etched Nazca Lines have puzzled and enthralled visitors for decades.

The magnificent Andes are justifiably the country's main draw, delivering history, culture, and adventure by the bucketload. Omnipresent is the enduring legacy of the Inca Empire – and even earlier cultures – from imposing ruined citadels to joyous traditional festivals. While the beauty of Cusco's elegant squares and cobbled streets is renowned, the resplendent plazas of Arequipa, Ayacucho, and Cajamarca ooze plenty of old-world charm. Lose yourself in the cloud-forested eastern flank of Peru's mountainous spine, brimming with dazzling birds, orchids, and butterflies, as it plunges into the lowland rainforest and majestic Amazon River. However you choose to experience Peru's natural beauty, its snow-crusted peaks, glacial lakes, and yawning canyons will not disappoint.

Peru's vastness can feel overwhelming, so we've broken the country down into easily navigable chapters, with detailed itineraries and comprehensive maps to help plan the perfect adventure. Whether you're staying for a week, or longer, this DK travel guide will ensure you see the very best of Peru. Enjoy the book, and enjoy Peru.

REASONS TO LOVE
PERU

From Andean peaks to Amazon rainforest, Peru promises variety. With its stunning ancient ruins, lively entertainment, and fascinating wildlife, there are so many reasons to love Peru. Here, we pick some of our favorites.

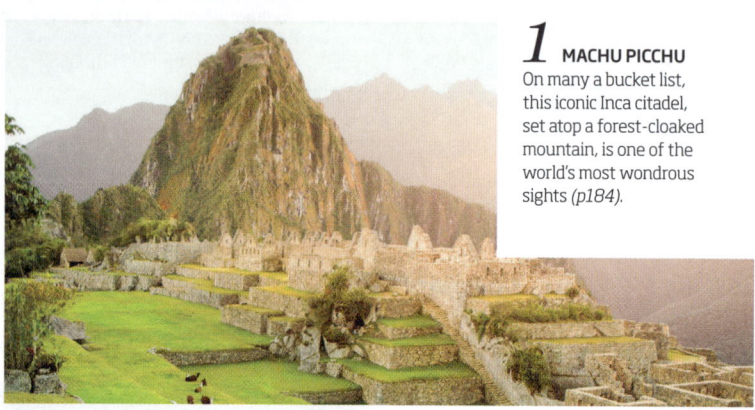

1 MACHU PICCHU
On many a bucket list, this iconic Inca citadel, set atop a forest-cloaked mountain, is one of the world's most wondrous sights *(p184)*.

AMAZON RIVER ADVENTURES 2
Whether dolphin-spotting from the deck of a luxury riverboat or fishing for piranha from a motorized dugout, adventure is guaranteed in the Amazon *(p248)*.

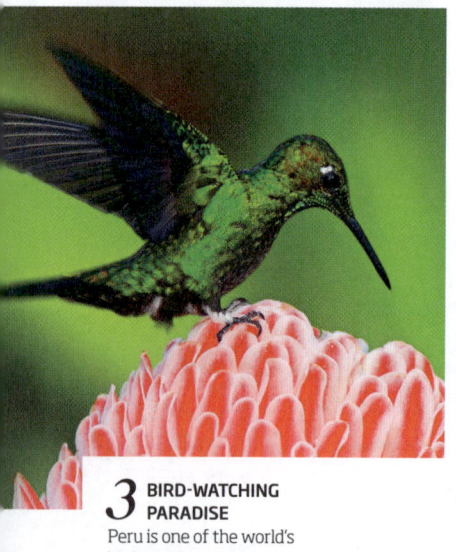

3 BIRD-WATCHING PARADISE
Peru is one of the world's bird-watching hot spots, with over 1,800 species, including the cock-of-the-rock, hummingbirds, and the Andean condor *(p56)*.

PERUVIAN FOOD 4

Lima hosts several of the world's top restaurants, but toasted sweet corn from a street grill in Ayacucho or a tangy ceviche in Máncora will excite foodies just as much.

WILD HIGHLAND FESTIVALS 5

A fusion of Catholic and ancient Andean beliefs, traditional festivals are a riot of dancers and musicians, colorful costumes, and paraded saints (p40).

PRE-COLUMBIAN CIVILIZATIONS 6

Peru harbors impressive remains of ancient cultures: from the adobe walls of the Chimú citadel of Chan Chan (p232) to Nazca's puzzling geoglyphs (p140).

HIKING IN THE ANDES 7

Many spectacular hikes across the Andes afford breathtaking views, punctuated by encounters with alpacas, traditional communities, and crumbling ruins *(p38)*.

PISCO SOUR 8

The tangy taste of fresh lime juice on ice, a spirit with a kick, and a whisked egg white on top together make up Peru's delicious national drink: pisco sour *(p50)*.

9 DIVERSE CULTURES

Indigenous people make up around 20 per cent of the Peruvian population, representing a rich diversity of languages and cultures. The vast majority are Quechua *(p74)*.

10 JUNGLE LODGES
Whether you're being lulled to sleep by chirping crickets or awakened by squawking parrots, a stay in a lodge in the heart of the rainforest is an unmissable experience.

THE WORLD'S DEEPEST CANYONS 11
Deeper than the Grand Canyon, the Cañón del Colca *(p166)* and the more remote Cotahuasi *(p168)* feature excellent hiking terrain and relaxing thermal pools.

PEÑAS 12
An essential part of Lima's nightlife and popular in other cities, these informal and intimate bars are the place to go to soak up live folk music *(p84)*.

EXPLORE
PERU

This guide divides Peru into nine color-coded sightseeing areas, as shown on this map. Find out more about each area on the following pages.

GETTING TO KNOW
PERU

Beyond the iconic citadel of Machu Picchu, Peru is a country of extreme geographical contrasts, comprising dry desert coast, sweltering jungle, and snow-frosted peaks. Its diverse wildlife and ancient pre-Hispanic ruins attest to its significance as one of the cradles of American civilization.

LIMA

Situated on the steep, cliffside edges of the barren Pacific coast, Peru's capital city is a clash of the old and new. Here, pre-Inca temples lead to trendy boulevards, while 16th- to 19th-century architecture features priceless, millennia-old artifacts. With an internationally renowned dining scene and a mix of sophisticated and traditional nightlife, Lima offers its own take on what defines a modern Latin American city.

Best for
Museums, colonial architecture, and fine dining

Home to
San Francisco, Huaca Pucllana, Museo Larco

Experience
Bar-hopping in the bohemian Barranco neighborhood

THE SOUTHERN COAST

Home to one of Peru's most famous archaeological sites, the Southern Coast is a long stretch of desert scattered with coastal towns reaching as far as the Chilean frontier. Despite its aridity, its biggest attraction is the wildlife reserve of Islas Ballestas. This is a region of surprising fertility, and, further inland, centuries-old vines cultivated on river plains play an important role in the production of the nation's favorite spirit, pisco.

Best for
Desert landscapes and vast pre-Columbian sites

Home to
Nazca Lines, Reserva Nacional de Paracas

Experience
An early morning flight over the Nazca Lines

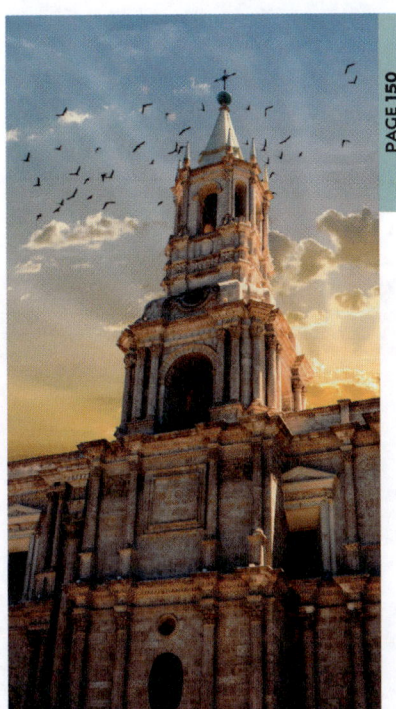

AREQUIPA, CANYONS, AND LAKE TITICACA

This Andean territory is home to a volcano-speckled cordillera that meets two of the world's deepest canyons and the dazzling glare of Lake Titicaca. With proximity to colonial and Indigenous cultures, the dramatic white city of Arequipa is a standout attraction. It also grants access to remote communities steeped in tradition and encounters with the soaring, sacred bird of the Inca, the Andean condor.

Best for
Breathtaking landscapes, hiking, and traditional Andean culture

Home to
Monasterio de Santa Catalina, Lake Titicaca, Cañón del Colca

Experience
The views of El Misti volcano from a rooftop café in Arequipa

CUSCO AND THE SACRED VALLEY

Extravagant colonial mansions and religious buildings crowd the old center of Cusco, but it's the mountainside remains of expertly built temples that loom most tangibly over the city. The extraordinary Inca ruins of Machu Picchu are inescapable and the region's ultimate drawcard, but the photogenic villages scattered across the Sacred Valley offer a compelling glimpse into the robust connection between ancient and modern Indigenous life.

Best for
Andean textiles, trekking, and discovering Inca culture

Home to
La Catedral, the Inca Trail, Machu Picchu

Experience
Strolling around an Andean market in Pisac

CENTRAL SIERRA

PAGE 196

The Andes are the backbone of the Central Sierra, a region of surprisingly lush valleys and attractive remote towns where mountain traditions hold fast. Ayacucho is the most photogenic of these, rivaling even Cusco with its 17th- and 18th-century architecture and 33 churches. It is here, and in villages near Huancayo, where the country's finest handicrafts are produced.

Best for
Stark Andean scenery, handicrafts, and traditional festivals

Home to
Ayacucho, Mantaro Valley

Experience
One of the world's highest train journeys from Huancayo to Huancavelica

CORDILLERA BLANCA

PAGE 206

Stretching north and inland of Lima, the Cordillera Blanca is Peru on a superlative scale. Its angular landscapes are crowned by frosted 20,000-ft (6,000-m) peaks, attracting mountaineers and hikers in their droves. But the most wonderful sights in this region are found at lower altitudes: the ancient archaeological sites of Chavín de Huántar, once home to a feline worshipping cult, and Caral, the oldest urban center in the Americas, rank among the most important in Peru.

Best for
Spectacular snowcapped peaks, trekking, and mountaineering

Home to
Parque Nacional Huascarán, Chavín de Huántar, Caral

Experience
A hike to a remote glacial lake in the Cordillera

THE NORTHERN DESERT

PAGE 222

This long, thin slice of desert reaches all the way to the border with Ecuador. Its powder-soft sand beaches are considered the finest in Peru and offer some of the freshest ceviche you can find anywhere. Yet the Northern Desert is more than just sand and sea; the weathered, dusty remains of ancient, pre-Inca cultures, along with fine archaeological museums, are among the continent's best attractions.

Best for
Beaches, pre-Inca archaeological sites, and museums

Home to
Trujillo, Museo Tumbas Reales de Sipán

Experience
The beach at Máncora, a lively beach resort and surfer's paradise

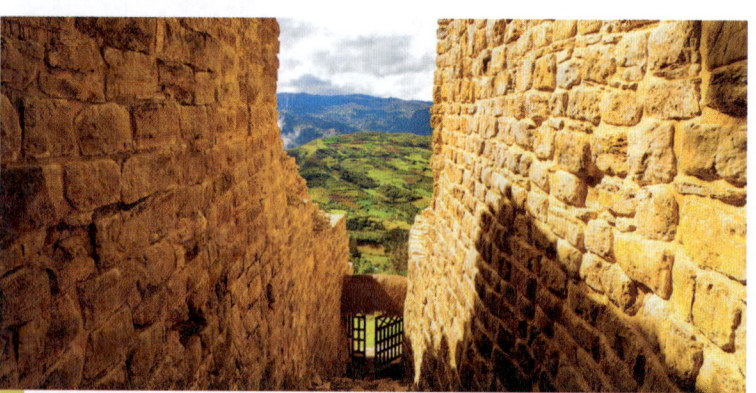

THE NORTHERN HIGHLANDS

PAGE 236

Peru's typically wild blend of deep river valleys and soaring mountain peaks characterizes the Northern Highlands. This was once the stronghold of the Chachapoya culture, who left their mark with Kuélap, a fortress that rivals Machu Picchu in magnificence. Nonetheless, the human impact on these landscapes pales in comparison with the drama of the natural world, with hiking being just one way of appreciating waterfalls that pound the earth from colossal heights and lush cloud forest that blooms with orchids.

Best for
Getting off the beaten path and the Chachapoya culture

Home to
Cajamarca, Kuélap

Experience
Sampling traditional cheese dishes in Peru's dairy heartland, Cajamarca

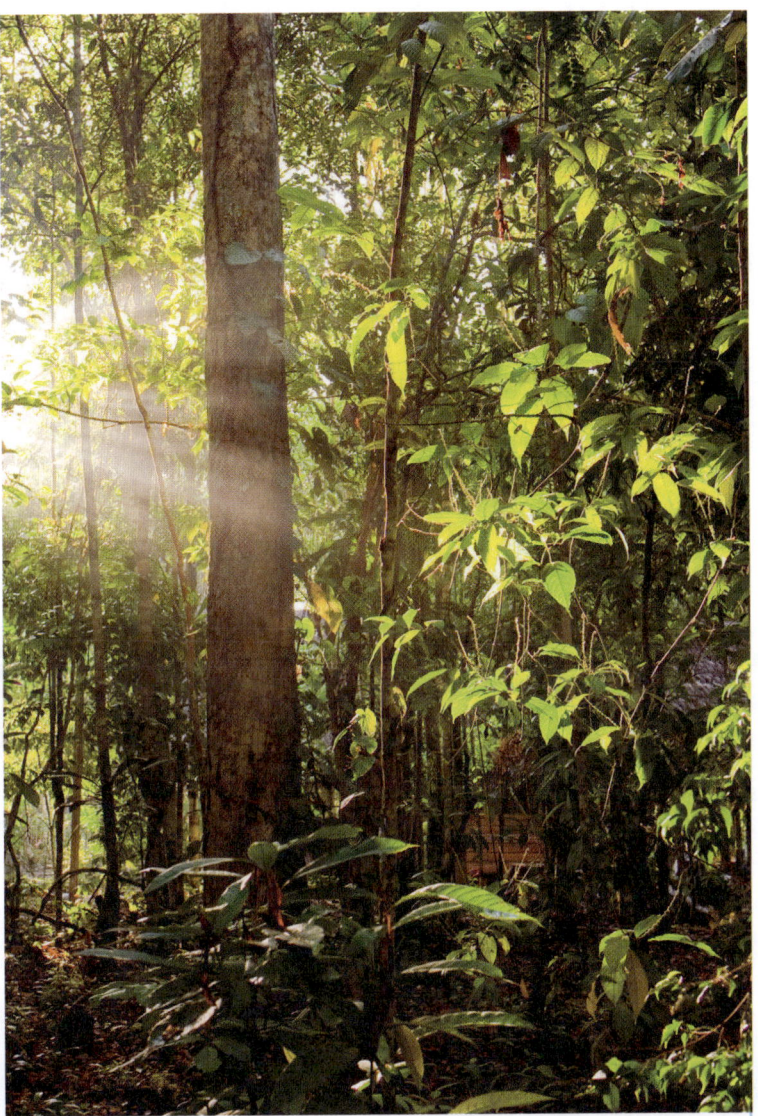

THE AMAZON BASIN

Just under two-thirds of the country is covered by the dense, damp foliage of the Amazon jungle, a place where nature is wholly in charge. As the most biodiverse corner of the planet, the rainforest provides the perfect cover for myriad species: from vibrantly colored macaws that flit through the canopy to capybaras slinking into muddy waterways. Gateway towns – Iquitos in the north and Puerto Maldonado further south – offer unforgettable jungle adventures by languid riverboat.

Best for
Jungle wildlife, Amazonian cultures, and riverboat trips

Home to
Iquitos, Reserva Nacional Pacaya-Samiria, Reserva de la Biósfera de Manu

Experience
A stay in a cozy lodge deep in the Amazon jungle

2 WEEKS

across Peru

Peru brims with travel possibilities, from four-day tours around the big cities to grand odysseys across the entire region. These itineraries will help you to chart your own course through this vibrant and varied country.

Day 1

Spend a day soaking up Lima's rich cultural history, impressive architecture, and live entertainment *(p80)*.

Day 2

Catch an early morning bus for the three-hour journey to the town of Paracas *(p144)*, a scenic coastal resort once popular among wealthy Limeños. After a late breakfast at a restaurant by the pier, visit the Islas Ballestas *(p144)*, home to a swarming mass of Humboldt penguins and sea lions. Back on dry land, fill up on a seafood lunch at Nautilus *(nautilusrestaurant.wixsite.com)*, before taking a tour to explore the Reserva Nacional de Paracas *(p142)*. For an unbeatable fresh fish dinner in the town of Paracas, scout out a simple restaurant near the jetty.

Day 3

The sunny city of Ica *(p144)*, an hour south, is surrounded by a fertile valley dotted with Peru's oldest vineyards. Begin your day getting to grips with the local spirit by hopping between artisanal pisco *bodegas* and lunching at a winery restaurant. Back in Ica, tour the Museo Regional Adolfo Bermúdez Jenkins *(p145)* with its textiles from the Paracas culture. Travel to Nazca in the evening by a bus for two hours and dine on criollo-style food at Los Angeles *(p146)* on arrival.

Day 4

Board an early flight for the clearest conditions for observing the mysterious geoglyphs that are the Nazca Lines *(p140)*. Despite numerous theories about

1. Lima's stunning cathedral.
2. Humboldt penguins on the Islas Ballestas.
3. Volcano behind Arequipa.
4. Passage in Monasterio de Santa Catalina.
5. Boats on Lake Titicaca.

why they were etched into the desert some 2,000 years ago, there's still no consensus. After your flight, catch an afternoon bus for the nine-hour journey to Arequipa (p154), a volcano-ringed city prized for its dazzling architecture. Upon arrival, wind down after the journey in the easygoing pisco bar Museo del Pisco (p169).

Day 5

Start the day by exploring Arequipa's historic and elegant UNESCO World Heritage center, constructed from the white volcanic sillar stone that's given it the nickname "the white city." To further appreciate Arequipa's singular architectural style, amble through the pretty cloisters of the Monasterio de Santa Catalina (p158). Continue on a self-guided tour of Arequipa's finest churches, including the Iglesia de la Compañía (p156) with its lavishly carved facade. As the evening approaches, sample local cuisine, such as *rocoto relleno* (spicy stuffed pepper), at one of the city's typical *picantería* restaurants.

Day 6

Leave Arequipa on a 3am bus for a three-hour journey to the Cañón del Colca (p166), the world's second deepest canyon. Have your camera at the ready at the Mirador Cruz del Cóndor (p166), where, if you're lucky, you may see Andean condors floating gracefully in the skies between 7am and 9am. Back on the eastern rim of the canyon, relax in Chivay, home to the iron-rich La Calera thermal baths (p166). After dinner at Maray (*Avenida Salaverry N-103, Chivay*), catch the overnight bus to Puno (p164).

Day 7

In the morning, head to the port and take a boat across the sparkling waters of Lake Titicaca (p162), considered by the Inca to be the birthplace of the sun. Spend an hour on the Islas Uros (p163) – islands constructed entirely from buoyant reeds. In the afternoon, arrive at Isla Amantaní (p164), an island admired for its colorful textiles. Stay overnight in a snug homestay with a Quechua-speaking family.

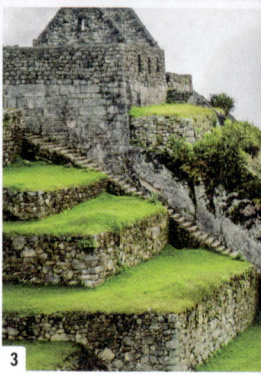

Day 8

As you land the next morning on the smaller Isla Taquile (p164), take the 500 or so steps up to the square slowly to avoid feeling the altitude. At the top, do not miss the expertly crafted garments for sale in a community-run shop. Dine on simple food at a restaurant overlooking the lake, before hiking back to the boat. Return to Puno and catch an overnight bus to Cusco (p174).

Day 9

Spend your first morning touring the Plaza de Armas (p174), home to La Catedral (p178) with its painting of the *Last Supper* featuring a roasted guinea pig as the table's centerpiece. Later, marvel at the paintings from the Cusco School (p179) in the Museo de Arte Religioso (p177) and find the famous 12-sided Inca stone that forms part of the museum's exterior wall. Take a taxi up to Sacsayhuamán (p175) and spend the afternoon exploring this Inca fortress. For dinner, dive into Andean food at Greens Organic (Santa Catalina Angosta 135).

Day 10

Begin the day with a glimpse of the Inca at Koricancha (p176), a once golden-walled temple to the Sun god. The temple was sacked by the Spanish, who took its priceless treasures and rebuilt it as the beautiful church and convent of Santo Domingo (p176). In the afternoon, admire the prettiest part of the city, the San Blas (p176) neighborhood. If visiting at the weekend, its crafts fair presents opportunities for buying traditional Andean textiles and other souvenirs. Go on the hunt for alpaca steaks for dinner in one of the tiny restaurants in the San Blas district.

Day 11

Hop on a *colectivo* (shared minibus) northwest to reach Pisac (p194) for its famed artisans' market, held daily but liveliest on Sundays. Continue along the valley to Ollantaytambo (p195), considered the last living Inca town. Here, cobbled streets lead to Araqama Ayllu (p195), a fortress used successfully by Manco Inca against the Spanish. For dinner, try inventive,

1. Stone archway on Isla Taquile.
2. Cusco's San Blas district.
3. Ruins of Machu Picchu.
4. Textiles in Pisac market.
5. Family of capybaras.

organic Andean cuisine at El Albergue (elalbergue.com/restaurant) before an early night in preparation for your train ride to Machu Picchu the next day.

Day 12

Wake at first light to make a pilgrimage to the spectacular Inca citadel of Machu Picchu (p184); be sure to reserve your train ticket and route online in advance. This UNESCO World Heritage Site is perched between two mountains, with agricultural terraces carved into the hillsides and flawless Inca stonework visible at the Templo del Sol (p188). Board the train back to Ollantaytambo and then the bus back to Cusco and wind down back at your lodgings.

Day 13

Take a 30-minute flight from Cusco to Puerto Maldonado (p258), and the Amazon rainforest. Travel up the Río Tambopata (p258) and stay at the wilderness lodge Refugio Amazonas (rainforestexpeditions.com), on the right bank of the river. As part of your tour, you'll visit a nutritious clay lick (p259) for the perfect opportunity to spot and photograph bright-colored parrots and trek to a nearby lake for sightings of rare giant otters. Take a night walk in the jungle for a chance to see a poison dart frog before falling asleep to the sounds of the forest.

Day 14

Take a four-hour boat journey from your lodge through rainforest on a sight-seeing hunt to spot colorful macaws, capybaras, howler monkeys, river otters, and even piranha. Return downriver by boat to Puerto Maldonado. To end your two weeks, catch a flight back to Lima.

To extend your trip

Spend four days and three nights hiking the Inca Trail (p180) from Cusco to Machu Picchu; note that it's essential to reserve at least six months in advance as tickets are limited. The alternative five- to seven-day Salkantay to Machu Picchu trail is an option only for acclimatized, experienced hikers due to its high-altitude passes.

→
1. Stunning facade of the Hacienda San José.
2. Reserva Nacional de Paracas.
3. Painting a clay pot.
4. Impressive Acueducto de Cantalloc.

4 DAYS
on the Southern Coast

Day 1
Morning Start your tour in Chincha Alta, the hub of Afro-Peruvian culture. Take in the Hacienda San José *(casahaciendasanjose.com)*, a former sugar plantation built in the 17th century.

Afternoon Heading south, stop at Tambo Colorado *(p145)*, one of the best-preserved adobe cities in Peru. From there, it's an hour's bus journey to reach Pisco *(p145)*. Unfortunately, many of the city's buildings were destroyed by the 2007 earthquake; visit the main square to see the remaining monuments.

Evening Take a bus to Paracas *(p144)* for a stroll along the harborside. Keep an eye out for pelicans as you indulge in a sundowner at an oceanside bar.

Day 2
Morning Board a motor boat for a spin around the Islas Ballestas *(p144)*, home to Humboldt penguins and sea lions. Back in Paracas, rent a bike to explore the Reserva Nacional de Paracas *(p142)*, a protected area where desert cliffs meet Pacific waters. Stop for lunch at the ramshackle fishing community of Lagunillas *(p142)*.

Afternoon A one-hour bus journey southeast brings you to Ica *(p144)*, a taxi ride from the oasis of Huacachina *(p145)*. Here, ramp it up a notch with an adrenaline-fueled dune buggy ride up and down the surrounding sand dunes.

Evening Back in Huacachina, grab an outside table for dinner at a restaurant overlooking the oasis.

Day 3
Morning Reserve a tour around Destilería La Caravedo *(caravedopisco.com)*, one of the top pisco *bodegas* in the countryside surrounding Ica. Take a horseback ride around its vineyards – some of the oldest in Peru – before enjoying a gourmet lunch.

Afternoon Head two hours southward to explore the desert town of Nazca *(p146)* and Museo Antonini *(p146)* with its collection of mummies uncovered from the nearby pyramids of Cahuachi *(p146)*. Next, dive into the ceramic workshops in San Carlos, where local artisans create high-quality replicas of Nazca pottery.

Evening To learn more about the town's most famous archaeological site – the Nazca Lines *(p140)* – stay overnight at the DM Hotel Nazca *(p145)*. A 45-minute lecture here introduces the theories regarding the geoglyphs' origins and uses.

Day 4
Morning Take a flight over the Nazca Lines, the giant collection of geoglyphs etched into the desert floor around 2,000 years ago. The nearby Acueducto de Cantalloc *(p146)*, a series of spiraled aqueducts built by the Nazca, are also worth a visit.

Afternoon Tour La Reserva Nacional Pampa Galeras Barbara D'Achille *(p146)*, home to several thousand wild vicuña.

Evening To finish off the day, spend a final evening in Nazca browsing the restaurants along Jirón Bolognesi for a taste of traditional food.

←

1 Arequipa's cathedral.
2 Weaving textiles at Mundo Alpaca.
3 Entrance to Chivay.
4 Souvenirs from the Islas Uros, Lake Titicaca.

5 DAYS
in Canyon Country

Day 1

Morning Start on Arequipa's Plaza de Armas *(p154)* to appreciate one of Peru's most majestic squares. Cross the square to the Iglesia de la Compañía *(p156)* and wander next door for souvenir shopping.

Afternoon Stop for a savory crepe on the patio of Crepísimo *(p155)* and then head to the Convento de la Recoleta *(p155)* to admire Arequipa's architectural style.

Evening Indulge at Zig Zag *(zigzagrestaurant.com)*, which serves alpaca steaks on sizzling slabs of volcanic rock.

Day 2

Morning Go behind the scenes of Inca sacrifice at the Museo Santuarios Andinos *(p157)*, home to Juanita, the mummified girl found frozen on a nearby volcano.

Afternoon For a look at Peru's weaving traditions, trot along to Mundo Alpaca *(p156)*, where alpacas graze on the lawns as you learn about turning wool into textiles; you can even buy some samples.

Evening Take in a contemporary art exhibition at Casona Iriberry *(p154)*, before heading to Chicha *(p155)* for the ultimate fine-dining experience.

Day 3

Morning Catch a bus for Chivay (taking three and a half hours) *(p166)* – keep an eye out for vicuñas as you travel through the high-altitude plateaus of the Reserva Nacional de Salinas y Aguada Blanca, found 73 miles (117 km) north of Arequipa.

Afternoon Stop in Chivay for a quick lunch before relaxing at one of the five pools at La Calera hot springs *(p166)*.

Evening Travel west for 15 minutes by bus to Yanque *(p166)*, a traditional farming village and a good base for a tour of the rim of the Cañón del Colca *(p166)*.

Day 4

Morning Rise early to admire the snow-white Iglesia de la Inmaculada Concepción *(Plaza de Armas, Yanque)* built from sillar stone. Next up is Mirador Cruz del Cóndor *(p166)*, a viewpoint over the canyon where Andean condors glide on thermal currents.

Afternoon Continue to the trailhead for the hike into the canyon. Along the 4,000-ft (1,300-m) descent, admire the Collagua terraces *(p166)* on the hills.

Evening At the Valle de Sangalle, an oasis deep within the valley, relax overnight in rustic accommodation.

Day 5

Morning Start the steep, four-hour hike back out of the canyon early to avoid the height of the day's heat. At Cabanaconde *(p166)*, travel back to Chivay to connect with a six-hour bus to Puno *(p164)*, passing dazzling, high-altitude scenery.

Afternoon From the jetty, join a tour of the Islas Uros *(p163)*, a group of islands constructed from buoyant totora reeds, before landing on Isla Taquile *(p164)*.

Evening Stay overnight in a homestay *(p163)* with one of the island's families.

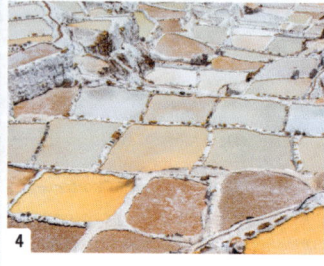

←

1 Tambomachay ruins and platforms in Cusco.

2 Selection of fruit and vegetables at Pisac market.

3 Impressive Moray terraces.

4 Salinas de Maras salt pans.

5 DAYS
in Cusco and the Sacred Valley

Day 1

Morning Start your tour of Cusco at the Museo Inka *(p174)*, a must for Inca-philes. Once you've had your fill of Inca history, wander along Calle Hatunrumiyoc *(p177)*, where the famous 12-angled stone built into a wall demonstrates the culture's skill.

Afternoon Cacao originated in the Amazon jungle, so there's no better place to try your hand at chocolate making than in a workshop at the Choco Museo *(p176)*.

Evening Stop off at the Museo de Arte Precolombino *(p174)* for Moche pottery masterpieces before settling in next door in the MAP Café *(p177)* for Peruvian fine dining.

Day 2

Morning Hail a cab from Cusco to Tambomachay, an area famed for its ruined Inca terraces. Hike down and follow the road back to Cusco, stopping on the way at Sacsayhuamán *(p175)*, a former Inca fortress.

Afternoon Back in the city, visit the Iglesia de Santo Domingo *(p176)* atop the Koricancha ruins. Cross the gardens behind to buy handwoven gifts at the Centro de Textiles Tradicionales de Cusco *(p176)*.

Evening As night falls, enjoy a pisco sour overlooking the square from the balcony of Calle del Medio *(p177)*.

Day 3

Morning Start early for a trip to the gates at Rumicolca *(p192)*, used by the Inca to control entry into Cusco. Finish your morning at San Pedro de Andahuaylillas *(p192)*, a church known as the "Sistine Chapel of the Americas" for its interior.

Afternoon Returning in the direction of Cusco, stop in Tipón *(p193)* for an Andean lunch: roasted guinea pig. Afterward, marvel at the Inca water canals of Tipón.

Evening Sink into a soundtrack of criolla music in the lively Museo del Pisco *(p169)*.

Day 4

Morning Catch an early *colectivo* to Pisac *(p194)*, followed by a taxi up to the hillside ruined fortress here. Back in the village, spend a few hours wandering around the artisans' market, one of the region's largest.

Afternoon Settle into the Spirit of the River Lodge *(spiritoftheriverlodge.com)* near Urubamba and join a horseback ride or bike ride in the valley's fertile river plains.

Evening Enjoy a mouthwatering dinner at the cozy Tres Keros *(p193)*.

Day 5

Morning Hire a taxi up to the circular Moray terraces *(p194)* and take the path to the Salinas de Maras *(p194)*, pans where local people have been extracting salt for centuries.

Afternoon A *colectivo* back into the valley brings you to Ollantaytambo *(p195)*, a village with excellent ice-cream parlors.

Evening Settle down in front of a fire back in your lodge and prepare for an early morning train to Machu Picchu *(p184)*.

←

1 Trujillo's striking cathedral.

2 A traditional reed boat on Huanchaco beach.

3 Fresh ceviche dish topped with chili.

4 Ceramic at the Museo de las Tumbas Reales de Sipán.

10 DAYS
in Northern Peru

Day 1

Morning Start by touring the colorfully painted mansions of Trujillo's colonial center. Stop at the mustard-yellow facade of the restored 17th-century cathedral (p226) on the Plaza de Armas, the largest central square in Peru.

Afternoon To better understand the region's pre-Inca history, take a bus to Chan Chan (p232), the biggest adobe city in the world and the former capital of the Chimú Empire. Elaborate friezes decorated with marine motifs that have been painstakingly restored its former grandeur.

Evening End your day at El Mochica (elmochica.com.pe) to sample the local dish *cabrito con frijoles* (goat and bean stew), and to catch a performance of Trujillo's traditional dance, the *marinera* (p52).

Day 2

Morning Take a bus south of the city and spend a few hours touring Huaca de la Luna and Huaca del Sol (p232), two adobe temples constructed by the Moche culture. Look out for the fascinating and somewhat grizzly multicolored friezes that narrate religious sacrifice rituals.

Afternoon Next, head to Huanchaco (p233), a quiet beach town with a fishing village ambience just outside of Trujillo. Choose from one of the seafront restaurants to enjoy a lazy, languid lunch of fresh fish or ceviche (p49).

Evening Catch a ride out on the waves aboard a traditional *caballito de totora* ("reed horse" sea raft) and appreciate a picturesque sunset from Huanchaco's fine golden sands.

Day 3

Morning Slip on a wetsuit and wake up with a dip in the chilly waters of the Humboldt current; or rent a surfboard to dive right into the action. Finish with a well-deserved stint soaking up the sunshine on the beach.

Afternoon Join a tour to the unparalleled Complejo Arqueológico El Brujo (p233), a Moche complex where the 1,500-year-old mummified body of a female shamanic leader was discovered in 2006 – the only ancient female ruler ever found in Peru. You can view her tattoo-covered body in the on-site museum.

Evening Continue back to Trujillo and grab a spot for dinner at El Celler de Cler (Jirón Independencia 588) on its atmospheric 18th-century balcony with views of the pretty Iglesia San Francisco nearby.

Day 4

Morning Take the three-hour bus journey north to reach Chiclayo (p233), once a small colonial town and now the second-largest city in northern Peru.

Afternoon A local *colectivo* brings you to Lambayeque and the unique pyramid structure of the Museo de las Tumbas Reales de Sipán (p230), crammed with over 1,400 precious artifacts. Many belonged to the Lord of Sipán's burial chamber (p230), a site that now ranks among Peru's most important archaeological discoveries.

Evening Reserve a table at Fiesta Chiclayo Gourmet (p235) and indulge in a night of fine traditional Peruvian dining at the original restaurant of celebrity chef Hester Solís.

→

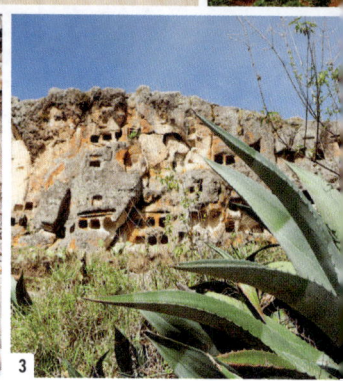

Day 5

Morning Fields clustered with sugar cane line the roads to Túcume *(p235)*, a group of 26 adobe pyramids that acted as the capital of the Lambayeque culture. As part of a circuit of the site, climb to the top of the 646-ft (197-m) El Purgatorio hill for all-encompassing views of the complex.

Afternoon Continue east to the nearby temples of Batán Grande *(p234)*, tucked within a forest of algarrobo trees and where 80 per cent of all pre-Columbian gold artifacts now on display in Peru are thought to have originated.

Evening Return to Chiclayo and spend the evening in Cuatro Once *(Calle Juan Cuglievan 411)*, a restobar serving Peruvian craft beer and typical local specialties such as ceviche.

Day 6

Morning Take a six-hour bus journey to the colonial city of Cajamarca *(p240)*.

Afternoon Few cities can compete with the historic atmosphere of Cajamarca's pretty cobblestone streets, which bore witness to the Spanish conquistadores' capture and later execution of Inca emperor Atahualpa *(p69)* in the early 16th century. To learn more about this event, El Cuarto del Rescate (the Ransom Chamber) *(p241)* is worth a visit. Later, explore the Museo Arqueológico y Etnográfico in Belén *(p241)*, with its engaging displays of ceramics, weavings, everyday utensils, and other artifacts from diverse pre-Inca cultures.

Evening Drop in on one of Cajamarca's typical *peñas*, Peña Usha Usha *(Cinco Esquinas 512)*. In such intimate and often hidden local bars, live music and friendly company are on the cards.

Day 7

Morning Catch an early bus to the striking Ventanillas de Otuzco *(p244)*, ancient cemeteries carved into a cliff of volcanic rock, located 5 miles (8 km) outside of Cajamarca.

Afternoon From the Ventanillas, a pleasant path follows the river south to join up with Los Baños del Inca *(p244)*,

1. Túcume site.
2. Cajamarca's cathedral.
3. Ventanillas de Otuzco.
4. Main square in Chachapoyas.
5. Kuélap ruins.
6. Stunning Catarata Gocta.

thermal baths once used for relaxation by Atahualpa and ideal for a few hours' soaking in a private pool.

Evening Try the regional delicacy *caldo verde* (green soup filled with chunks of soft cheese) at Salas *(Jr Amalia Puga 637)*, a classic Cajamarca restaurant.

Day 8

Morning Embark on the 12-hour journey to Chachapoyas *(p245)* via Celendín and Leymebamba *(p244)*. Skirting plunging valleys and chugging up to 13,000-ft (4,000-m) passes, the road is hair-raising.

Evening Upon arrival in Chachapoyas, stretch your legs with a walk along the pedestrianized street Jirón Amazonas, heading east of the Plaza de Armas, and dine at one of its cozy restaurants.

Day 9

Morning Rise early to catch the cable car up to the mountaintop citadel of Kuélap *(p242)*, a huge stone fortress built by the Chachapoya people some 1,500 years ago. Study the ground inside the 400 circular houses on the site and look out for the stone runs used for keeping guinea pigs.

Afternoon Back in Chachapoyas, wander over to the municipal-run Museo el Reino de las Nubes *(p245)* on the main square. This small museum houses excellent exhibitions on most of the ancient sites surrounding the city and their cultures.

Evening Wind down over a glass of *macerado* (a fermented fruit liquor) made on the premises at lively Licores la Reina *(Jr Jirón Ayacucho 544)*.

Day 10

Morning Bus out to the trailhead for the 4-mile (6-km) hike through verdant forest to the base of the Catarata Gocta *(p247)*, one of the tallest waterfalls in the world. It dramatically cascades down over 2,525 ft (770 m) in two tiers.

Afternoon Post-hike, pop into Café Fusiones *(p245)* for heavenly organic meals and coffee cultivated on nearby farms.

Evening Catch a flight back to Lima.

↑ Dramatic scenery around the impressive Machu Picchu ruins

EXPERIENCE
INCA PERU

The Inca Empire left behind a trail of magnificent cultural treasures throughout the Andes, stretching beyond the renowned Machu Picchu. A host of lesser known, little-visited remains and experiences beckon, allowing you to follow in the footsteps of, and even eat like, the Incas.

Food Markets

Bustling Andean markets are an exciting blend of smells and textures, and sell much the same vegetables as they did in Inca times. Browse sacks of local quinoa, *kiwicha* (a staple grain for the Inca), and potatoes – some of the 3,000 plus varieties of spud that originated from the area around Lake Titicaca can be sampled in the food stalls of Puno's popular markets *(p164)*.

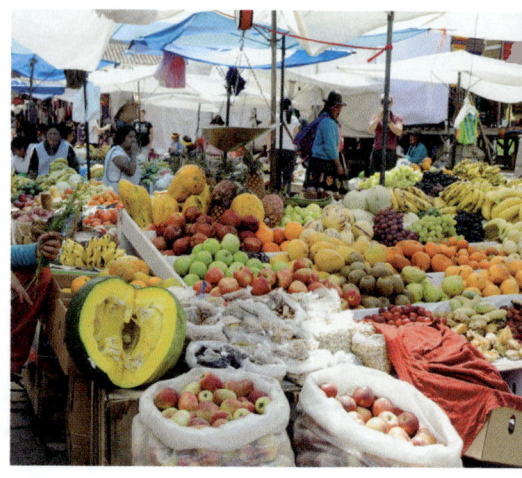

→ Mounds of multicolored fruit and vegetables at Písac market

Inca Icons

Top of any visitor's list, and often their main reason for traveling to Peru, Machu Picchu *(p184)* does not disappoint. The remarkably restored ruins of this iconic Inca citadel are undoubtedly impressive, but the stunning natural setting is what makes this site truly magical. Other highlights along the Inca Trail *(p180)* include the ruined town of Phuyupatamarca and the complex of Wiñay Wayna *(p182)*. Elsewhere, the sprawling archaeological site at Tipón (said to be the remains of a royal Inca estate) is well worth a visit, too *(p193)*.

← The well-preserved ruins at Tipón

> **THE LAST BRIDGE STANDING**
>
> Rope bridges were a common sight in Inca Peru – an estimated 200 along the Cápac Ñan; today only one remains. Located near Huinchiri (a community south of Cusco) the spectacular 500-year-old Q'eswachaka Rope Bridge is made from woven straw and spans the raging Río Apurimac. It's an imposing structure, but it's far from indestructible: every June a replacement bridge is woven and hung during a joyous community festival. Tours to this historic bridge can be organized from the city of Cusco.

Marvellous Museums

Peru's numerous ruins might provide an atmospheric encounter with history, but for a deep dive into Inca culture, head to one of the country's acclaimed museums. Cusco's Museo Inka *(p174)* is a popular choice, with its vast collection of Inca mummies, textiles, and artifacts. In Lima, the Museo Larco *(p128)* is another go-to – it's famed for its excellent display of Inca gold and silver, among other ancient treasures – while the Museo de Arte de Lima has a smaller collection of artifacts, including some Inca cups.

→ An ancient carved figure on display at Lima's famed Museo Larco

Gaze at Glaciers on the Salkantay Trek

The favorite alternative to the Inca Trail centers on snowcapped Mount Salkantay – the jewel in the crown of the Cordillera Vilcabamba in Cusco. Whether taking the high road that skirts the sacred mountain's glittering glacier, or opting for the classic trek, the mountain vistas are breathtaking. Soften the five-day challenge by swapping your tent and sleeping bag for the comfort of a rustic lodge, complete with gourmet food and muscle-soothing hot tubs.

→ Rock-strewn path leading to the snow-topped Mount Salkantay

SPECTACULAR
INCA TREKS

There's no need to feel disappointment if the oversubscribed Inca Trail is fully reserved. Other equally exciting treks await, with the lure of stunning scenery, memorable cultural encounters, and impressive Inca ruins – all without the crowds and easily organized in Cusco at the last minute.

Encounter Ancient Traditions

The top choice for the less experienced hiker is the three-day Lares Trek. At 20.5 miles (33 km) long, this glorious route passes through traditional Andean villages, providing a precious glimpse of everyday life in local weaving communities. It also offers fabulous hot springs and scenic highland valleys dotted with picturesque lakes and waterfalls.

← Carrying a heavy load down Calle Lares, Ollantaytambo

GREAT VIEW
Casa Andina Observatory

The Casa Andina hotel *(casa-andina.com)* in the Sacred Valley *(p171)* offers a great planetarium and observatory. At this magical spot you can marvel at the Milky Way and appreciate the importance of the night sky to Inca cosmology.

Did You Know?

The best time to hike is from May to September, when the days are usually dry and sunny.

Keep Your Adrenaline Levels High

The three-day Jungle Trek, a blend of thrilling activities and hiking, calls out to all adventure-lovers. A daring descent by mountain bike precedes a trek along a flourishing subtropical valley, with rafting and ziplining as optional extras. Before setting off on the final day's hike along the railroad tracks to Machu Picchu Pueblo (Aguas Calientes) *(p183)*, a dip in the thermal baths at Cocalmayo is the perfect pick-me-up. To find out more, visit cocalmayo.com.

↑ Ziplining over the canopy of the Peruvian jungle

Challenge Yourself on Choquequirao

Perched on an isolated mountaintop, Choquequirao is a cousin to the busier Machu Picchu, with ruins and views to match. Since much of the site remains buried beneath tropical forest, it retains an atmospheric air reminiscent of when Machu Picchu was rediscovered over a century ago. The ruins lie at the end of a tough seven-day hike, so you'll likely have the place to yourself.

←

Choquequirao, nestled within mountains covered with stunning Amazonian flora

PERU FOR FANTASTIC FESTIVALS

Peru's 3,000 annual festivals are a dazzling fusion of the heritage of Indigenous cultures and colonial Spanish Catholicism. From the spiritual to the musical, traditional festivals are laden with symbolism, and energetic visitors can dance for days regardless of the time of year.

Carnaval in Cajamarca

Though the riotous pre-Lenten festivities are celebrated countrywide, the highland city of Cajamarca (p240) throws one of the best parties. Expect water-balloon fights, allegorical floats, and the ceremony of the "yunza" – a large decorated tree covered in gifts, symbolizing abundance – which is cut down in a ritual dance to mark the end of the fun. The Queen Carnival and the satirical Rey Momo (or Ño Carnavalón) preside over events, with an effigy of the king burned on Ash Wednesday.

→

One of the colorful masked parades in Cajamarca's Plaza de Armas

Fiesta de la Virgen de la Candelaria

Head and shoulders above all Peruvian folkloric festivities is this annual 16-day cultural extravaganza. Taking place in February, it fuses veneration of the Virgin with ancient Andean rituals related to harvesting and fertility. Though celebrated in other parts of Peru, nowhere are the costumes as dazzling as in Puno *(p164)*, where some 40,000 dancers gather. Once an effigy of the Virgin has been paraded around town, the dance troupes compete for prizes before spilling into the streets in a riot of technicolor and sound. The La Diablada, which symbolizes the victory of good over evil, is the festival's most famous dance, featuring armies of devils in elaborate costumes pursued by angels.

↑ Dancers performing choreographed routines in their glittering finery

TOP 4 FUN FESTIVALS

Inti Raymi
Held on June 24 in Sacsayhuamán, Cusco, to celebrate the winter solstice, it features a dramatic reenactment of the Inca festival in honor of the Sun god.

Virgen del Carmen
Three days in July with outlandish masked costume parades in Paucartambo in honor of the town's patron saint.

Perú Mucho Gusto
A movable feast (quite literally) in September, this event showcases regional food and drink, with plenty of music and dancing, too.

Selvámonos
This fun music festival and culture week in the small Tyrolean-Peruvian town of Oxapampa is held at the end of June.

← Acting out the scene of Christ on the cross during Semana Santa

Semana Santa

Known as Holy Week, Easter is the most important event in Peru's religious calendar. Ayacucho *(p200)* stages the most elaborate devotions, with fabulous carpets of flowers depicting iconic Easter scenes and many candlelit processions. On Good Friday the Señor de Santo Sepulcro and the Virgen Dolorosa are carried on towering litters adorned with white roses and illuminated with thousands of white candles.

→ Carrying effigies of Mary Magdalene to Lima's Catedral

DISCOVER Peru Your Way

Sandy Stretches

Peru may not be famed for its beaches, but there are plenty along its northern coastline. Máncora and Chicama are a paradise for surfers, while Punta Sal is favored by sunseekers. Along the southern coast, desert landscapes can be found in the Reserva Nacional de Paracas *(p142)*, a golden expanse of sand by the sea; and in the high desert plateau between Nazca and Palpa, where the otherworldly Nazca Lines *(p140)* are best viewed by plane.

↑ Chicama beach, a well-known destination among surfers

PERU FOR NATURAL WONDERS

From snow-frosted summits to sweltering jungle, vast canyons to desert sand dunes, Peru has a plethora of diverse and awe-inspiring landscapes. Some can be marveled at from afar; others require persistence to reach: either way, the rewards are truly spectacular.

> **INSIDER TIP**
> **Sorting the Seasons in Peru**
>
> The coastal desert strip is dry year-round but hotter in summer (Dec-Mar/Apr). In the Andes and the Amazon the rainy season (Oct-Apr) is called winter, but it does rain in the Amazon to some extent all year.

Wonderful Waterfalls

Peru has many waterfalls, from the Catarata Gocta *(p247)* to the Catarata Bayoz *(p264)*, but the most spectacular is the Catarata de Yumbilla in Chachapoyas *(p245)*. Plunging 2,952 ft (900 m) over a cliff into verdant forest, these breathtaking falls in northern Peru are one of the world's highest.

→ Stunning Catarata de Yumbilla, falling over a sheer cliff

Amazon Rainforest

Few places capture the imagination quite like the Amazon. Covering well over half the country, and teeming with wildlife, Peru's vast jungle is a patchwork quilt of towering trees, swamps, mangroves, and floodplains, united by its life-force, the Amazon River. Within its sprawl, a number of reserves – including Reserva de la Biósfera de Manu *(p256)* and the Ríos Tambopata and Madre de Dios Area *(p258)* – offer access to the jungle.

← Splendid Amazon River, and *(above)* exploring the rainforest

Picture-Perfect Peaks

Other than the mountains surrounding Machu Picchu, Peru's most photographed peak is Vinicunca, or Rainbow Mountain *(p192)*. As the name suggests, this dazzling site is famed for its colorful striations, which were revealed in 2013 by a retreating glacier. It gets busy, with many tourists hiking from Cusco. Looking for quieter high-altitude landscapes? Head further north to Parque Nacional Huascarán *(p210)*, where hulking, snow-tipped peaks and striking glacial lakes await. Stunning views are a dime a dozen – though some require a lengthy hike to get there.

→ Astonishing colors of Vinicunca (Rainbow Mountain), located in Cusco

Hands-On Experience

Textiles are integral to Quechua culture, with ancestral narratives woven into the fabric. Specialist tour operators in the Sacred Valley (p170) offer workshops on the traditional weaving techniques passed down through generations. In Cusco, the Centro de Textiles Tradicionales del Cusco *(textilescusco.org)* is a popular spot for travelers to learn from locals. In Ollyantaytambo, visitors can also try weaving on a backstrap loom at Awamaki *(awamaki.org)*, which partners with local artisans.

→

Learning from crafters in the Centro de Textiles Tradicionales del Cusco

PERU FOR
CRAFTS

From pots and ponchos to masks and miniatures, Peru's traditions of handmade, high-quality crafts have evolved with its various cultures over thousands of years. Whether you're looking to pick up an original souvenir or learn from the experts, Peru's crafts scene offers something for everyone.

US$1,700

Is the price of a vicuña scarf, made from the world's finest and rarest animal fiber.

Picking Up a Bargain

Browsing bustling highland markets and bartering is half the fun of shopping in Peru, though it's worth remembering that profit margins are already slight. Prices are lower than in the smart stores of Lima – especially if you get a reduction by buying several items from the same vendor – but the choice can be overwhelming and the quality variable. The local markets in Pisac (p194) and Chinchero (p194) are known for their quality textiles, while Feria Dominical in Huancayo (p202) is famed for Mantaro Valley crafts. On the hunt for filigree jewelry? The scenic town of Catacaos, in northern Peru, offers some of the country's best.

←

Colorful souvenirs adorning a shop in Ollantaytambo

←

Intricately patterned ceramic pots at Pisac market

Learning From the Experts

Peru's artisans use their immense skill, passed down through generations, along with great patience to create stunning works of art. A large, intricately carved gourd or a finely woven shawl can take months to complete, but many artisans are keen to demonstrate their techniques to visitors and answer questions, especially if they secure a sale. For workshops, head to the city of Ayacucho (p200); for weaving cooperatives, Isla Taquile (p164) is a go-to; and for on-site artisans working on backstrap looms, the museum of Mundo Alpaca is a great choice (p156).

↑ Backstrap loom weaving at Mundo Alpaca in Arequipa

TOP 5 PERUVIAN CRAFTS

Textiles
Weavings and knitwear from the Sacred Valley, Arequipa, and Taquile are highly prized.

Ceramics
Pottery ranges from Nazca reproductions to delicate Shipibo pots.

Jewelry
Natural Amazonian seed-based necklaces sold in Iquitos are particularly popular.

Woodwork
Ayacucho's painted folk-scene *retablos* (portable altarpieces) are highly sought after.

Painted Gourds
Exquisitely produced and engraved in the Mantaro Valley.

Flying High in the Sky
Whether ziplining in the Sacred Valley or paragliding amid the Cordillera Blanca, you're guaranteed incredible mountain vistas. Yet paragliding over Lima offers an altogether different view of the capital's dramatic clifftop skyline. For those wanting an even bigger rush of adrenaline, South America's highest bungee jump is located just outside of Cusco (actionvalley.com.pe).

← Paragliding over Lima's extensive coast, with a great view over the capital

PERU FOR
ADVENTURERS

With the world's highest tropical mountain range, the Andes, giving rise to the world's mightiest river, the Amazon, Peru is a playground for thrill-seekers. Travelers can take to the skies, sail down rushing rivers, or explore the country by mountain bike, and that's just the beginning.

Explorations by Bike
While many choose to explore Peru's majestic landscapes on foot, there is another exciting way to do it. Take to two wheels, and you'll see a lot more in a lot less time. In the vast desert of Reserva Nacional de Paracas (p142), travelers can ride through the stunning sandy landscapes via a popular cycle circuit. Looking for more elevation? Try mountain biking down the hairpin bends of the Abra Málaga route (amazonas-explorer.com), part of the Machu Picchu Jungle Trail. Speeding through this breathtaking alpine scenery is nothing short of exhilarating and offers a unique perspective on the beauty of Peru.

→ Hiking trail with the sun setting over beautiful mountain scenery

STAY

Sky Lodge
Clinging to the rock face, hanging 1,312-ft (400-m) above the Sacred Valley, are the transparent pods of the unique Sky Lodge. Just reaching your bed entails a rock-climbing challenge, and is only the start of the adventure. This one-of-a-kind experience offers impressive views of the valley below and the twinkling night sky above for those who are brave enough.

🅰F6 📍Valle Sagrado, Pista 224 km 🌐naturavive.com

ⓢ ⓢ ⓢ

↑ Fishing for piranhas at Tambopata National Reserve

Deep in the Jungle
Taking a cargo boat from Pucallpa to Iquitos *(p252)* may be enough adventure for some, but serious explorers should consider taking part in an exciting jungle survival training course. Check out Amazon Explorer *(amazonexplorer.com)* and hone your bush skills by constructing shelters and balsa rafts while seeking out fresh water and fishing for piranha. You can also learn about the Amazon rainforest's unique ecosystem and its fascinating wildlife.

On the Water
With raging torrents and a beach-laden northern coast, Peru has plenty to offer for water thrillseekers. The Cañón de Cotahuasi *(p168)* offers exhilarating multiday rafting fun for the adventurous, while kayaking on Lake Titicaca *(p162)* offers a more sedate and relaxing experience. The weeklong Andes-to-Amazon rafting and camping trip also promises an unforgettable adventure.

→ Scenic white-water rafting trip on Río Urubamba

PERU FOR FOODIES

Renowned for its succulent seafood, home to super grain quinoa, and possessing more than 3,000 varieties of potato, Peru's culinary landscape is as diverse as its scenery. Whether dining off damask in Arequipa or snacking on ceviche on a beach in Máncora, your taste buds are in for a treat.

Lima's Food Scene

Thanks to Gastón Acurio, the superstar chef who brought Novoandina cuisine (traditional Andean ingredients given a modern twist) to international attention, Lima is synonymous with culinary innovation. If you can't get a reservation at the legendary Central Restaurante *(centralrestaurante.com.pe)*, you can give a culinary tour or cooking class a go, offered by Lima Gourmet Company *(limagourmetcompany.com.pe)* and Sky Kitchen *(skykitchen.com.pe)*.

→

Peruvian chef Virgilio Martínez Véliz at Central Restaurante, offering exquisite fine dining

Fabulous Fruits

Peruvian markets offer a colorful abundance of fruits, equally delicious as freshly squeezed juices or in cocktails. Alongside tropical favorites such as mango, papaya, and pineapple, you'll find heavenly chirimoya, camu-camu, and lúcuma. Known as Inca Gold and associated with fertility, lúcuma's creamy, caramel texture makes it Peru's favorite ice-cream flavor.

← Pitahaya – a fruit native to the Americas – on sale at a Peruvian market

CEVICHE

With possible origins in pre-Inca culture 2,000 years ago, ceviche is the country's national dish and the number one meal to try when visiting. The classic seafood recipe comprises chunks of raw fish marinated in lime juice, onions, and chilies, served with toasted maize and sweet potato. The Northern Desert *(p222)* is where you'll find some of the best ceviche in the country.

Food Festivals

Peru's food festivals are a treat – the free food and drink extravaganza Perú Mucho Gusto is a highlight. Usually held over several days in September or October, it allows Peruvians and tourists to sample regional dishes in a casual picnic-style setting, accompanied by music and dance. Also in Lima, the indulgent Salon de Cacoa y Chocolate, held in July, features local chocolate tastings and demonstrations.

← Fresh grapes coated in chocolate and candy, a popular delicacy

TOP 3 MUST-TRY PERUVIAN DISHES

Lomo Saltado
Sautéed strips of beef with onions, chilies, tomatoes, spices, fries, and rice.

Rocoto Relleño
Spicy roasted red peppers stuffed with meat, topped with melted cheese.

Suspiro a la Limeña
For the seriously sweet tooth, a blend of egg yolks, condensed milk, cinnamon, and port, topped with meringue.

↑ Dining at the Mercado Central in downtown Cusco

Dine Like a Local

Offering a chance to interact with the locals, hole-in-the-wall traditional *picanterías* or market stalls often serve an inexpensive *menú* (lunchtime set menu). Generally including a soup, main course, and a drink, it is as agreeable to the wallet as it is to the stomach, but get there early for the freshest fare.

From Chicha to Craft Beer

Most often sold during highland festivals, *chicha de jora* (fermented maize beer) is a potent homebrew that has been in existence since Inca times. *Chica* may still be the tipple of choice for the rural populations, but downing the popular bottled Pilsen Callao, Cristal, and Cusqueña is infinitely more refreshing after a long day. To sample the burgeoning craft beer scene, head for the Cervecería del Valle Sagrado in Urubamba *(cerveceriadelvalle. com)*, Nuevo Mundo in Cusco *(Portal de Confituria 233)*, Miraflores in Lima *(C. Manuel Bonilla 103)*, or Sierra Andina in Huaraz *(sierraandina.com)*.

← Draft beer available to sample at Cervecería del Valle Sagrado

PERU FOR
HOME BREWS

Crossing desert, clambering up mountains, and traipsing through the jungle can easily leave you parched. Thankfully, Peru possesses a wealth of alcoholic and non-alcoholic beverages that hit the spot, from its world-renowned pisco to a cornucopia of delicious fruit- and vegetable-based drinks.

TOP 3 PISCO COCKTAILS

Pisco Sour
One of the most popular choices, a classic mix of pisco, lime, sugar syrup, and bitters, topped with whisked egg white.

Pisco Chilcano
A refreshing combination of pisco, lime, ginger ale, and bitters.

El Capitán
Resembling a Manhattan cocktail, comprising a blend of pisco, sweet vermouth, and bitters.

Pisco Reigns Supreme

When it comes to alcohol, pisco is king in Peru. Appearing in a number of popular drinks, it is consumed with particular pomp and partying twice yearly: on its national day, the fourth Sunday in July, and on the first Saturday in February, when pisco sour – the renowned cocktail – is also celebrated. Expect fun tastings, food stalls, and music in the major pisco-producing regions, particularly Ica *(p144)* and Lima. Year-round you can learn all about this emblematic *aguardiente* (grape brandy) on a fascinating tour of Ica's major *bodegas* (wineries), accompanied by a tipple or two.

→ Classic pisco sour cocktail with bitters and fresh lime

Staving Off the Highland Chill

Visitors to the Andean highlands are likely to be offered *maté de coca* (coca leaf tea), an ancient Indigenous remedy believed to counteract altitude sickness. Tastier *matés* (herbal teas) include *manzanilla* (camomile), *canela* (cinnamon), and *anis* (aniseed). Coffee addicts may need to manage their expectations. As Peru's reputation for coffee continues to grow, Peruvians are increasingly leaving behind the traditional *café pasado* (percolated coffee mixed with hot water) and developing a taste for Americano, espresso, and cappuccino.

← Dried coca leaves for coca leaf tea, great for counteracting altitude sickness

Quenching the Thirst

Though the fluorescent-yellow color and bubblegum flavor of Inca Kola, Peru's top-selling soft drink, is not to everyone's taste, *chicha morada*, concocted from boiled purple corn/maize, pineapple, apple, lime, and cloves, is always gaining new fans. In Peru's many markets, juice stalls flourish. Ask for the "jugo especial" to sample the house special blend.

↑ Wine-colored *chicha morada*, said to have medicinal properties

> **INSIDER TIP**
> **Ley Seca (Dry Law)**
>
> During national elections and in Semana Santa (Holy Week) the sale of alcohol is prohibited in Peru. Yet in the rural district of Tuti, in the Valle del Colca, *ley seca* prevails year-round, except on two days of riotous local celebrations: May 12 and December 12.

Andean Huayno

The panpipe is the archetypal Andean instrument, which together with flutes, harps, and *charangos* (small lutes) forms the core of *huayno* bands, whose decibel count is often bolstered by drums, brass, and other wind instruments. A central feature of any Andean festival, you can hear *huayno* bands accompanying joyful dance troupes as they sashay through the streets.

→ Playing the panpipe at the market in Pisac

PERU FOR
MUSIC
AND DANCE

Music and dance are integral to Peruvian life, reflecting the fusion of Hispanic, African, and Andean roots. While folk traditions are still thriving in the highlands, the infectious rhythms of criolla and salsa music, alongside the throbbing beats of local rock, hold sway in the clubs of lowland cities.

Do the Marinera

With regional variations, Peru's national dance is a flirtatious courtship ritual of waving white handkerchiefs. The woman performs barefoot, swishing her voluminous skirt while the man seduces with his sombrero. One of the best chances of seeing this dance is at the Festival Nacional de la Marinera *(p66)*.

→ Dancing the *marinera*, performed countrywide

Did You Know?

The 1960s Peruvian band Los Saicos is widely believed to have been the world's first punk rock group.

Afro-Peruvian and Criolla

With its origins in the enslaved communities on the central coastal strip, the infectious rhythm of Afro-Peruvian and criolla music is a favorite in Lima's *peñas (p84)*. Powered by *cajónes*, rectangular wooden box-drums, in tandem with a grating *quijada de burro*, an instrument made from a donkey's jawbone, the pulsating beat of *festejo* (uptempo beat) incites dancers.

↑ *Cajón* players at an international music festival

Modern Sounds

Hit any club in Lima and you'll find proof that Peru's urban youth are into a variety of modern music. Electronica, Latin hip-hop, rap, rock, and the insistent beat of reggaeton (rapping and singing, typically in Spanish) all have their fans. You can also find this music blaring out of any beach bar in Máncora *(p234)*.

← Olaya Sound System, a Peruvian indie band, performing at a festival

Supaypa Wasin Tusuq (Scissors Dance)

The all-male scissors dance is a spectacle. In this historical symbol of resistance against Spanish colonialism, dancers perform eye-popping cartwheels, somersaults, and aerial jumps, all the while clicking giant scissors in time to the music. See this dance performed at any festival round Ayacucho *(p200)*, but especially during Yaku Raymi *(p67)*, the Big Water Festival, in the Ayacucho region.

→ Vibrant costumes and towering headdresses of the scissors dance

TOP 3 SECLUDED PARADISES

Arennas, Las Pocitas
B2 arennasmancora.com
Stylish boutique oceanfront hotel that includes villas with a private pool.

Kichic, Las Pocitas
B2 kichic.pe
Rustic luxury in nine uniquely styled rooms made from natural materials.

Yemaya, Punta Sal
B2 yemayaperu.com
Thai-style stone-and-thatch accommodations with all mod cons.

Beautiful night sky above the bustling party town of Máncora →

THE NORTHERN DESERT'S BEAUTIFUL BEACHES

Peru's desert coastline provides endless stretches of sand and year-round sun, but the best beaches and warmest waters lie in the north. From Trujillo to Tumbes, there are beach scenes to suit all tastes, be it surfing, fishing, snorkelling, partying, or simply kicking back and watching the waves.

Play in the Waters of Punta Sal

The shallow rippling waters of Punta Sal, near Zorritos (p234), are perfect for safe swimming or trying out a new watersport. Sea kayaks, windsurfers, and stand-up paddleboards are all available for rent, with instruction on hand. You may even glimpse migrating humpback whales, visible from the shore between July and October.

←

Broad belt of flat sand on Punta Sal, arguably Peru's most attractive beach

Party on the Shores of Máncora

Surf-and-party central, Máncora *(p234)* is one of South America's best-known holiday resorts. Packed with beach bars and fun-seeking Limeños who fly up for the festive season between December and March, this is the spot to dance and drink the night away. Bask on the soft sands during the day, hit the waves surfing, or learn to dive at Peru's first PADI-affiliated school.

> **INSIDER TIP**
> **Whale Watching**
>
> Responsible whale-watching trips led by marine biologists set out from Los Órganos, south of Máncora, in search of humpbacks in the migration season. Visit pacificoadventures.com for more details.

Unwind on the Sands of Las Pocitas

Máncora's palm-fringed satellite strand is distinctly more luxurious and tranquil than the raucous resorts – the only nighttime rhythms to reach your oceanside cabaña are those of breaking waves. Las Pocitas is a heavenly spot to relax: feast on succulent seafood, laze in a hammock, or stroll along the beach at sunset.

→ Rows of palm trees along the blissful beach of Las Pocitas

Surf on the Waves of Chicama

On the bucket list for all serious surfers, Chicama claims to have the longest left-breaking wave in the world, providing over 2 miles (3 km) of surfing heaven. For non-surfers, the splendid Chicama Surf Resort *(waterwaystravel.com)* nonetheless offers plenty of entertainment, from the swimming pool to ping-pong or table soccer, as well as day trips to Trujillo *(p226)* and the surrounding ancient sites.

↑ Riding a wave at the splendid Chicama beach

Colorful Displays at Madre de Dios

The dawn spectacle of macaws descending on an Amazon clay lick to eat the mineral-rich earth is truly breathtaking. Although they depart as quickly as they arrive, it is not difficult to seek out other impressive birds: bright-billed toucans or the extraordinary hoatzin spend much of their time here. Lodges and camps in Manu (p256) organize visits to clay licks, though they are a lot more accessible from Tambopata (p258).

→ A moving kaleidoscope of macaws on a clay lick in Madre de Dios

PERU FOR BIRD-WATCHING

Peru is home to over 1,800 bird species, making it a magnet for wildlife enthusiasts. The jungle offers some fantastic areas to witness the dazzling colors and extraordinary behaviors of Peru's tropical birdlife, so be sure to pack some binoculars.

HIDDEN GEM
Chaparrí Lodge

Peru's first privately owned reserve, the splendid Chaparrí Reserva Ecológica is home to 70 endemic bird species. Experience the reserve with a stay in the rustic cabins at Chaparrí Ecolodge (chaparrilodge.com).

Close Encounters on a Canopy Walkway

Since most animal activity occurs in the rainforest canopy, it pays to join them up in the treetops. You can find a number of canopy towers or walkways in several places, but for something spectacular, check out Explorama Lodges (explorama.com) near Iquitos or Rainforest Expeditions in Tambopata (rainforestexpeditions.com).

→ Bird-watching from a canopy walkway deep in the rainforest

Seabird Central on Islas Ballestas

In a deafening cacophony of squabbling and squawking, millions of seabirds jostle for position on these crowded rocky islets. Visitor favorites include the comical Humboldt penguins and the smart grey Inca terns, sporting white whiskery moustaches and scarlet beaks. Boats to the Islas Ballestas *(p144)* leave Paracas daily.

→ Cormorants gathering on rock formations on the Islas Ballestas

Giant Condors at the Cruz del Cóndor

A close encounter with a condor will surely amaze. Usually a distant black speck soaring high over a remote Andean valley, at the Cruz del Cóndor - a viewpoint overhanging the Cañón del Colca *(p166)* - these avian giants rise up majestically from the canyon floor, mesmerizing the spellbound crowds.

← Condor flying over the Cañón del Colca

↑ A cock-of-the-rock (male), Peru's national bird, perching on a branch

Star Attractions in the Yungas

Two private patches of reforested land safeguard rare Andean treasures. Owlet Lodge in the Reserva Abra Patricia protects the Long-whiskered Owlet - a tiny bird that was for many years thought to be extinct. Nearby Reserva Huembo's star resident is the marvelous spatuletail hummingbird, dazzling visitors with its shimmering racket-tail feathers in a magical acrobatic display. Visit the reserves' shared website *(owletlodge.org)* for more details on both spectacular spots.

Hiking Off the Beaten Path

While the dramatic peaks of the Cordillera Blanca *(p206)* are a magnet for both casual and experienced hikers, the undeniably challenging 12-day circuit of the neighboring Cordillera Huayhuash *(p221)* promises equally magnificent Andean scenery without the tourists. High mountain passes afford breathtaking panoramas across snow-frosted peaks and sheer rock faces that plunge into glacial lakes. Meanwhile, a break at the hot springs near the midway point provides welcome relief and a massage for your sore muscles. Sign up with a tour operator in Huaraz *(p220)*, or hire a guide locally.

→ Camping amid the picture-perfect landscapes in the Cordillera Huayhuash

PERU FOR
HIDDEN GEMS

The vast, varied, and challenging terrain in Peru makes it possible to escape the tourist track without too much effort. There are bountiful treasures to be discovered, from crashing waves in secluded coves to stunning mountain-top vistas that are all yours.

Homestay with an Indigenous Family

Rich in ancient traditions, the majestic Lake Titicaca offers a host of homestay options. With a smattering of Spanish, visitors can delve deeper into the culture by staying with a local family. Learn about medicinal plants, turn your hand to fishing, or help prepare a tasty *pachamanca* (meal cooked in an earth oven). Eschewing the more visited islands of Taquile and Amantaní *(p164)*, a warm welcome is guaranteed in the mainland communities of Chucuito *(p165)* or Llachón.

→ Gathering beside a reed boat on one of the Islas Uros on Lake Titicaca

The Dirt Road Less Traveled

Impassable at times during the rainy season, which lasts from October to March or April, the unpaved road north from Oxapampa *(p264)* provides a spectacular, hair-raising ride as it plunges down to charming subtropical Pozuzo *(p265)* – a small Tyrolean-Peruvian settlement. Skirting the edge of a ravine for much of the way, the road spans countless streams, offering tantalizing glimpses of cascading falls, lush forested slopes, and the raging river below. To experience an even greater adrenaline rush, rent a mountain bike.

← Oxapampa-Asháninka-Yanesha Biosphere Reserve

TOP 3 REMOTE RETREATS

Tapiche Jungle Reserve
249 miles (400 km) S of Iquitos · tapichejungle.com
Rustic accommodations in a private reserve brimming with wildlife deep in the rainforest.

Cordillera Blanca Lodge
22 miles (36 km) N of Carhuaz · cblodge.com
Luxurious mountain hiking lodge with stunning views in the Cordillera Blanca.

Wayqecha Lodge
26 miles (42 km) N of Paucartambo · amazonecolodge.com.pe
Simple wooden cabins for bird-watchers set in dreamy cloud forest.

Dining Afloat in the Amazon

For a unique culinary experience, take a ferry from Iquitos *(p252)* out to Al Frio y Al Fuego *(alfrioyalfuego.com)* – a floating upscale restaurant. Sip a jungle-juice cocktail, soak up a glorious Amazonian sunset if dining in the evening, and sample the local mouthwatering gourmet cuisine.

↑ The picturesque setting of Al Frio y Al Fuego, complete with a pool and sun deck

59

Treasures inside the Museo de las Tumbas Reales de Sipán, and a spider necklace *(inset)*

Glorious Gold
All that glitters really is gold in the Museo de las Tumbas Reales de Sipán *(p230)* at Lambayeque, home to some of Peru's most notable treasures, which were unearthed in an imperial Mochica tomb. Gold and silver breastplates, goblets, and exquisite jewelry inlaid with semi-precious stone are superbly displayed in a darkened pyramid, alongside an impressive reconstruction of the grave site.

PERU FOR ARCHAEOLOGY ENTHUSIASTS

Machu Picchu and the Incas may hog the headlines, but a host of earlier cultures have left a monumental mark on the Peruvian landscape. From the impressive northern citadel of Kuélap to the enigmatic Nazca Lines in the southern desert, there's no shortage of fascinating archaeological wonders.

Ancient Remains
A common practice among pre-Columbian cultures, mummification has always held a macabre fascination. In the Cementerio de Chauchilla *(p147)*, seated skeletons well over a thousand years old stare back at you eerily. Remarkably preserved in elaborate shrouds, their hair and even fragments of skin remain intact due to the arid desert climate. The Museo Regional Adolfo Bermúdez Jenkins in Ica *(p144)* also houses a fascinating collection of mummies.

Mummies on display at the Cementerio de Chauchilla, near Nazca

Historic Ruins

Looming out of the Northern Desert, the vast adobe Huaca del Sol (Temple of the Sun) *(p232)*, center of the ancient Mochica Empire, is an imposing sight. Yet the real thrill is examining the lavishly painted friezes of the sibling Huaca de la Luna (Temple of the Moon), depicting an array of natural spirits and the fierce face of ruling deity Ai-Apaec. A visit to one of Peru's best-preserved adobe ruins, Tambo Colorado *(p145)*, is extraordinary.

> **TOP 3 ARCHAEOLOGY MUSEUMS**
>
> **Museo Larco**
> Private collection in Lima laden with gold, silver, and Mochica erotic art *(p128)*.
>
> **Museo de Arte Precolombino**
> Superb wide-ranging set of ancient artifacts in Cusco *(p174)*.
>
> **Museo Arqueológico Nacional Brüning**
> An impressive private collection of Lambayeque *(p233)* that examines Peru's early northern coastal cultures.

← Evocative painted frieze at Huaca de la Luna in Trujillo

SEÑOR DE WARI

The discovery of the Lord of Wari's tomb in 2011 in Espiritú Pampa was proof that it had been occupied by the Wari before the Incas made their last stand there against the Spanish. Objects found are held in the museum at Pikillacta *(p192)*.

↑ Familia Real, Palpa Lines, featuring the eye-boggling *dios oculado*

Desert Etchings

Peering out of the plane window as you sweep over the mysterious Nazca Lines *(p140)* – including the giant monkey, hummingbird, and spider – is an exhilarating experience. Now the thrill can be extended to include the more recently unearthed Palpa Lines *(p140)*, even older geoglyphs etched into hillsides by the Paracas culture. The best known, Familia Real (Royal Family), features the *dios oculado* deity.

Charming Spectacled Bear

The inspiration for children's favorite Paddington, the spectacled bear gets its name from the rings around its eyes. South America's only species of bear is a shy, mild-mannered creature that prefers chewing bamboo to eating meat. The best chance of spotting one is the Reserva Nacional Chaparrí *(chaparrilodge.com)*, which also runs a rehabilitation center.

←

Spectacled bear, also known as the Andean bear, native to South America

PERU FOR
ASTOUNDING WILDLIFE

One of the top spots in the world for wildlife, Peru is home to an array of species. Many can be found on the coastal deserts and in the mountains, but most inhabit the eastern slopes of the Andes and the lush Amazon.

Majestic Jaguar

Much revered by Peru's Indigenous populations, this powerful cat is the Amazon's supreme predator, equally at home on land, up a tree, or in water. Staying at a remote lodge or camp in Tambopata *(p258)* or Manu *(p256)*, accompanied by a naturalist guide, increases your chances of catching a rare glimpse of this magnificent beast.

→

A jaguar perfectly camouflaged in a tree

Comical Camelids

Llamas and alpacas are synonymous with the Andes, their faintly humorous appearance – long necks and camel-like faces – making them the stars of many a photo. Llamas are larger, with longer ears and coarser coats, while alpacas are smaller and fluffier. Their threatened wild relative, the vicuña, can be seen grazing the plains in Pampa Galeras *(p146)*.

↑ Herd of elegant wild vicuña in the Andes in Arequipa

Beautiful Butterflies

Flitting around Peru's tropical forests are stunning butterflies adding splashes of color and ethereal elegance. The spectacular blue morpho is especially dazzling, its iridescent wings shimmering in the sunlight. Lepidoptera enthusiasts tend to head for the Pakitza region of the Manu National Reserve *(p256)*, which has the richest butterfly environment of anywhere on the planet.

←

Morpho peleides, or blue morpho butterfly

↑ Beautiful spider monkey perched on a tree branch

Marvelous Monkeys

Fabulous treetop entertainers, monkeys top the must-see list of most visitors to the rainforest. Over 30 species cavort in the canopy, from the rare scarlet-faced uakari, to the more commonly spotted acrobatic troupes of spider monkeys and mischievous capuchins. At almost any jungle camp or lodge, you'll be woken by the pre-dawn chorus of bellowing howler monkeys, who may oblige with an encore before dusk.

AMAZON ADVENTURES

The enticing prospect of a boat trip is guaranteed in the rainforest. Whether in a motorized dugout bound for a jungle lodge, or on a converted steamship cruising up the Amazon, the possibilities for adventure along the splendid waters in Peru are endless.

Great Views by Riverboat Cruise

Riverboat cruises are a wonderful way to unwind on the Amazon. For those craving action, land excursions promise forays into the undergrowth while explorations by dugout involve close encounters with aquatic life. Most vessels head out of Iquitos to explore the Reserva Nacional Pacaya-Samiria *(p254)*, but consult Rainforest Cruises *(rainforestcruises.com)* for options.

Exploring the lush environs of the Amazon River by a small boat

Explorations by Dugout

It's much easier to navigate narrow tributaries and shallow lagoons by dugout. What's more, it enables closer encounters with wildlife, drifting right up to dazzling kingfishers ready to plunge after prey, basking caimans, or even a family of watchful giant river otters. Most lodges organize trips by dugout as part of their package; otherwise, simply turn up at your chosen dock to begin the adventure.

← Boat gliding along the Madre de Dios River, tributary of the Amazon River

> **INSIDER TIP**
> **Wildlife Photography**
>
> The best time to photograph wildlife is at dusk or dawn, when light is just above the horizon. If shooting in cloudy conditions, the light will be more even and provide the perfect atmospheric shot. Remember not to shoot with flash, as this may frighten the wildlife.

↑ A passenger ferry crossing the Amazon River near the port of Iquitos

Lazy Journeys by Lancha

Swinging in a hammock on a *lancha* (chugging cargo boat) is a no-frills way to travel downriver and experience river life first-hand. Timetables can be vague, and it's best to bring your own food. The main routes lie between Yurimaguas *(p260)* or Pucallpa *(p262)* and Iquitos *(p252)*; just roll up at the dock the day before.

↑ Hanging out in a hammock on a *lancha*, a local way to travel

A YEAR IN PERU

JANUARY

△ **Festival de la Marinera** *(Jan/Feb)*. Couples of all ages compete in Trujillo to be named Peru's best *marinera* dancers.

Aniversario de Lima *(Jan 18)*. Celebrations for Lima's anniversary involve fireworks and music.

FEBRUARY

△ **Fiesta de la Virgen de la Candelaria** *(Feb 2–mid-Feb)*. Religious parades, folk music, and dancing honor the patron of Puno, the Virgin of Candelaria.

Festival del Verano Negro *(Feb/Mar)*. A celebration of Afro-Peruvian culture takes place in Chincha and El Carmen.

MAY

Corpus Christi *(May/Jun)*. Statues of 16 saints are carried to the cathedral in Cusco in this religious celebration.

△ **Qoyllur Rit'i** *(late May/early Jun)*. During this religious festival, people hike overnight to a shrine at Mount Ausangate in Cusco.

JUNE

△ **Inti Raymi** *(Jun 24)*. The Festival of the Sun celebrates the Inca Sun god, Inti, with a procession up to Sacsayhuamán in Cusco.

Festival de San Juan *(Jun 24)*. Celebrating St. John the Baptist, this festival in Iquitos features purification rituals, traditional dancing, and feasting.

SEPTEMBER

△ **Fiesta de la Primavera** *(Sep/Oct)*. Spring is marked across the country with houses decked with flowers and the procession of the city's new beauty queen in Trujillo.

OCTOBER

△ **Fiesta del Señor de los Milagros** *(Oct 18–28)*. Tens of thousands of penitents follow an image of the Lord of Miracles on its 24-hour journey across Lima.

Día de la Canción Criolla *(Oct 31)*. Creole music is honored with concerts in Lima.

MARCH

Festival de la Vendimia *(early Mar)*. Expect to see live grape-stomping from the Harvest Queen and her handmaidens in Ica.

△ **Domingo de Ramos** *(Mar/Apr)*. A donkey is led by children dressed as angels at this Palm Sunday festival in Cruces de Porcón, mixing Andean and Catholic traditions.

APRIL

△ **Semana Santa** *(Mar/Apr)*. The week leading up to Easter ushers in religious processions countrywide.

Concurso Nacional del Caballo Peruano de Paso *(mid-Apr)*. Celebrated in Lima, more than 700 animals and horse breeds are presented at the National Peruvian Paso Horse Contest.

JULY

Fiesta de la Virgen del Carmen *(Jul 15–18)*. Virgin del Carmen, patroness of the mestizo people, is paid tribute to in Paucartambo.

Fiestas Patrias *(Jul 28–29)*. Independence Day is celebrated across the country.

△ **Día Nacional del Pisco** *(last Sun)*. Bars and restaurants throw pisco-themed parties in Lima, Arequipa, and in vineyards around Ica to celebrate the national drink.

AUGUST

Selvámonos *(end Jun–Aug)*. Enjoy national and international bands and DJs at Peru's largest alternative music and art festival in Oxapampa.

△ **Aniversario de Arequipa** *(Aug 15)*. Head to the Plaza de Armas to see colorfully dressed folk-dancing troupes on Arequipa's anniversary.

Yaku Raymi *(end Aug)*. Offerings are made to goddess Pachamama amid striking dances such as the *Supaypa Wasin Tusuq* (Scissors Dance) during this Big Water Festival across the Ayacucho region.

NOVEMBER

△ **Día de Todos los Santos and Día de Los Difuntos** *(Nov 1–2)*. Picnics are held at cemeteries across Peru to commemorate All Saints' Day and All Souls Day.

Semana Jubilar de Puno *(first week Nov)*. Dancing, processions, and fireworks celebrate the founding of Puno.

DECEMBER

△ **Vispera de Navidad and Día de Navidad** *(Dec 24/25)*. Cusco's Plaza de Armas hosts the Santurantikuy market, with handcrafted Nativity scenes for sale.

A BRIEF HISTORY

The origins of civilization in Peru can be traced back 20,000 years before the Incas, making the country one of the cradles of ancient cultures. Peru today is the result of a collision between the Andean and Western worlds, a process that began with the arrival of the Spanish in 1532.

First Human Traces
Peru's earliest settlers arrived via the Bering Strait during the last Ice Age (40,000 to 20,000 BCE), leaving evidence of human civilization in Cueva de Pikimachay in around 20,000 BCE. Later, the planting of crops established a system of agriculture and founded permanent settlements. Excavations of Caral, north of Lima, revealed a complex urban center in the Central Andes. Radiocarbon dating indicates that it was built around 2600 BCE – 4,000 years before the appearance of the Incas. After 500 years of occupation, Caral was abandoned for reasons unknown.

[1] A map of Peru from the 16th century.

[2] Ruins found at the vast site of Caral, an impressive complex.

[3] Golden mask from a Chimú jewelry collection.

[4] The defeat of Huáscar by his brother Atahualpa during the civil war.

Timeline of events

11,000 BCE
First nomadic communities roam the highlands hunting giant animals.

20,000 BCE
Nomadic groups cross the Bering Strait from Asia to the Americas, gradually spreading south.

8000 BCE
Potatoes are first cultivated by farmers near Lake Titicaca.

2627 BCE
Caral, the oldest city in the Americas, is built in the Supe Valley.

900–300 BCE
Coastal societies disintegrate while the Chavín cult flourishes.

Major Early Cultures

The Early Horizon (1000 BCE–200 CE) saw the Chavín cult unite coastal and highland societies, but as their influence waned, various regional cultures arose, from the Nazca (100 BCE–700 CE) in the south, to the Moche (100–700 CE) in the north. By the Middle Horizon period (600–1000 CE) two expansive states had emerged: the Wari, from Ayacucho and the Tiwanaku, based around Lake Titicaca. It was not until 1197, though, that a group in the Cusco Valley known as the Inca came to prominence.

The Inca

Little is known about the early Inca leaders, although legend tells that the first, Manco Cápac, founded the city of Cusco. The most important was the ninth, Pachacútec (1438–71), under whose leadership the Tahuantinsuyu (Land of the Four Quarters) expanded and covered nearly a third of South America, making it one of the largest empires in history. In the 16th century, civil war broke out when Huayna Cápac, the 11th Inca, died. The kingdom was divided between his son, Huáscar, and illegitimate son, Atahualpa, though the latter finally seized control.

> **THE CÁPAC ÑAN (ROYAL ROAD)**
>
> Roads were crucial to Pachacútec's program of unification. During his reign alone, the Inca built some 18,600 miles (30,000 km) of stone roads, some scaling passes 16,500 ft (5,000 m) high. This Cápac Ñan network connected all four regions of the empire, running 3,500 miles (5,500 km) from Quito in Ecuador right down to Santiago in Chile.

---

650 — The Wari-Tiahuanaco period begins.

220–600 CE — Moche culture thrives.

1200 — Cusco is founded by the first Inca, Manco Cápac.

1400 — Maximum expansion of the Chimú kingdom.

1438–71 — The ninth Inca Pachacútec's 33-year reign begins.

The Spanish Conquest

In 1524, the conquistador Francisco Pizarro set out to conquer "Birú," a kingdom rich in gold and silver situated south of present-day Colombia. Returning to Spain with goods to prove the existence of "El Dorado," Pizarro was appointed Governor and Captain-General in 1529, and authorized to conquer Peru.

The Spanish invasion was one of the first and bloodiest clashes between European colonizers and people in the Americas. Pizarro and fellow conquistador Diego de Almagro landed in Tumbes in 1532 during the civil war between Atahualpa and Huáscar over succession. Pizarro later executed Atahualpa and took over the leaderless empire.

Life Under the Spanish

The original leaders of the Spanish conquest perished in a bitter feud, with the execution of Almagro by Pizarro in 1538, which led to the assassination of Pizarro in 1541. Colonization and exploitation of the country's natural and human resources continued nonetheless. The conquistadors introduced new economic classes, as well as Catholicism and the Spanish language, which Peruvians

↑ Francisco Pizarro, Spanish conqueror of the Inca Empire

Timeline of events

1525
Huayna Cápac dies and his son Huáscar succeeds; war with Atahualpa.

1532
Pizarro lands in Tumbes with 168 men and captures Atahualpa.

1533
Atahualpa is tried and executed; Cusco is sacked.

1535
Pizarro founds Lima on January 18.

still adhere to and speak today. The feudal *encomienda* system they introduced produced immense inequalities, and to reduce these, the Spanish king issued new laws. From 1542, civil war broke out between the conquistadors, who saw their livelihoods as under threat, and the Viceroyalty, the Spanish administrative district that had been newly established by the Spanish Crown. After ten years of conflict, the Viceroyalty triumphed. In 1574, Viceroy Francisco de Toledo reintroduced the Inca mit'a tax, forcing people to work unpaid, to their death, in mines.

Push for Independence

With the abdication of Spain's King Charles IV in the early 1800s, thoughts of independence spread throughout South America. In 1821, José de San Martín defeated the royalist forces in Peru and proclaimed its independence. After trying to introduce a new constitution, San Martín ceded control to Venezuelan general Simón Bolívar. The first elected president in Peru did not enter office until 1827. In the first 40 years after independence, the presidency changed hands 35 times, of which only four presidents were constitutionally chosen.

[1] Spaniards burning Atahualpa in 1538.

[2] Almagro loyalists murdering Francisco Pizarro in 1541.

[3] General San Martín proclaiming Peru's independence.

15

The number of different constitutions written in the first 40 years after independence.

1600
Potosí mines reach population peak with 160,000 workers.

1767
Jesuits are expelled from the Spanish Empire.

1780–82
A descendant of Atahualpa, Túpac Amaru II, stages the final Inca rebellion and is executed.

1821
San Martín proclaims Peru's independence.

Post-Independence and the Modern Era

The War of the Pacific (1879–83) was sparked by a dispute over control of nitrate-rich land in the northern Atacama Desert. Following a rising global demand for nitrates, a key ingredient in explosives and fertilizers, Bolivia attempted to tax Chilean companies operating in their territory. When Chile refused, Bolivia declared war, asking for aid from neighboring Peru. Much of the conflict played out at sea, through warships such as the iron-clad *Huáscar*. By 1883, Chile had won; Bolivia had lost its sea access, while Peru ceded substantial territory.

Early 20th Century

After the war, Peru oscillated between democracy and military dictatorship. In 1919, Augusto Leguía assumed the presidency in a coup, introducing a new constitution which gave the state wide-ranging powers. In 1968, a military dictatorship was again enforced when General Juan Velasco Alvarado seized control. Democracy was restored in 1980 by Fernando Belaúnde. Intent on privatizing industry, his term was hampered by high inflation and the threat of guerrilla movements.

↑ Augusto Leguía, who served as president of Peru from 1919 to 1930

Timeline of events

1879–83
War of the Pacific.

1919–30
Leguía's 11-year civil dictatorship, marked by strong foreign investment and restrictions of civil rights.

1938
María Luisa Aguilar, Peru's first professional astronomer, is born.

1968–80
Period of military dictatorship under General Juan Velasco Alvarado.

1980
Belaúnde is re-elected; Sendero Luminoso (Shining Path) initiates the guerrilla struggle.

Shining Path, Fujimori, and Civil Conflict

The growth of the extremist guerilla movement Sendero Luminoso (Shining Path), led by Abimael Guzmán, and the Marxist Movimiento Revolucionario Túpac Amaru (MRTA), resulted in a brutal guerrilla conflict. From 1980, vast stretches of the sierra and Amazon were cut off from the rest of the country, with 70,000 mainly rural Indigenous Peruvians killed. In 1990, the Cambio 90 party was elected and their leader Alberto Fujimori, initially popular, was sentenced to 25 years in prison in 2007 for corruption and human rights abuses during the civil conflict.

Peru Today

Between 2001 and 2013, Peru became one of the fastest growing economies in Latin America. However, many – especially rural Indigenous people – have not benefited from the wealth. The adverse health and economic impacts of the COVID-19 pandemic have disproportionately affected the 70 per cent of workers in informal employment. Combined with corruption at high government levels, with five former presidents implicated in major scandals, this has led to continued public protests demanding change.

[1] The Battle of Angamos during the War of the Pacific.

[2] Juan Velasco Alvarado's presidency tour in 1971.

[3] Workers cleaning up a bomb explosion in Miraflores in 1992, for which Guzmán was captured and tried.

[4] Alejandro Toledo, Peru's first Indigenous president, at a traditional blessing ceremony at Machu Picchu in 2001.

1999–2000
Fujimori elected president for a third term, then resigns amid scandal.

2016–19
Odebrecht bribery scandal implicates four former Peruvian presidents.

2020–23
220,000 Peruvians die in the COVID-19 pandemic, which also damages the economy and widens social inequalities.

2022
Former vice-president Dina Boluarte becomes the country's first female president.

PERU'S INDIGENOUS POPULATION

Speaking 47 different languages, Peru's Indigenous population comprises around a fifth of the country's 34 million people. Most inhabit the Andes, dominated by Quechua groups, or the Amazon Basin, where the Asháninka make up the majority community. Common to all is the struggle to maintain their traditional customs and ways of life while trying to adapt to modern living on their own terms. Significant numbers have migrated to the big cities in recent decades, initially fleeing the violence of the 1980s, and latterly in search of employment. A visit to the highlands or the rainforest affords unique opportunities to learn from these ancient societies.

ANDEAN PEOPLES

Quechua and Aymara groups dominate Peru's Andean spine, and their beliefs permeate everything from labor practices to festivals, and food to fabric. *Pachamama* (Mother Earth) reigns as the supreme deity and guiding force, and ritual offerings made every August 1 kickstart a month of celebrations across the Altiplano. Since colonial times, the three-million plus Quechua and half a million Aymara have often worshipped *Pachamama* along with the Virgin Mary.

AMAZONIAN PEOPLES

Around 40 Indigenous groups inhabit the forested Amazon Basin, with some 55,000 Asháninka the most numerous. They, along with many others, are increasingly being forced off their lands by oil exploration, illegal logging, mining, and drug trafficking. Widespread among Indigenous Amazonian groups are animism and shamanism, the belief that all nature is imbued with spirits that can be contacted via spiritual leaders in altered states of consciousness.

↑ Feeding a llama in the Cusco area of Peru

> **INSIDER TIP**
> **Homestays**
>
> Avoiding the voyeuristic visits to Indigenous villages offered by tour operators, homestays *(p163)* offer a deeper intercultural exchange. Visit the website peru.travel/es/experiencias/vivencial to find the best places for homestays.

↑ Islas Uros on Lake Titicaca, a great place to do a homestay

THE IMPORTANCE OF PLANTS

Plants have been crucial to traditional societies for centuries, whether making clothing, homes, and utensils, or used as medicines and during shamanic rituals.

Coca Since pre-Columbian times sacred coca leaves have fulfilled social, ritual, and medicinal functions, combating diverse ailments such as hunger, fatigue, and altitude sickness.

Ayahuasca This giant vine with hallucinogenic and purgative properties is used by shamans for medicinal and spiritual purposes.

Achiote As well as possessing antibacterial properties, the crushed seeds of this tropical shrub's flowers produce a red dye, used for fabrics.

1. A colorful handmade bag used to hold coca leaves.
2. Ayahuasca leaves, found at a healing center in Peru.
3. The stunning flowers on an Achiote tree.

↑ Members of the Amazonian Yagua entering a traditional *maloca*

EXPERIENCE LIMA

Enjoying the Circuito Mágico del Agua

3 Days in Lima 80

Lima Your Way 82

Central Lima 88

Miraflores and San Isidro 104

Barranco 116

Beyond the Center 126

PERU

Río Rímac
AVENIDA MORALES DUAREZ
AVENIDA ARGENTINA
AV. REPÚBLICA DE VENEZUELA
Parque de las Leyendas
AVENIDA LA MARINA
LA PERLA
AVENIDA LA PAZ
AVENIDA COSTANERA
SAN MIGUEL
AV. UNIVERSITARIA
MAGDALENA

EXPLORE
LIMA

This guide divides Lima into four sightseeing areas: the three shown on this map and Beyond the Center.

CENTRAL LIMA
p88

MIRAFLORES AND SAN ISIDRO
p104

BARRANCO
p116

EXPERIENCE Lima

←

1. Lima's majestic main square.

2. Paragliding over Larcomar shopping mall.

3. Goldenberries on sale at Mercado de Surquillo, Lima.

4. Illuminated fountain at the Circuito Mágico del Agua.

3 DAYS
in Lima

Day 1

Morning Begin your day in Central Lima's Plaza Mayor *(p102)*. This bustling square is lined with grand buildings, and visitors can also watch the changing of the guard at 11:45am outside the Palacio del Gobierno *(p97)*. Continue one block north to the Casa de Aliaga *(p97)*, the oldest colonial mansion in the city and, allegedly, South America. Continue south to reach Chinatown *(p100)* for a traditional lunch at a *chifa*.

Afternoon Catch a cab across the city to the Museo Amano *(p112)*, which displays a dazzling array of ancient Peruvian textiles. After gazing upon the colorful textiles, hop in another cab to the collection of pre-Columbian ceramics covering 3,000 years of history at the renowned Museo Larco *(p128)*.

Evening For souvenir shopping, take a taxi south to Miraflores and browse the handicraft and antiques stalls clustered in the cat-filled Parque Kennedy *(p110)*. Stroll south for dinner at one of the modern restaurants in the Larcomar shopping mall, which come complete with expansive ocean views.

Day 2

Morning One of the city's loveliest parts is Miraflores' Malecón *(p114)*, a cliff-side path punctuated by manicured parks and plenty of benches. Rent a bike for an early-morning spot of exercise. Continue on foot along the coast to reach Barranco *(p116)*, strolling along Avenida Sáenz Peña to take in the neighborhood's exquisite 20th-century mansions.

Afternoon Head further north and grab lunch on the go as you explore the bustling Mercado de Surquillo, an unmissable Peruvian market experience. Pick your way between stalls laden with mouthwatering fruit, mountains of vegetables, and hook-slung meat. Afterward, take a *metropolitano* bus north for the Museo de Arte de Lima *(p98)*, a museum with 34 galleries.

Evening For dinner, reserve a table at one of the branches of the perpetually rammed Punto Azul *(puntoazulrestaurante.com)*, a chain of *cevicherías* offering some of the city's finest and most affordable dining.

Day 3

Morning From central Lima, hop on a bus heading south along the Pan-American Highway to reach Pachacámac *(p133)*. A guided tour takes you around this temple complex, which dates back to 200 CE.

Afternoon Back in Miraflores, grab a sandwich at La Lucha Sanguchería *(p111)* before taking in the Huaca Pucllana *(p108)*, a pre-Inca adobe pyramid that offers excellent views across the city. Browse the neighborhood's boutique stores as you weave your way north into San Isidro for even more stylish shopping.

Evening Drop by the Parque de la Reserva for the Circuito Mágico del Agua *(p95)*, an interactive water show where 15 lit fountains dance to music. Make a reservation for dinner at the renowned Astrid & Gastón *(p111)*, one of the city's finest restaurants, owned by celebrity chef Gastón Acurio and his wife Astrid.

El Beso sculpture epitomizing the love theme in the Parque del Amor

LIMA FOR ART LOVERS

Lima's thriving contemporary art scene continues to gain momentum as small private galleries showcase exciting new talent in Miraflores and Barranco, while street art flourishes organically. With a wealth of sculpture, public art, and traditional paintings, Lima has pieces to suit every taste.

Painting: Puka Wamani

Bold shapes and colors rooted in Indigenous Andean motifs are the hallmarks of Fernando de Szyslzo's paintings. Szyslzo is considered one of Latin America's greatest abstract artists, and his work is well worth a visit. *Puka Wamani* (1968) - part of a series of the same name - is one such oeuvre, which hangs in the Museo de Arte de Lima *(p98),* alongside some of his other works.

Museo de Arte de Lima, where Szyslzo's paintings are on display

Sculpture: El Beso

One of Lima's most photographed sights, *El Beso* (The Kiss) is a gigantic stone sculpture in Miraflores by Limeño artist Victor Delfín, modelled on himself and his wife locked in a passionate embrace. Inaugurated on Valentine's Day in 1993, it remains the star attraction in the themed clifftop Parque del Amor (Park of Love) *(p111)*. More of his work is exhibited in his nearby studio-gallery *(Jirón Domeyer 368)*, where he gives tours.

TOP 3 CONTEMPORARY ART GALLERIES

Museo de Arte Contemporáneo
This gallery hosts both permanent and temporary collections *(p122)*.

Palacio de las Artes Miraflores
w visitamiraflores.com
Municipal palace with works by national and international artists.

Wu Galería
w wugalleria.com
Encouraging emerging artists in all media.

Street Art: Hogar de un Suspiro

Sprawling across walls, bridges, and shopfronts, up steps, or tucked away in courtyards, murals are a big deal in bohemian Barranco. Jade Rivera's *(museojaderivera.com)* striking *Hogar de un Suspiro* (Home of the Sigh), located near the Puente de los Suspiros *(p121)*, is one of the main sights in Barranco and celebrates human freedom. If a camera snap is not enough, his art gallery on Avenida Bajada de los Baños sells prints. For mural enthusiasts, Tailored Tours *(tailoredtours-peru.com)* will guide you through the pick of Barranco's graffiti.

↑ The impressive *Hogar de un Suspiro* mural, painted in 2015

> **INSIDER TIP**
> **Circuito Mágico del Agua**
>
> For something different, catch the Magic Water Circuit (p95) in the Parque de la Reserva, a great technicolor sound and light fountain show.

LIMA
AFTER DARK

The capital's vibrant nightlife scene holds something for everyone, with little need to stray from the sophisticated clifftop *barrios* of Miraflores and Barranco. Whether you opt for a moonlit stroll along the malecón, indulge in a gourmet meal, or hit the bars, clubs, and *peñas*, Lima has it covered.

Experience Peñas

Originally community venues celebrating a shared heritage of great food and musical traditions, Lima's modern *peñas*, such as La Candelaria (lacandelaria peru.com), are now more visitor-oriented, putting on well-choreographed shows of Afro-Peruvian or Andean folk music and dance. For a much more intimate experience, catch an unadulterated slice of criolla culture at Don Porfirio's on a Friday night *(Manuel Segura 115, Barranco)*.

←

Dancers performing at Barranco's popular *peña* Don Porfirio

An Evening at the Theater

Lima's two standout venues offer plenty. The Teatro Municipal *(Jirón Ica 377)*, with its top-notch acoustics, is the perfect spot for fans of modern dance and classical music. The striking Gran Teatro Nacional de Peru *(granteatronacional.pe)* serves up a more varied program, staging everything from rock to opera, and Broadway to ballet.

←

Dancers rehearsing for a performance at the Gran Teatro Nacional

DRINK

Mango's
For a stellar sundowner, bag a clifftop table at this Miraflores bar with fantastic ocean views.

🅐 D5 📍 Larcomar, Malecón de la Reserva 610 🌐 mangosperu.com

Ayahuasca
Trendy bohemian restobar set in a gloriously restored colonial mansion with creative cocktails and superb snacks.

🅐 D5 📍 Av San Martin 130 🌐 ayahuascarestobar.com

Bar-Hop in Barranco

When it comes to bar crawls, Barranco is the place to be, offering all manner of watering holes. Hip bars such as Café Victoria *(Pedro de Osma 135)* inhabit glorious mansions, while family-run Juanito Barranco *(Av Almte Miguel Grau 270)* with its sedate decor attracts a more local crowd. All are conveniently packed round the Parque Municipal *(p122)*.

→

The bohemian Bajada de los Baños in Barranco

Dance Until You Drop

While dance venues abound in Lima, all require stamina, as the action only hots up around midnight and continues at full speed until almost dawn. Take your pick from intimate dance floors to vast laser-lit caverns, contemporary to retro, rock to reggaeton, and salsa to hip-hop. Miraflores in particular hosts a number of clubs, many within walking distance of Parque Kennedy.

←

Larcomar shopping center and surroundings lit up at night

LIMA'S COLONIAL ARCHITECTURE

A designated UNESCO World Heritage Site, the historic center of the "City of Kings" is known for its 16th to 19th-century architecture. Spanish and Indigenous design often merge in colonial architecture, resulting in a kind of Creole style seen all over Lima. The two grandiose main plazas and neighboring streets overflow with fine churches, palaces, and mansions. Though ravaged by earthquakes, many have been rebuilt in more earthquake-resistant adobe (bricks made from organic materials) and *quincha* (wood or cane covered in mud and plaster).

CASA DE ALIAGA

The opulence and artistry on display in Lima's oldest and best-preserved mansion *(p97)*, dating from 1535, are omnipresent, seen in the magnificently carved wooden coffered ceilings, pediments, and mouldings. *Azulejos* (painted tin-glazed ceramic tiles adapted from Islamic architecture) found here are a key decorative feature of both religious and secular colonial buildings.

PALACIO DE TORRE TAGLE

This 18th-century palace *(Jr Ucayali, 363)* was commissioned by the then treasurer of the Spanish fleet, Don José Bernardo de Tagle y Bracho. It features two of the city's most ornate balconies – a key feature of the time. *Mudéjar* (North African Islamic) architectural features inside include lobed arches and fine *azulejos*. The building has been home to the Ministry of Foreign Affairs since 1918.

↑ Casa de Aliaga's impressive inner patio, complete with fig tree and fountain

CASA DE PILATOS

Built in 1590 for a Spanish merchant, the Casa de Pilatos *(Jr Ancash 390)* is based on the Sevillian house in Seville, Spain, of the same name. Currently housing offices of the Supreme Court, the mansion possesses a characteristic colonial courtyard, enclosed by a fine stone staircase. The original wooden balconies were replaced after an earthquake.

CASA DE OSAMBELA

Also known as Casa de Oquendo *(Jr Conde de Superunda, 298),* this was Lima's tallest *casona* (mansion) in the early 1800s. It uniquely has three stories and is topped with a *mirador* (observation tower). The original owner, shipping merchant Martín de Osambela, would watch his galleons rolling into port from this *mirador*. Though the house was built in the early 19th century, the current facade displays later Neo-Classical characteristics with Rococo embellishments.

Casa de Osambela's splendid facade lined with wooden balconies ↑

LIMA'S CHURCHES

Iglesia San Pedro Relatively restrained on the outside, Iglesia San Pedro *(p98)* is jaw-droppingly ornate on the inside, and saturated in gold leaf. Built in its third, and current, incarnation in 1636, Churrigueresque *(p156)* ornamentation was added over time. Gold embellishes everything, from the altarpieces and pulpit to the lateral naves and glorious coffered ceiling and cupola.

Iglesia de San Francisco Dating from 1664, the imposing facade of the Iglesia de San Francisco *(p92)* is a sight to behold. Flanked by twin towers, the facade presents a fine example of Spanish Baroque style, comprising a stone altarpiece-portal decorated with niches, statues, and pilasters.

1 Stunning gold embellishment inside San Pedro.

2 San Pedro's cupola, a common feature in religious buildings.

3 San Francisco's splendid facade.

Did You Know?

Pablo Andrade, Lima's former mayor, launched an "Adopt a Balcony" campaign to rescue them.

Elegant courtyard of Convento de Santo Domingo

CENTRAL LIMA

The area on which present-day Lima is located had been populated for thousands of years before the Spanish arrived. It was once home to a confederation of rural fiefdoms, which were later absorbed into the Inca Empire. The Incas also established three urban centers here: Carabyll to the north, Maranga in the center, and Surco, south of what is today Miraflores.

Lima, as we know it, was founded by Francisco Pizarro in 1535, and was the capital of the Spanish Empire in South America for almost two centuries. Dubbed the City of Kings, it was at the time the most important metropolis in the region, the center of power and wealth. Its coat of arms bears three crowns, representing the three kings of the Nativity, and the motto proclaiming, "This is truly the sign of kings." Based on a Roman plan, the original 117 city blocks radiate out from Plaza Mayor, where the imposing presence of both church and state accent its pivotal role. Many of the buildings date from the 18th and 19th centuries, as an earthquake in 1746 razed most original structures. Private homes have since morphed into museums or government offices. Fervent devotion to the Catholic doctrine, introduced by the Spanish, means there is a Baroque-, Renaissance-, or Rococo-inspired church or convent on almost every street corner, from the beautiful Santo Domingo to the grand San Francisco.

CENTRAL LIMA

Must See
1. San Francisco

Experience More
2. Estadio Nacional
3. Circuito Mágico del Agua
4. La Catedral
5. Museo de Sitio Bodega y Quadra
6. Casa de Aliaga
7. Palacio de Gobierno
8. Museo Andrés del Castillo
9. San Pedro
10. Parque de la Muralla
11. Museo de Arte de Lima
12. Santo Domingo
13. Convento de los Descalzos
14. Chinatown
15. Plaza San Martín
16. Las Nazarenas
17. Museo de Arte Italiano
18. Museo Nacional de la Cultura Peruana

Eat & Drink
1. L'Eau Vive
2. Restaurant Bar Cordano

Map Labels

Grid D1–F1:
- AVENIDA TACNA
- GUARDIA REPUBLICANA
- CALLE 7
- Convento de los Descalzos [13]
- JIRÓN PALLASCA
- FRANCISCO PIZARRO
- JIRÓN PRESA
- JIRÓN VIRU
- JIRÓN RAMO ESPINOZA
- JIRÓN TRUJILLO
- JIRÓN MADERA
- JIRÓN PAITA
- JIRÓN CHICLAYO
- JIRÓN ATAHUALPA
- CALLE 10
- 29 DE AGOSTO
- SAN CRISTÓBAL
- JIRÓN LETICIA
- AL MAGRE EL JOVEN

Grid D2–F2:
- Santa Rosa
- CHANCAY
- CALLAO
- AYABACA
- JIRÓN CAJAMARCA
- JIRÓN LIBERTAD
- JIRÓN CAJAMARCA
- AVENIDA PANAMERICANA NORTE
- JIRÓN LORETO
- MARAÑON
- LORETO
- AV. PANAMERICANA NORTE
- VÍA EXPRESA LÍNEA AMARILLA
- Río Rímac
- Santo Domingo [12]
- CDE DE SUPERUNDA
- Casa de Aliaga [6]
- Estación Desamparados
- Parque de la Muralla
- [5] Museo de Sitio Bodega y Quadra [10]
- [7] Palacio de Gobierno [2]
- PLAZA MAYOR
- AMAZONAS
- ABANCAY
- San Francisco [1]
- Las Nazarenas [16]
- San Agustín
- CALLAO
- TORRICO
- HUANCAVELICA
- La Merced
- HUALLAGA
- La Catedral [4]
- Hotel Maury
- PLAZA BOLÍVAR
- JIRÓN ANCASH
- JIRÓN ANCASH
- AYACUCHO

Grid D3–F3:
- convention center
- AV. EMANCIPACIÓN
- MOQUEGUA
- UNION
- MIRO QUESADA
- CENTRO [1]
- UCAYALI
- JUNIN
- JIRÓN HUANTA
- JIRÓN PARURO
- CANGALLO
- JIRÓN
- HUALLAGA
- N. DE PIEROLA
- OCAÑA
- Plaza San Martín [15]
- CARABAYA
- LAMPA
- AZANGARO
- San Pedro [9]
- PUNO
- AV. ABANCAY
- AV. CUZCO
- ANDAHUAYLAS
- Chinatown [14]
- JUNIN
- CANGALLO
- CUZCO STREET
- LUCANAS
- JIRÓN HUANUCO
- Museo Andrés del Castillo [8]
- QUILCA
- TAMBO DE BELÉN
- APURIMAC
- AYACUCHO
- Parque Universitario
- AV. N. DE PIEROLA
- PARURO
- Jardín Botánico
- JIRÓN HUAMANGA
- JIRÓN HUANUCO
- LÓPEZ
- AV. ROOSEVELT

Grid D4–F4:
- Sheraton
- PASEO DE LA REPÚBLICA
- Central Station
- Museo de Arte Italiano [17]
- PLAZA GRAU
- Museo de Arte de Lima [11]
- Parque de la Exposición
- AV. J. GALVEZ
- SANDIA
- COTABAMBAS
- LETICIA
- MONTEVIDEO
- AV. ZAVALA
- AV. MANCO CAPAC
- RAIMONDI
- J. CANTA
- GARCÍA NARANJO
- JIRÓN ANDAHUAYLAS
- OBREROS
- PJ. RAIMONDI
- JIRÓN MENDOZA MERINO
- AVENIDA GRAU
- AVENIDA GRAU
- HUAMANGA
- JIRÓN LA MAR
- AV. ABTAO
- GARCÍA NARANJO
- AVENIDA 28 DE JULIO
- PROLONGACIÓN PARINACOCHAS
- AV. BAUZATE Y MEZA

Grid D5–F5:
- PLAZA JORGE CHÁVEZ
- AV. AREQUIPA
- AV. PETIT THOUARS
- DIAZ
- Estadio Nacional [2]
- Circuito Mágico del Agua [3]
- AV. J. GALVEZ
- J. CANTA
- AV. BAUZATE Y MEZA
- Plaza Manco Cápac
- AVENIDA 28 DE JULIO
- AV. BAUZATE Y MEZA
- JIRÓN IQUITOS
- JIRÓN S. PEÑA
- AV. MANCO CAPAC
- JIRÓN HUASCARAN
- HUMBOLDT
- RENOVACIÓN
- LUNA PIZARRO
- SAN CRISTÓBAL
- JIRÓN ANDAHUAYLAS
- AV. ISABEL CATÓLICA

0 meters 500
0 yards 500
N

SAN FRANCISCO

◎ E2 ◎ Jirón Ancash, block 3 ◎ Church: 7–11am & 4–8pm daily; Museum & Convent: 9am–6pm daily ⓦ museocatacumbas.com

The striking yellow-and-white complex of San Francisco comprises a church, a convent, the chapels of La Soledad and El Milagro, and eerie catacombs. The facade alone is one of the best examples of 17th-century Baroque architecture in Peru. Inside, the complex also houses superb examples of Baroque sculpture as well as a valuable collection of treasures, from art with Andean touches to the first dictionary published by the Real Academia Española.

The original mud and wood church built in 1557 was destroyed in the 1656 earthquake, and the reconstructed church was completed in 1672 by Portuguese architect Constantino de Vasconcellos. With the exception of the stone altarpiece-portal and the lateral portal, the church is made of earthquake-resistant *quincha* (rushes, mud, and plaster). The church itself is built on underground tunnels or catacombs, which were used as a cemetery until the early 19th century.

Being the preferred place of worship for the Spanish viceroy and his court, the church received generous donations, especially from the gold and silver mines of Peru. Some of these treasures vanished during the wars of independence in the 19th century, though many remarkable works of art, architecture, and literature remain. The Religious Museum is especially worth a visit, housing a series of the "Passion of Christ" paintings by the 17th-century Flemish painter Peter Paul Rubens. Portraits of the apostles from the studio of the Spanish painter Francisco Zurbarán hang in the Zurbarán Room.

↑ Dramatic circles of skulls and femur bones in the crypt

↑ The splendid convent library, home to centuries-old manuscripts and books

Highlights

The High Altar
△ Designed by the renowned Spanish architect Presbitero Matías Maestro, this impressive structure is carved in a Neo-Classical style.

Convent Library
△ This 17th-century library houses around 25,000 books from the 15th to 18th centuries, including many first editions and parchments.

Baroque Church Facade
△ Two towers flank a stone altarpiece-portal, a lavish mass of sculptures, niches, and more dating from 1664.

Convent Cloister and Garden
△ The tiled patio has a stunning ceiling made from mahogany, and the walls are painted with frescoes.

Must See

70,000

The estimated number of bodies in San Francisco's bone-packed crypt.

↑ Stunningly ornate Baroque facade of the Complejo de San Francisco

Building San Francisco

In 1535, Emperor Charles I ordered Francisco Pizarro to put aside two sites in Lima so that the Franciscans could build a church and convent. Located on the banks of the Río Rimac, the sites were approximately one-eighth the area of the city, the largest church complexes in the Americas. The best artists of the day, from silversmiths to sculptors, were brought in to add decoration. A factory was organized to produce *azulejos* (painted tiles). The impressively detailed decorative patterns can best be seen on the altarpieces, facade, domes, and towers in the church.

↑ Tiled walls, paintings, and ornate woodwork in the colorful *azulejos* hallway in the cloisters

The convent cloisters feature a wall fresco on the life of St. Francis of Assisi.

Convent Library

The original wooden dome was constructed in 1625.

Fountain

The High Altar

GUINEA PIG SUPPER

Guinea pigs are integral to Peruvian life and millions are eaten every year. The Incas reportedly sacrificed 1,000 guinea pigs and 100 llamas in Cusco's plaza each year for the safety of their fields. Small wonder that Diego de la Puente's *Last Supper*, displayed in San Francisco's Dining Hall, shows Jesus and his 12 disciples sitting down to *cuy chactado* (roast guinea pig). This painting is often mistaken for Marcos Zapata's of the same name *(p179)*.

Must See

↑ Spectacular ceiling of the High Altar, in San Francisco

The church interior features three seven-span aisles, a transept, and a presbytery.

Quincha *was used to construct most of the church.*

↑ Layout of the grand San Francisco complex, with its church, convent, and chapels

Did You Know?

Lima's largest collection of *azulejos*, from Seville, Spain, dating back to 1620, lines the cloisters.

EXPERIENCE MORE

② Estadio Nacional

📍D5 🏛 Calle José Díaz 📞 01 431 6190 🕐 For fixtures and events

The Estadio Nacional is a 40,000-capacity stadium and home ground of the Peruvian national soccer team. Built in 1952, it hosts international matches, including three of the six Copa America (South American Championship) tournaments held on Peruvian ground. It's also one of Lima's main music venues, hosting big international names.

On May 24, 1964, the stadium saw one of the most tragic soccer disasters in history. During an Olympic qualifying match against Argentina, tear gas was used to dispel pitch invaders and caused a stampede of spectators toward the exit, killing 300 people.

③ Circuito Mágico del Agua

📍D5 🏛 Between Av Arequipa and Av Paseo de la República 🕐 2-10pm daily (water shows at 7:10, 7:50, 8:30 & 9:10pm) 🌐 circuitomagicodelagua.com.pe

The spacious Parque de la Reserva, designed by French architect Claude Sahut, is one of Lima's most enticing public areas. In 2007, after lengthy and controversially costly remodeling, 13 cybernetic fountains were installed to create the Circuito Mágico del Agua, an enchanting circuit of ornamental water features. At night, its splendid illuminated water show is Lima's most spectacular entertainment. The fountains are choreographed to light and music. Some spray water 260 ft (80 m) into the air, while others, such as the Túnel de las Sorpresas, form archways through which you can walk.

> **INSIDER TIP**
> **Laberinto del Ensueño**
>
> Be sure to protect your valuables when making your way through this fountain at the Circuito Mágico del Agua, as the vertical shots of water are likely to soak you.

↑ The Circuito Mágico del Agua's Túnel de las Sorpresas

Gilded vaulting above the naves of La Catedral

④

La Catedral

◉ E2 📍 Plaza Mayor
📞 01 427 9647 🕐 9am-1pm & 2-5pm Tue-Sat

With its imposing twin towers, the cathedral dominates the eastern side of Plaza Mayor. Founder of Lima Francisco Pizarro (1478–1541) carried the first log for the construction of the original adobe wall and the straw roof structure on this site in 1535.

Construction began on the current Baroque-Renaissance-style structure in 1564. Work stalled due to lack of funds and the devastating earthquakes of 1687 and 1746 but was finally completed in 1758. Further rebuilding followed the earthquake of 1940.

The cathedral has five naves and ten side chapels, the smaller ones dedicated to religious figures. The chapel of John the Baptist has a carving of Jesus said to be the most beautiful in the Americas. The remains of Francisco Pizarro lie in the mosaic-covered chapel to the right of the entrance. Highlights include the ornate choir stalls, carved by Spanish sculptor Pedro Noguera, and the museum of religious art.

⑤

Museo de Sitio Bodega y Quadra

◉ E2 📍 Jirón Ancash 213
📞 01 428 1644 🕐 10am-3pm Tue, Thu & Sat

Behind an unassuming exterior lies a journey into the past: a painstakingly excavated 17th-century colonial house. Stripped walls and floors allow you to wander the layout and imagine how life was lived in that era. It was the home of Spanish merchant and Lima consul Thomas de la Bodega y Quadra and his Peruvian-born son Juan Francisco, the famous explorer and naval officer in the Spanish Armada. Juan Francisco explored California and traveled to the Canadian Quadra Island (named after him) and Vancouver Island. The museum includes ten interesting exhibition rooms, audiovisuals,

→ Grandiose facade of the president's residence, Palacio de Gobierno displays of china and pottery, and cutlery found in the excavations.

6
Casa de Aliaga

D2 **Jirón de la Unión, 224** **10am–4pm daily, for pre-reserved tours with an authorized guide only** **casadealiaga.com**

This *quincha* (earthquake-resistant material) mansion was built by Jerónimo de Aliaga, one of Pizarro's lieutenants. It is the oldest and best-preserved colonial-era home in the continent and is owned by the same family 17 generations later.

The ornate timber balcony offers the only external clue to the lavish 66-room house that lies within. Marble stairs lead to the second-floor patio and the main entrance. The part that is open to the public showcases a wide range of colonial art and decor from the 16th to 18th centuries, such as Louis XIV mirrors and furniture, family portraits, and Cusco School paintings *(p179)*. One of the two Andalusian patios has a bronze fountain.

> **INSIDER TIP**
> **Take a Food Tour Downtown**
>
> Go on a walking tour through the colorful Mercado Central to devour delicious *papas rellenas* (spicy meat-filled potato croquettes) from a street stall, and sample citrusy ceviche. Check the website for details *(limawalking tour.com/foodie-tour)*.

7
Palacio de Gobierno

E2 **Plaza Mayor** **01 311 3900** **PR office, Jirón de la Unión** **For pre-reserved tours only: 9 & 10am Sat & Sun; call 01 311 3900, ext 523, to reserve (Mon–Thu)**

Known as the Casa de Pizarro, the Government Palace was built by Pizarro on the land once owned by Taulichusco, a pre-Hispanic chief of the Rimac Valley. It has been the seat of political power in Peru ever since, undergoing major reconstruction in the 1920s and 1930s following a fire.

Inaugurated in 1938, the palace is a grand example of colonial affluence. Rooms are adorned with mahogany and cedar carvings, French glass, Carrara marble, and Czech crystal. A marble staircase dominates the Grand Hall, flanked by busts of key figures in Peru's history. The gilded Salón Dorado (Golden Room) is modeled on the Palace of Versailles' Hall of Mirrors.

The interior is open for tours only, on weekend mornings, but the Changing of the Guard in front of the palace, which takes place daily at noon, is well worth seeing.

8
Museo Andrés del Castillo

D3 **Jirón de la Unión 1030** **9am–5pm Mon–Sat** **madc.com.pe**

This beautifully restored 19th-century house is home to a private museum set up in memory of Andrés del Castillo, a young student of mining engineering who died tragically in 2006. The exhibits reflect Andrés' studies and interests, with a unique and vast collection of crystallized minerals from the Peruvian Andes; exceptional Chancay ceramics dating from 900 CE to 1500 CE; and a collection of pre-Hispanic clothing and accessories, with robes, corsets, shoes, belts, hats, wigs, and jewelry.

9
San Pedro

◆E3 ◆Jirón Azángaro 451 ◆01 428 3010 ◆7:30am-12:30pm daily, 5-8pm Mon-Fri (to 7pm Sat & Sun)

The only church in Lima with three entrances (usually a feature of cathedrals), the Iglesia de San Pedro is a fine example of early colonial architecture in the city. Built in 1636, it was consecrated two years later. Inspired by the Jesuits' Chiesa del Sacre Nome di Gesù in Rome, it has three naves.

The restrained exterior is adorned with Churrigueresque (Spanish Baroque) and gilded altars, carvings of the founders of various religious orders, and North African Islamic-style balconies. The side chapels, with their glazed tiles, are awash with paintings from the Lima, Quito, and Cusco schools.

The impressive golden main altar, designed by priest Matiás Maestro (1760–1835), features columns, balconies, and sculpted figures.

A painting depicting the coronation of the Virgin Mary by Bernardo Bitti (1548–1610), who worked with Michelangelo in Italy and supervised the construction of San Pedro, hangs in the sacristy.

10
Parque de la Muralla

◆E2 ◆Jirón Amazonas and Jirón Lampa ◆01 433 1546 ◆7am-6pm daily

Once a deprived area, this park has become a popular spot to exercise for locals and visitors. Situated behind the Iglesia San Francisco, next to the Río Rimac, it exhibits the remains of a 17th-century wall that once protected the city from pirates and enemies of the Spanish crown. The park has an outdoor gym, library, a small exhibition of maps, prints, and artifacts, and a statue of Francisco Pizarro.

11
Museo de Arte de Lima

◆D4 ◆Paseo Colón 125 ◆10:30am-1pm & 2-6pm Tue-Sun (to 5pm Sat) ◆mali.pe

Nestled in the Parque de la Exposición and surrounded by statues and gardens, the Neo-Renaissance Palacio de la Exposición (the Palace of the Exhibition) was built for the big industrial expo held in the city in 1872. The palace, once at the heart of Lima's most important 19th-century urban projects, is home to the city's Art Museum. Its collection of Peruvian art from the past 3,000 years ranges from ancient ceramics and textiles to contemporary jewelry, furniture, and paintings.

Highlights of the Colonial Art Gallery on the second floor include paintings by Juan de Santa Cruz Pumacallao, Diego Quispe Tito, and Juan Zapata Inca. These paintings of the Cusco School (p179) combine Andean mythology with Catholic symbols and contrast marvelously with

Did You Know?

San Martín de Porras was South America's first Black saint.

the conventional religious parables depicted by Bernardo Bitti (1548–1610).

The collection includes Nazca ceramics, Inca cups, and colonial dresses. Also on view are portraits of wealthy 19th-century families by José Gil Castro (1785–1841) and Carlos Baca Flor (1867–1941), renowned for his paintings of eminent people such as Pope Pius XII, US banker J.P. Morgan, and fashion designer Charles Frederick Worth. Challenging works by 1960s vanguardists, such as Jesús Ruiz Durand, are also on display.

Parque de la Exposición, also known as the Parque de la Cultura, provides a welcome respite from Lima's traffic. The park houses an amphitheater, a children's puppet theater, and other performance areas. There is a peaceful Japanese garden and an artificial lake with paddleboats. Monuments here – such as the Chinese fountain, the Byzantine Pavilion, and the attractive North African Islamic-style Pavilion – all celebrate Peru's centenary of independence. Avoid visiting after dark as thieves have been known to frequent the park.

SANTA ROSA DE LIMA

The Americas' first saint, Lima-born Isabel Flores de Oliva, was nicknamed "Rose" due to her beauty. She rubbed hot peppers on her cheeks to make herself less attractive, and used the pain to focus solely on God. Isabel joined the Third Order of St. Dominic and her penances became more rigorous. She worked tirelessly for Lima's poor and advocated rights for Indigenous people. On her feast day, thousands flock to the Sanctuario de Santa Rosa de Lima, built near the house she was born in. Letters asking for her help are thrown into the same well that she threw the key of the iron chain she wore around her waist.

12

Santo Domingo

D2 Jirón Camaná 170
01 426 5521 9:30am-1pm, 2-5:30pm Tue-Sat, 2-7pm Sun

Construction of the Basílica de Santo Domingo began in 1540, a few years after Francisco Pizarro granted the land to Dominican friar Vicente de Valverde, who was with him during his conquest of Peru. Pizarro had sent Valverde to meet the Inca ruler Atahualpa *(p190)* in order to persuade the Inca to convert to Christianity or face a war with the Spanish. However, Valverde was unsuccessful.

Completed in the late 16th century, the basilica features an imposing dome and the Retablo de las Reliquias, an altar with relics of three Dominican Peruvians who attained sainthood – Santa Rosa de Lima (1586–1617), San Martín de Porras (1579–1639), and San Juan Masías (1585–1645).

To the right of the basilica tower are the chapel and the convent cloisters, said to be the best preserved in Lima.

←

A riot of gilded Baroque decoration in the vestry of the Iglesia de San Pedro

13

Convento de los Descalzos

E1 Calle Manco Cápac 202-A, Alameda de los Descalzos **01 481 0441**
10am-12:30pm & 2-5pm Tue-Fri, 10am-3pm Sat & Sun

Founded in 1592 by Andrés Corso, a Corsican priest, the Convent of the Shoeless Ones was named after the barefooted Franciscan monks who lived a silent, spartan life in this spiritual retreat, relying on donations to meet their needs. Missionaries who took over the convent in 1852 said it breathed "poverty, orderliness and thrift, in contrast to the ostentation of other religious establishments."

Today, it is home to a priceless collection of religious and colonial paintings from the 17th and 18th centuries, which includes a work by Murillo (1617–82), of St. Joseph with Jesus. The convent regularly holds music and art events.

The chapel has a gold-leaf altar, a kitchen, a refectory, an infirmary, and monks' cells. Seville tiles adorn the patio walls and Cusco School *(p179)* paintings hang in the chapel dedicated to Nuestra Señora de la Rosa Mística.

Take a taxi and ask it to wait as assaults have been known to happen in this area.

↑ Colorful curios displayed in a shop in Lima's Chinatown district

Did You Know?

It took José de San Martín 21 days to cross the Andes. The journey claimed the lives of one in three of his men.

EAT

L'Eau Vive
A French order of nuns serves delicious cooking in a beautifully restored 18th-century home. The fixed-price lunch is a bargain. Proceeds go to charity.
◘E3 ◙Jirón Ucayali 370 ☏01 427 5612 ◷12:30–3pm Mon–Sat

⑤⑤⑤

Restaurant Bar Cordano
This is one of the oldest bars in the country. While dining options here are limited to traditional ham sandwiches loaded with criolla sauce, this restaurant delivers a perfect slice of Limeño history.
◘E2 ◙Jirón Ancash 202 ☏01 426 0072 ◷8am–8pm Tue–Sun

⑤⑤⑤

⑭
Chinatown

◘E3 ◙Calle Calpón, between Jirón Andahuaylas and Jirón Paruro

Covering a few blocks of downtown Lima, Chinatown is one of the city's most intriguing neighborhoods. Chinese immigrants arrived in waves during the late 1800s, enticed by the offer of jobs building Peru's new railroad. Today, the Chinese-Peruvian community numbers around 14,000.

The entrance to Chinatown is marked by an ornate, 26-ft- (8-m-) high Chinese archway where Jirón Ucayali and Jirón Andahuaylas converge. While few tourists venture to the area, it's home to some of Lima's best *chifas* (Chinese restaurants), and is unmissable at Chinese New Year.

⑮
Plaza San Martín

◘D3

Built in 1921 to commemorate 100 years of independence, Plaza San Martín has a distinct French architectural influence which can be seen in the exclusive men-only Club Nacional and the Gran Hotel Bolívar, of 1924. At its center is a statue of the Argentinian liberator of Peru, General José de San Martín, crossing the Andes on horseback. A statue of Madre Patria, the symbolic mother of Peru, stands beneath the nation's protector. She should have been adorned with a *llama*, or crown of flames. Instead she has a little Peruvian llama – the animal – sitting on her head. The double meaning of the word was obviously lost on the artist, who crafted the image in Spain.

⑯
Las Nazarenas

◘D2 ◙Jirón Huancavelica 515 ☏01 423 5718 ◷7am–1pm & 3:50–8pm Mon–Fri & Sun, 7am–noon & 3:50–8pm Sat

The Church of the Nazarene was built in the 18th century outside the city's walls in Pachacamilla, a neighborhood then inhabited by people from Angola who had been freed from enslavement and Pachacámac people. It was constructed around a local freed person's painting of Christ on an adobe wall, *El Señor de los Milagros* (Lord of Miracles), which inexplicably survived three major earthquakes, in 1655, 1687, and 1746. Sensing a miracle, people began to flock to see the painting, and the church sprang up at the site. Today, behind the altar, is a replica in oils of *El Cristo de la Púrpura*, as it is also known.

A copy of the image is paraded through Lima's

EARTHQUAKES IN LIMA

Peru is prone to earthquakes due to its location on a geological fault and Lima has endured its fair share over the centuries. On October 28, 1746, a colossal tremor rattled the country for four minutes. More than 15,000 people died in the capital, many vanishing in the tsunami that swallowed Callao, sinking all the boats in the harbor and reportedly carrying one vessel a mile (2 km) inland. Lima was in ruins, its 74 churches, 12 monasteries, and all but 20 of its 3,000 private houses severely damaged. In the aftermath of the quake, one account said of Lima's 40,000 survivors that "it was not life they were living but death they were enduring." Most of the buildings seen today date from after 1746. Lima's last major earthquake, in May 1940, demolished 23 per cent of its buildings.

streets on a one-ton silver litter during the El Señor de los Milagros procession in October (p66). The procession, which takes different routes on three different days, draws thousands of devout believers dressed in purple robes.

17

Museo de Arte Italiano

D4 ▪ **Paseo de la República 250** ▪ **9:30am-4:30pm Tue-Sat** ▪ **museos.cultura.pe**

The Italian Art Museum was gifted to Peru in 1921 by the Italian community living in Lima to mark the centenary of the country's independence. Designed by the Milanese architect Gaetano Moretti (1860–1938), it has a grand, white Renaissance-style facade that features the coats of arms of major Italian cities and reliefs made of marble. Two detailed mosaic panels depict illustrious figures from Italian history.

Inside, there are decorative details inspired by Italian masters such as Donatello, Michelangelo, and Botticelli. More than 300 works by about 100 Italian artists of the 20th century include paintings, engravings, sculptures, and drawings, as well as ceramics.

18

Museo Nacional de la Cultura Peruana

C2 ▪ **Av Alfonso Ugarte 650** ▪ **9am-4:30pm Tue-Sun** ▪ **museos.cultura.pe**

The National Museum of Peruvian Culture was set up in 1946 to conserve Peru's ethnographic heritage. The building's design was inspired by the iconography of the Tiahuanaco culture, which flourished around Lake Titicaca in 300 BCE.

Folkloric and ethnographic exhibits gathered from all over the country include objects from the 40 different groups that inhabit the Amazonian jungles, and from the Andes are works from Ayacucho, Cusco, Cajamarca, and Puno. Other sections are devoted to functional and traditional objects, including musical instruments. Folk art lovers should not miss the miniature *retablo* depicting the *marinera*, Peru's national dance, by Joaquín López Antay (1897–1981). The engraved gourds, particularly the donkey pen by Alicia Bustamante, and the ceramics of the Shipibo people, are also spectacular.

→ Italianate garden in front of the decorated facade of the Museo de Arte Italiano

A SHORT WALK
PLAZA MAYOR

Distance 2 miles (3 km) **Time** 30 minutes
Nearest station Desamparados

Formerly called the Plaza de Armas, it was here that Francisco Pizarro founded Lima. A stroll around this part of the city takes you to various major institutions established here, and which today form part of Lima's historic center, such as La Catedral, the Palacio Arzobispal (Archbishop's Palace), the Municipalidad (City Hall), and the Palacio de Gobierno (Government Palace). The plaza has witnessed many significant historical events, including the declaration of Peru's independence *(p71)* in 1821. The large bronze fountain in the center, erected in 1651, is the square's oldest feature.

Palacio de Gobierno *was the president's residence and was remodeled and inaugurated in 1938.*

Casa de Aliaga *is the oldest piece of family-owned real estate on the continent; it was built on top of an Inca shrine in 1535 (p97).*

Municipalidad

This **bronze fountain** *was commissioned by the Count of Salvatierra, who was also the Viceroy of Peru, in 1650.*

Jirón de la Unión *links Plaza Mayor with Plaza San Martín via a busy thoroughfare (p100).*

Named after its original owner, writer Don José de la Riva Agüero, the 19th-century **Casa Riva-Agüero** *houses a fine library and the Museo de Arte Popular (Folk Art Museum). It is now run by Lima's Catholic University.*

↑ Relaxing outside the grand Palacio de Gobierno

Home to the Archbishop of Lima, **Palacio Arzobispal** was reconstructed in 1924. It is famed for the North African Islamic-style carved balconies that decorate its imposing facade.

Museo de Arte Religioso de la Catedral is housed inside the cathedral.

Did You Know?

The Spanish Inquisition used this square to execute its condemned.

Locator Map
For more detail see p90

Ambitious building plans combined with earthquakes saw the rebuilding of **La Catedral** several times, until it was finally reconstructed in 1758. The choir chairs are one of the greatest works of Peruvian art (p96).

The **Palacio Torre Tagle**, considered the best representation of 18th-century Lima architecture, was built in 1735. It is famed for its carved wooden balcony and stone entrance.

Museo del Banco Central de la Reserva specializes in pre-Columbian archaeology and displays 19th- and 20th-century Peruvian art. There is also an exhibition on Peru's currency.

Iglesia de la Merced is where Lima's first Latin mass was held.

Pre-Columbian *tumi* (ceremonial knife) at the Museo del Banco Central de la Reserva

103

Scenic pier with the Rosa Náutica restaurant

MIRAFLORES AND SAN ISIDRO

Officially established in 1857, Miraflores quickly developed into Lima's prosperous commercial hub. With a history dating back thousands of years, vestiges of the area's ancient past remain in the form of the Huaca Huallamarca and the Huaca Pucllana – ancient adobe pyramids constructed in 200 and 400 CE respectively. After Francisco Pizarro founded Lima in 1535, the area became known for leisure, with its flower-filled parks and the beaches that line Miraflores' Costa Verde or Green Coast.

Close to Miraflores, San Isidro is the city's garden district. An olive grove was planted here in 1560, and still thrives today. In the 1920s, the establishment of a country club, golf club, and polo field helped make the area the preferred address of Lima's upper echelons of society, and it still is today.

Map: San Isidro / Miraflores, Lima

Grid references: G, H, J (columns) × 7, 8, 9, 10 (rows)

Labeled points of interest
- (1) Huaca Pucllana
- (1) Paz Soldán
- (2) [Playa Makah area]
- (4) Miraflores Clifftops
- (4) [Parque Naciones Unidas area]
- (6) Museo Amano
- (7) Huaca Huallamarca
- (8) Lugar de la Memoria (LUM)
- (9) Bosque El Olivar

Neighborhoods
- SAN ISIDRO
- MIRAFLORES

Parks and green spaces
- Lima Golf Club
- Parque Roosevelt
- Parque La Redonda
- Parque Naciones Unidas
- Parque Blume
- Parque Correo Elías
- Parque El Faro
- Parque Raimondi
- Bosque El Olivar

Beaches / Coast
- Playa Los Delfines
- Playa 3 Picos
- Waikiki
- Playa Makah
- Circuito de Playas

Pacific Ocean

Major avenues and streets
- Avenida Javier Prado Oeste
- Av. 2 de Mayo
- Salaverry
- Alberto del Campo
- Av. Basadre
- Aurelio Miro Quesada
- Miró Quesada
- Augusto Bolognesi
- José Dionisio Anchorena
- Baltazar La Torre
- Juan Dellepiani
- Francisco Valle Riesta
- Octavio Espinoza
- Coronel Pedro Portillo
- Pezet
- Beaudiez
- Romanet
- Harris
- Santa Teresita
- Santa Margarita
- Maurtua
- Av. Pérez Araníbar
- Av. Ejército
- Villar
- Av. Mendiburu
- Gral. Córdova
- La Mar
- 8 de Octubre
- Tudela y Varela
- Salazar
- Vandergehen
- Sucre
- Retiro
- Triana
- Quiñones
- Av. Pardo y Aliaga
- Av. Camino Real
- Av. República
- Paseo Padre Bolívar
- Conquistadores
- Cervantes
- Yerovi
- Cavenecia
- Av. Santa Cruz
- Carrión
- Herrera
- Borgoño
- Meiggs
- Habich
- Arica
- Espinar
- Larco Herrera
- Chiclayo
- Rosario
- Piura
- Aguirre
- Enrique Palacios
- 2 de Mayo
- Av. José Pardo
- Berlín
- León
- Iglesias
- Plaza Morales Barros
- Jose Galvez
- Francia
- Madrid
- Italia
- Tripoli
- Venecia
- Lavalle
- Bolognesi
- Grau
- Av. Comandante Espinar
- Recavarren
- Av. Aviación
- Porta
- Santa Luisa
- Tamayo
- Habana
- Santo Toribio
- Alzamora
- Rosario
- Naranjos
- Cipreses
- Álamos
- Palmeras
- Sauces
- Bañón
- Belaunde
- Robles
- Cedros
- Choquehuanca
- Andes
- Nogales
- Laureles
- Flores
- Granda
- Castaños
- Eucaliptos
- Porras-Osores
- Edison
- Prescott
- Marconi
- Carrión
- Laureles
- Manuel S. Ugarte Moscoso

Scale
0 meters — 600
0 yards — 600

N ↑

MIRAFLORES AND SAN ISIDRO

Must See
1. Huaca Pucllana

Experience More
2. Parque Kennedy
3. Larcomar
4. Miraflores Clifftops
5. Casa Ricardo Palma
6. Museo Amano
7. Huaca Huallamarca
8. Lugar de la Memoria (LUM)
9. Bosque El Olivar

Eat
1. Astrid & Gastón
2. La Rosa Náutica
3. Mangos
4. La Mar
5. La Lucha Sanguchería

Stay
6. Westin Lima
7. Hostal El Patio
8. Lighthouse B&B

HUACA PUCLLANA

J8 Calle General Borgoño, block 8 01 617 71 48 9am–5pm Mon, 9am–9pm Wed–Sun

Right in the heart of the Miraflores district lie the ruins of the Huaca Pucllana, an adobe-brick pyramid thought to have served as both an administrative and ceremonial center for the Lima culture civilization. Several of the oldest mummies in Lima have been unearthed here, making it the most popular archaeological site in the city.

Huaca Pucllana was an important temple, constructed in the shape of a truncated pyramid in around 400 CE. While it was reserved for priests, the lower buildings and plazas at its base were open to all citizens.

It has been used by different civilizations over the centuries. After it was abandoned in 800 CE, likely due to the rise of new ideas and religions, the Wari occupation began. They destroyed much of the original architecture, turning it into a cemetery. After this culture collapsed around 1100 CE, the Ychsma arrived. They restored elements of the temple and used it as a cemetery and a spiritual place.

The museum contains artifacts uncovered since excavations began in 1967. Wari ceramics, many of which depict sea themes, and Ychsma pottery depicting women – potentially used as offerings in lieu of human sacrifices – are on display.

Did You Know?

Small handmade adobe bricks were arranged like books in shelves to build platforms for the main pyramid.

Must See

Highlights

Wari Textiles
▲ Wari fabrics were characterized by geometric and animal shapes. Wari textiles are among the most vibrant and finely woven in the world.

Ceramics
▲ The ceramics in the museum are mainly sea-themed. This two-headed shark was considered the bringer of life and death.

Wari Mummy
▲ The dead were buried in a sitting position, wrapped in elaborate bales of fabric and tied with rope. The oldest mummy found here is 1,300 years old.

Pyramid
▲ Religious rites and ceremonies were performed at the pyramid and plazas by the priests, who served as governors.

> **LIMA CULTURE RITUALS**
>
> Mannequins around the site *(pictured)* recreate ritual ceremonies that formed part of paying tribute to the gods. Religious rites were performed by the priests, and it was believed that breaking jars and sacrificing children and women helped maintain community cohesion. Many of the jars and ceremonial plazas were decorated with marine symbols, such as waves to symbolize movement, sea lions, and even two-headed sharks.

↑ Impressively arranged adobe bricks at Huaca Pucllana

EXPERIENCE MORE

2
Parque Kennedy

📍K9 📌Cnr of Av Benavides & Calle Schell, Miraflores

The shady, tree-lined Parque Kennedy and the adjoining Parque 7 de Junio offer a welcome escape from Lima's jostling crowds and lurching traffic. Its modern playground is a bonus for families. Local artists line the pedestrianized street in front of the Iglesia Virgen Milagrosa, proffering colorful canvases of Peru's landscapes and street scenes. Food vendors and shoeshiners ply their trade across the park.

The weekends are even more lively, with all kinds of entertainment. A small but colorful market springs up in the center of the park in the Rotonda de los Artesanos, selling a wide variety of Peruvian crafts, and the park's small amphitheater is transformed into a dance arena. Couples take to the floor, sashaying to everything from salsa beats and Andean pipes to Latin American pop.

3
Larcomar

📍K10 📌Av Malecón de la Reserva 610, Miraflores
🕐6am–10pm daily
🌐larcomar.com

Built in 2002, Larcomar is a shopping and entertainment mall, comprising three terraces carved into the Miraflores cliffs. It mainly hosts well-known international stores, but there are some boutiques with a more local flavor, too. The food scene comprises a fast-food court, various chain restaurants, smart bars, and independent restaurants – many with spectacular ocean views. There's also a 12-screen cinema and a theater, which regularly hosts live music events.

4
Miraflores Clifftops

📍J9 📌Malecón Cisneros & Malecón de la Reserva

The clifftops overlooking the Pacific Ocean form one of Lima's most popular outdoor destinations. The weekends are particularly crowded with picnickers, skaters, paragliders, ice-cream vendors, and rehearsing musicians and dancers. At the northern end, colorful flower beds in the shape of the Nazca Lines, the mysterious

Serpentine mosaic bench at the Parque del Amor on the Miraflores clifftops

Across the Puente Villena Rey bridge is the imposing *Intihuatana* sculpture by abstract artist Fernando de Szyszlo, celebrating the Incas' sacred stone *(p187)*. *Intihuatana* in Quechua translates as "hitching post of the sun."

5. Casa Ricardo Palma

📍 K8 📍 General Suárez 189, Miraflores 🔧 For renovation

Peruvian writer Ricardo Palma's witty historical anecdotes or *tradiciones* have won him a prominent place in Latin American literature. His love for writing and books was reflected in his efforts to rebuild Lima's National Library. He was director of the library from 1884 until his retirement in 1912. He is said to have recovered several books that had been removed by Chilean soldiers, which he found by chance in the possession of some street vendors.

Built at the beginning of the 20th century, the house where Palma spent his last years celebrates his life and works. Palma became such an institution in Lima that a pilgrimage to his home was deemed essential for connoisseurs of Latin American literature. His bookshelves were filled with Voltaire's works in particular. The writer's desk, favorite chair, manuscripts, letters, photographs, and even an X-ray of his hand, dating from 1899, have been preserved for posterity.

Visitors can explore the music room, study, and bedroom to get a glimpse of Palma's life. His binoculars and books are placed exactly where he left them.

"drawings" in the desert *(p140)*, dominate the view at the Parque Marïa Reiche. On summer Sundays, tango dancers gather in nearby Parque Grau on a paved area overlooking the sea to show off their skills.

Southward is the black-and-white striped La Marina lighthouse. The nearby skate park swarms with padded-up BMX bikers, boarders, and bladers on the weekends.

The pretty Parque del Amor, or Love Park, inaugurated on February 14, 1993, is devoted to the old Peruvian custom of courting in public gardens. In the center is a colossal sculpture of a kissing couple.

📷 **PICTURE PERFECT**
Sunset from the Miraflores Clifftops

Catch the sun setting from Parque Raimondi on the western edge of the Miraflores cliffs, where the sun slips beneath the sea horizon with the silhouettes of floating paragliders in the foreground.

EAT

Astrid & Gastón
Celebrity chefs Gastón Acurio and Astrid Gutsche blend contemporary and traditional Andean cuisine.

📍 J6 📍 Av Paz Soldán 290 🕐 1–3:30pm & 7–11pm Mon–Sat, noon–4pm Sun 🌐 astridygaston.com

Ⓢ Ⓢ Ⓢ

La Rosa Náutica
Enjoy great seafood on a charming pier.

📍 J10 📍 Espigón 4 🕐 Noon–9pm daily (to 11pm Mon–Sat) 🌐 larosanautica.com

Ⓢ Ⓢ Ⓢ

Mangos
Looking for brunch with a view? Bag a seat on the clifftop terrace here.

📍 K10 📍 Malecón de la Reserva 610 🕐 8:30am–midnight daily (to 1am Mon–Thu, to 2am Fri & Sat) 🌐 mangosperu.com

Ⓢ Ⓢ Ⓢ

La Mar
Arrive by noon at this seafood restaurant, or prepare to wait in line.

📍 H8 📍 Av La Mar 770 🕐 Noon–5pm daily 🌐 lamarcebicheria.com

Ⓢ Ⓢ Ⓢ

La Lucha Sanguchería
Fantastic, inventive sandwiches and crusty rolls. Wait in line for a table or opt for takeout.

📍 K9 📍 Diagonal 308 🕐 8am–10pm daily 🌐 lalucha.com.pe

Ⓢ Ⓢ Ⓢ

Ancient slopes of San Isidro's Huaca Huallamarca

⑥ Museo Amano

📍J8 🏛 Retiro 160, Miraflores ⏰10am–5pm Tue–Sun; Mon: by appt only 🌐museoamano.org

The house of Yoshirato Amano (1898–1982), and his collection of exhibits, was opened to the public in 1964 as the Museo Amano. A Japanese businessman turned archaeologist who settled in Peru, Amaro traveled the country in search of cultural artifacts, amassing what is one of the most comprehensive private collections of pre-Hispanic textiles and handicrafts in Lima.

The ceramics section has objects from the Kotosh, Moche, Chimú, Cupisnique, and Nazca cultures and charts the development of pottery in Peru through the ages. The exhibits are organized chronologically, illustrating the differences, and the advances made, between one culture and the next. They reveal how people in the north, such as the Moche, focused more on sculptural images, while those in the southern areas, the Nazca for example, used vibrant and vivid colors.

However, the section dedicated to pre-Hispanic textiles is what draws the crowds. Among the myriad items on display are beautiful woven pieces by the Chancay people, some of which resemble fine lacework, and an ancient Inca *quipu*, their unique system of recording events and keeping track of livestock with multicolored threads and knots.

Ceramic bottle with geometric patterns in the Museo Amano

⑦ Huaca Huallamarca

📍J6 🏛 Nicolás de Ribera 201, San Isidro 📞01 222 4124 ⏰10am–3pm Tue, Thu & Sat

Also known as the Sugar Loaf or Pan de Azúcar, the Huaca Huallamarca is a fully restored ancient adobe pyramid dating from 200 to 500 CE. In the Quechua language, *marca* denotes "region or town" and consequently *huallamarca* means the "place or residence of the Hualla people."

Experts believe it to be a ceremonial center. The floors show little sign of wear, indicating that it was used only by the religious elite.

The tombs uncovered in the *huaca* (shrine) show the changes in funerary practices from 300 CE up to the 15th century, when the center was finally abandoned. During the Early Intermediate Period (200–600 CE), bodies were laid on their backs on reed mattresses. Later, the dead were put in a fetal position and wrapped in fine fabrics. During the Middle Horizon (600–900 CE), burials became more

> **INSIDER TIP**
> **Catch Some Culture**
>
> In six branches across the city, the Instituto Cultural Peruano Norteamericano *(icpna.edu.pe)* organizes events and exhibitions of photography, painting, sculpture, and ceramics. One of the branches is a 30-minute walk south from the Bosque El Olivar.

elaborate and wrapped bodies had a mask of wood or painted fabric placed over the head.

Archaeologists have recovered farming tools, children's games, crockery, woven cotton, and sewing baskets from the tombs. The presence of the latter emphasizes the importance of women within these ancient communities.

Some of the mummies, as well as the artifacts found with them, are on display at the on-site museum. The ceremonial platform located on top of the *huaca* provides a vantage point for an excellent view of San Isidro.

⑧
Lugar de la Memoria (LUM)

◘ G7 ◘ Bajada San Martin 151, Miraflores ◘ 10am–5pm Tue-Sun ◘ lum.cultura.pe

This museum examines the 20 years of internal conflict instigated by the Sendero Luminoso (Shining Path) rebel group in the 1980s and 1990s that resulted in the deaths or disappearances of 70,000 Peruvians at the hands of both the rebels and the Peruvian military. The exhibition comprises a powerful collection of texts, photos, and videos of interviews with survivors (some with English subtitles), alongside multimedia exhibits from the Truth and Reconciliation Commission. It provides a vital, sobering insight into modern Peruvian history and the lasting effects of the conflict on the country's ongoing political tensions.

⑨
Bosque El Olivar

◘ J7 ◘ Av La República, San Isidro

Spread over a large area in central San Isidro, the beautiful Bosque El Olivar (Olive Grove) was declared a national monument in 1959. Antonio de Rivera, a former mayor of Lima, introduced the olive tree to Peru in 1560. Of the numerous saplings he brought from Seville, only three survived the journey, and he planted them here.

By 1730, Nicolás de Ribera, a descendant, expanded the grove to over 2,000 trees while building his hacienda – Los Condes de San Isidro. Today, the garden contains over 1,600 ancient olive trees, and over 200 other species. The grove is also home to around 25 species of birds. It's a perfect spot for picnicking under the trees during the day, or taking a leisurely stroll in the evening.

STAY

Westin Lima
High-rise hotel with contemporary decor, a luxury spa, an indoor pool, and a fine-dining restaurant.

◘ K6 ◘ Calle Las Begonias 450 ◘ westin.marriott.com

S/ S/ S/

Hostal El Patio
A welcoming, central B&B offering self-contained mini-suites, all set around a pretty terrace.

◘ K10 ◘ Diez Canseco 341 ◘ elpatio.pe

S/ S/ S/

Lighthouse B&B
Charming guesthouse in a safe residential district of Miraflores, within walking distance of all attractions.

◘ K9 ◘ Cesareo Chacaltana 162 ◘ 01 446 8397

S/ S/ S/

↑ Olive trees, some four centuries old, in the Bosque El Olivar

A SHORT WALK
MALECÓN DE MIRAFLORES

Distance 2 miles (3 km)
Time 45 minutes **Terrain** Easy, mostly flat **Nearest bus and coach station** Hostal Torreblanco

Clinging to the coastal edge of the city, the Malecón de Miraflores is a manicured, park-lined promenade showcasing Lima's greener side. Following the curve of the coastline, this clifftop walk connects palm- and sculpture-studded parks and fine sweeping views of the Pacific Ocean below. Popular among joggers, families, and those on a romantic stroll, this route is even more spectacular at sunset.

Locator Map
For more detail see p106

Parque Grau Miraflores, a leafy park named after Peru's most esteemed naval figure, often displays brilliant art exhibitions.

The striking Entre El Tiempo sculpture by Limeño artist José Tola in **Parque El Libro** has two faces: one watches the sunrise, the other the sunset.

The iconic, black-and-white striped **La Marina Lighthouse** started life at Punta Coles near Tacna, but was moved to its present location in 1973.

↑ The black-and-white striped La Marina lighthouse

Did You Know?

The Paddington Bear statue was designed by British comedian Stephen Fry and wears a Union Jack coat.

Victor Delfín's sculpture *El Beso* in the themed Parque del Amor, or Love Park

Known as the green belt of the city, **Parque Antonio Raimondi** has fine sea views and is the spot for watching paragliders leaping into the air.

Victor Delfín's El Beso, a sculpture of two lovers kissing, and Gaudí-inspired mosaics are among Lima's most emblematic art, found in **Parque del Amor** (p111).

Peruvian artist Fernando de Szyszlo's dramatic concrete sculpture **Intihuatana** represents an Inca stone thought to have been used for rituals or as a solar clock (p111).

The award-winning sculpture **El Amarre**, created in travertine marble by Limeña artist Sonia Prager, was accused of being "unintelligible" when installed in 1986.

Stop for a sweet or savory crepe at the **Beso Francés Crepería**, a coffee shack with sublime ocean views.

Honoring French priest St. Marcellin Champagnat, the **Parque San Marcelino Champagnat** overlooks a historic pier home to Lima's famed restaurant La Rosa Náutica.

The **Paddington Bear Statue** was a gift from the British embassy in July 2015.

Finish the walk by browsing the boutique stores of Lima's flashiest shopping center, **Larcomar** (p110).

Colorful buildings in bohemian Barranco

BARRANCO

Just a stone's throw from Miraflores, Barranco is located on the cliffs at the southern tip of Lima Bay. When the Spanish first arrived here in 1533, they encountered a community of Indigenous farmers and fisherfolk. The area was handed over to one of the companions of conquistador Francisco Pizarro, the leader of the Spanish invasion, and the local people were soon drawn into the colonizers' harsh *encomienda* labor system. It was a quiet, windmill-dappled hamlet until the 19th century, when Lima's elite moved in and began to build grand summer mansions, spurred on by the new fashion of bathing in the sea. Small communities of Europeans, mainly English, French, and Italians, settled here, adding their own stylistic traits to local architecture.

Barranco's most famous sights, the Bajada de los Baños footpath – a scenic walkway down to the beach – and the Puente de los Suspiros, or Bridge of Sighs, were constructed in the 1870s. During the 20th century, the district became a bohemian area, popular with Peruvian writers and artists. Today, the Parque Municipal and many of the area's cafés, restaurants, and bars retain a hint of the refined airs of days gone by.

BARRANCO

Experience
1. Museo de la Electricidad
2. La Ermita
3. Puente de los Suspiros
4. Bajada de los Baños
5. MATE – Museo Mario Testino
6. Museo de Arte Contemporáneo
7. Parque Municipal
8. Museo Pedro de Osma

Eat
1. Central
2. Isolina
3. El Muelle de Barranco

Drink
4. Invictus Taproom
5. Bodega Piselli
6. Del Carajo

MIRAFLORES AND SAN ISIDRO
p104

BARRANCO

Key locations:
- 6 Museo de Arte Contemporáneo
- Parque de los Héroes
- Parque de la Familia "Manuel Montero Bernales"
- 4 (Jirón Cajamarca / San Antonio area)
- 2 La Ermita
- 2 Puente de los Suspiros
- 3 Bajada de los Baños
- Museo Galería Arte
- 7 Parque Municipal
- 1 Museo de la Electricidad
- Parque Raimondi
- 5 MATE – Museo Mario Testino
- 8 Museo Pedro de Osma
- Unity Stadium
- San Pedro Cemetery
- Zona Agricultura

Playas:
- Playa Barranquito
- Playa Barranco
- Playa Los Yuyos
- Playa Sombrillas / Escuela aloja

0 meters 400
0 yards 400

N ↑

EXPERIENCE

① Museo de la Electricidad

📍 L12 📌 Av Pedro de Osma 105 📞 01 477 6577 🕘 9am–5pm daily

The charming restored tram outside the Museo de la Electricidad (Museum of Electricity) is the main draw at this museum. The tram was rebuilt from an abandoned car that was found in a city scrapyard. It bears the number 97 in honor of the year it was restored (1997), some 30 years after the last tram stopped running in Lima.

Photos and further details of Lima's trolley and tram system are found inside the museum. Lima's tram cars were built in the 1920s in Italy and operated in the center of the city, while larger carriages served Barranco.

Beyond electrically powered transport, exhibitions at the museum also cover the history of electricity both globally and locally. There are displays of a wide array of electrical appliances and machines that have been used by people of the area over the years, including an old Wurlitzer jukebox and vintage television, radio, and telephone models. The museum's interactive room is particularly popular with school groups.

② La Ermita

📍 L11 📌 Jirón Ermita 🚫 To the public

The Church of the Hermitage is a famous Barranco landmark, although one in desperate need of restoration. According to legend, a group of fishers, lost in a winter mist blanketing Lima's coast, prayed to be rescued. They rowed toward a glow that suddenly appeared in the distance and, once on land, they found only a wooden cross in the place from where the light had emanated. Believing that divine intervention had spared them, the fishers erected La Ermita on that spot.

In front of La Ermita is a statue commemorating Peruvian singer Chabuca Granda, most famous for her tribute to the Puente de los Suspiros. A pathway bordering the side of the church, built in 1988, leads past colorful houses and cafés to El Mirador Catalina Recavarren, a lookout point offering panoramic ocean views.

> **INSIDER TIP**
> **Barranco's Graffiti**
>
> To experience Barranco's art scene, stroll down Calle 28 de Julio, which is lined with murals. Many of the paintings offer political commentary, with several works by artist Jade Rivera *(p83)*. Check freewalking tourbarranco.com for guided tours.

> **BARRANCO, THE SEASIDE RESORT**
>
> The early 20th century saw Barranco transform from a simple seaside hideaway into the most popular summer address for aristocratic Peruvians and expatriates escaping Lima's heat. Its pier, built in 1906, has a huge restaurant with a dance floor that played host to the best orchestras of the day. Postcards from 1915 show women in extravagant hats and white dresses promenading on the pier, escorted by men in straw boaters and crisp, pressed suits. A funicular took patrician families from the clifftops to the beach. Windmills, used to draw water for the houses, dot the area.

Colorful and bustling Puente de los Suspiros

3
Puente de los Suspiros

L11 **Between calles Ayacucho and La Ermita**

The 19th-century "Bridge of Sighs," which survived the earthquake of 1940, is steeped in legend. It derived its name from the thwarted love of a beautiful girl who lived on the Bajada de los Baños. She fell in love with a lowly street sweeper, but her father forbade her to see the boy and she spent the rest of her days gazing out of the window hoping for a glimpse of him. People crossing the bridge used to hear her sighing for her lost love.

4
Bajada de los Baños

L12

The Bajada de los Baños, a pretty 19th-century walkway, slopes gently to the sea, connecting the streets of Ayacucho and La Ermita. Built to give Barranqueños access to the beach, the walkway starts below the Puente de los Suspiros and leads down to the sea in a combination of steps and sloping pathway. Bustling with locals at weekends, the path is bordered by small cafés and ice-cream shops, interspersed with crumbling buildings, colorful vegetation, and jewel-bright murals and graffiti. Closer to the sea, a viewing platform provides the perfect spot to watch the surfers bobbing like seals in the bay below.

During the late 19th and early 20th centuries, many upper-class Peruvian families built fancy country homes in Barranco. Wooden baths were built in 1876, and then rebuilt in 1906 following their destruction during the War of the Pacific *(p72)*. Unfortunately, the baths were razed in the 1960s to make way for a coastal road.

Today, most of these homes have been transformed into restaurants, cafés, and bars, but their balconies and carved ceilings are a reminder of their former grandeur.

← Bright paintwork of La Ermita, typical of the Barranco district

DRINK

Invictus Taproom
Set within a renovated mansion, this trendy bar offers a selection of craft beers on tap.

L11 **Av Pedro de Osma 215**
934 112 429

Bodega Piselli
Largely unchanged since 1915, this is a great spot for a quiet pisco sour among the locals.

L12 **28 de Julio 297**
01 252 6750

Del Carajo
A classic *peña*, with criolla dancing, performances from top Peruvian musicians, and inexpensive beer.

L10 **Jirón Catalino Miranda 158**
delcarajo.com.pe

EAT

Central
World-class tasting menus take inspiration from across Peru; reserve ahead.

📍L12 🏠Av Pedro de Osma 301 🕐12:45–1:45pm & 7–8:30pm Mon-Sat 🌐centralrestaurante.com.pe

S/ S/ S/

Isolina
Dishes draw on creole cooking at this shabby chic tavern.

📍L11 🏠Av Prolongación San Martín 101 🌐isolina.pe

S/ S/ S/

El Muelle de Barranco
Perfect for inexpensive seafood dining.

📍L11 🏠Av Alfonso Ugarte 225 📞01 252 8643

S/ S/ S/

5
MATE – Museo Mario Testino

📍L12 🏠Av Pedro de Osma 409 🕐10am-7pm Tue-Sat 🚫Public hols 🌐mate.pe/en

Lima-born Mario Testino, one of the most influential photographers in the world, founded this museum in 2012. Set in a 19th-century townhouse, MATE reflects the history of Barranco as the cultural hub of Lima. Its mission is to promote Peru's artists, their culture, and their heritage. MATE also showcases iconic works by Testino, including his popular *Alta Moda* series and portraits of Diana, Princess of Wales and other international celebrities.

Latin American art at the Museo de Arte Contemporáneo →

6
Museo de Arte Contemporáneo

📍L10 🏠Av Grau 1511 🕐10am-7pm Tue-Sun 🌐maclima.pe

This modern, glass-walled museum set within a public park houses a permanent collection of more than 120 contemporary paintings, sculptures, and installations by some of today's leading Peruvian and Latin American artists, including Fernando de Szyszlo, Ramiro Llona, Oswaldo Guayasamín, Sonia Praga, Lika Mutal, and José Tola. The museum also hosts temporary exhibitions and events, and has a research library. Visitors to the museum also have access to the gardens, where sculptures are displayed. The "Sundays in the MAC" program offers weekend art workshops and guided tours for children.

7
Parque Municipal

📍L12 🏠Av Grau

Inaugurated in February 1898, Barranco's Parque Municipal, with its wooden benches, towering palms, and colorful flower beds, is a favorite stop for locals, especially after Mass in the nearby Iglesia de la Santísima Cruz.

During the late afternoon, resident artists often display their canvases under the watchful gaze of the Carrara marble statue of *La Donaide* (Daughter of Venus). She floats over the waters of the central pool alongside two small angels, or *putti*. An exquisite Etruscan vase – Barberini's *Candelabro* – also in marble, sits nearby.

The striking Biblioteca Municipal, constructed between 1895 and 1899 and opened in 1922, dominates this popular park. The tower,

> **During the late afternoon at Parque Municipal, resident artists often display their canvases under the watchful gaze of the Carrara marble statue of *La Donaide*.**

> **HIDDEN GEM**
> **Inside Víctor Delfín's House**
>
> A 30-minute tour of Víctor Delfín's house and studio at Jirón Domeyer 366 – just a five-minute walk from the Parque Municipal – grants insight into the life and work of one of Peru's most celebrated artists, who is often in residence. Visits by appointment only (victordelfin.com).

which was added in 1911, displays the Barranco crest and a clock. Designated a "historic monument of exceptional worth" by Peru's Ministry of Culture, the Biblioteca organizes regular lectures in Spanish, on diverse topics ranging from Peruvian identity and gastronomy to art and theater.

On weekends, a food market takes over the plaza opposite the park, where a number of Peruvian cooks show off their baking, roasting, frying, and selling skills.

Paintings from the Cusco School, melding Spanish Baroque with Andean imagery, offer fascinating examples of subversion, such as the Virgin Mary portrayed with dark Andean hair. Outstanding religious sculptures, many from the Lima School, also line its walls. Of particular interest are the bleeding head of John the Baptist and Adam and Eve reaching for the apple. The second building, set among palm trees, geranium beds, and marble sculptures in the back garden, was originally the dining room. It now houses photographs and dinnerware belonging to the Osma family. A third building is home to an impressive collection of silverware.

8

Museo Pedro de Osma

L12 **Av Pedro de Osma 423** **10am–6pm Tue–Sun** **museopedrodeosma.org**

This sugar-white structure is one of Barranco's oldest summer homes, built in the early 20th century for the Osma family. The main building houses a fine collection of colonial art and furniture and pre-Hispanic and colonial works and objects from the southern Andes.

BOHEMIAN BARRANCO

Barranco has long been a popular spot with artists and intellectuals. From 1913 through the 1950s, it saw memorable partying, especially during Carnaval. One of Peru's most beloved singers, Chabuca Granda *(right)*, lived here, praising it thus: "The founder of Barranco was none other than God." Today, it is Lima's evening haunt, with music spilling out of hole-in-the-wall bars, posh nightclubs, and busy *peñas*. Gian Marco, local pop icon and popular Latin music composer, honed his skills here with bar gigs, and after a stint abroad returned to live in his favorite *barrio* (district). While writer Mario Vargas Llosa's seafront house has been replaced by an apartment block, other homes remain, such as that of sculptor and artist Víctor Delfín.

A SHORT WALK
BARRANCO

Distance 1.2 miles (2 km) **Time** 25 minutes
Nearest bus station Estadio Unión

While wandering along the stately Avenida Sáenz Peña, dotted with mansions and leafy side streets, it is easy to visualize Barranco's previous life as an aristocrats' playground. Some of these old buildings, however, are crumbling; in response, Barranco is promoting private investment as a means of restoring the neighborhood's beauty. Colorfully painted facades along Calle Junín, Avenida Grau, and Bajada de los Baños merge the past with the present.

*The **Museo Jade Rivera** showcases the life and works of Peru's most famous graffiti artist and muralist. A gift shop on site sells prints of some of his best-known works.*

Avenida Sáenz Peña *is lined with graceful old mansions of sepia, rose, ochre, or lapis lazuli painted facades that recall a bygone era.*

*The exhibits at **80m2 Livia Benavides** are focused on Peruvian art.*

*The present-day bajada (slope) corresponds with the path of a stream once followed by fishers down to the ocean. Over time it has morphed into **Bajada de los Baños**, a lane of summer homes and restaurants (p121).*

*The devastating 1940 earthquake considerably damaged **La Ermita** church (p120); the disintegrating roof is a reminder of the tremor's ferocity.*

↑ Barranco's famous bridge, Puente de los Suspiros, lit up in the evening

↑ Distinctive yellow facade of La Ermita church, surrounded by abundant flora

Locator Map
For more detail see p118

PUNA Tienda Galería, *a small arts and crafts store and gift emporium, sells local art and plenty of other treasures.*

Did You Know?

Legend states La Ermita was built where a wooden cross guided lost fishers at sea.

Following the destruction of La Hermita in 1940, prominent local parishioners asked the Archbishop of Lima to authorize the building of a new parish church in the municipal plaza. The first stone of the **Iglesia Santisima Cruz** *was laid in 1944 and the church was finally consecrated in 1963.*

The **Puente de los Suspiros** *(p121), a symbol of romantic Barranco, was remodeled in 1921. Legend has it that anyone who crosses this bridge for the first time while holding their breath will be granted their wish.*

The **Biblioteca Municipal** *(Municipal Library) opened in 1922 and functioned as Barranco Town Hall for many years. The columns at the entrance and along the facade are repeated on each side of the elongated windows.*

Must See

1. Museo Larco

Experience More

2. Fortaleza del Real Felipe
3. Museo Naval del Perú
4. Museo de Sitio Submarino Abtao
5. Callao's Islands
6. Museo Nacional de Arqueología, Antropología e Historia del Perú
7. Museo de Oro del Perú
8. Pantanos de Villa
9. Pachacámac
10. Museo del Automóvil Colección Nicolini

BEYOND THE CENTER

Beyond the key areas of Central Lima, Miraflores, and Barranco, the sights of interest are somewhat dispersed. The village-like suburb of Pueblo Libre, to the south of Central Lima, is home to the world-famous Museo Larco that chronicles Peru's intriguing past. Far away from the confines of the city is the archaeological site of Pachacámac, once inhabited by both Wari and Inca cultures. Stately houses in the nearby district of La Punta in Callao, are a reminder of the area's popularity with Lima's aristocracy from the 19th century to the 1940s.

MUSEO LARCO

Av Bolívar 1515, Pueblo Libre ◷ **9am–7pm daily** ⓦ **museolarco.org**

A grand mansion built on a ceremonial site dating back to the 7th century CE provides a more than fitting home for this treasure trove of ancient history. Founded in 1926, Museo Larco houses the largest private collection of Peruvian pre-Columbian artifacts (a staggering 45,000 pieces), amassed by sugar baron and archaeologist Rafael Larco Hoyle.

The Main Collection

The Museo Larco provides an excellent chronological and geographical overview of Peru's early cultures, including the Chimú, Mochica, Paracas, Nazca, and Wari. Fascinating and beautifully crafted artifacts from these ancient peoples are displayed in illuminated cases and informatively curated throughout the museum. Highlights of the collection include a Mochica portrait vessel – which was Rafael Larco's first museum piece, given to him by his father – and a gleaming collection of Chimú funeral attire that includes the world's only known complete gold costume, found at the Chan Chan archaeological site (p232).

Mochica Ceramics

In a gallery separate from the main house, visitors can also see erotic ceramics made by the ancient Moche over 1,500 years ago. Some of the pieces symbolize the importance of fertility and procreation (among people, deities, or animals) while others graphically depict sexual pleasure.

← An ornament created by the Moche using shell, sodalite, and turquoise

Checking out the artifacts on show at the Museo Larco ↑

Must See

EAT

Café del Museo Larco
This high-end restaurant in the grounds of the Museo Larco has seating on a glorious floral terrace. It's the perfect place to treat yourself after exploring the museum.

🏠 Av Bolívar 1515, Pueblo Libre
🌐 museolarco.org

💲💲💲

1. The peaceful patio at Museo Larco, ideal for a quiet afternoon stroll.

2. A pre-Columbian statue depicting a loving couple, a part of the Mochica Ceramics collection.

3. Beautiful exterior of the museum.

RAFAEL LARCO HOYLE

Born in 1901 on a sugar plantation in Trujillo, Rafael Larco Hoyle rose to be one of Peru's most noted businessmen, as well as a renowned archaeologist; his family hacienda broke production records when he mechanized it after studying in the USA. He had a passion for collecting Peru's ancient artifacts – ceramics, metalwork, and textiles – exploring and excavating sites in northern Peru in search of the rarest and finest pieces. He once commandeered the largest swimming pool on the hacienda to wash salt from a newly acquired 8,000-piece collection.

EXPERIENCE

❷
Fortaleza del Real Felipe

🏛 Plazuela de la Independencia, Callao
📞 01 429 0532 🕘 9am-4pm daily (nighttime visits on Fri & Sat; reservations required) 🚫 Public hols

The stone-walled Royal Felipe Fort is one of the largest forts built by the Spanish in the 18th century. Of interest to both the visitor and the historian, it was designed by Frenchman Luis Gaudin. The fort was named in honor of Felipe V, the first Bourbon king of Spain, who died in 1746.

The austere, pentagon-shaped fort was intended to defend against pirate attacks. During the 19th century, Callao, where the fort stands, was considered to be the most protected port on the west coast of South America. Real Felipe had been "war-ready" since colonial times, and had repelled many attacks. The fort had been besieged five times but never conquered. It also played a pivotal role in Peru's War of Independence (p71), acting as the first line of defense.

Covering more than 84,000 sq yards (70,000 sq m), the fort contains brass and iron cannons, military tanks, the Governor's House, and Towers of the King and Queen, as well as the Museo del Ejército (Military Museum), with its impressive collection of weapons, documents, military uniforms, and relics.

❸
Museo Naval del Perú

🏛 Av Jorge Chávez 123, Callao 📞 01 429 4793
🕘 9am-4pm Tue-Sun

The Naval Museum, near the Fortaleza del Real Felipe, is a key site for seafaring history buffs. Instigated by Capitán de Navío Julio J. Elías Murguía, a Peruvian naval figure, the museum has an important collection of historical naval documents, oil paintings, uniforms, and relics from the 1879–83 War of the Pacific (p72). Also included are many personal objects of those involved in the conflict, photographs, weapons, and navigational instruments.

Prized items are the belongings of one of Peru's most famous military figures, Admiral Miguel Grau, who died in the Battle of Angamos. Also known as the Caballero de los Mares (Gentleman of the Seas), his letters, navigational charts, and medals, as well as a sarcophagus containing a fragment of his shinbone, his only remains found after the battle, are displayed here. One room is devoted entirely to model ships, showcasing vessels from different eras and several other countries.

↑ Remnants of the military past at the Fortaleza del Real Felipe, Callao

❹
Museo de Sitio Submarino Abtao

🏛 Jorge Chávez 120-A, Callao 🕘 9:30am-4:30pm Tue-Sun 🌐 museosub marinoabtao.com

A short walk away from Museo Naval del Perú and moored against the quayside lies a unique museum housed in a Sierra Class submarine which was built at the Electric Boat Company shipyard in the United States. It was launched in New London, Connecticut, in 1953 as the BAP *Tiburón*.

The submarine was one of four commissioned by the Peruvian Navy, and was rechristened later as the BAP *Abtao* in commemoration of the Battle of Abtao, off the coast of Chile in 1866. The submarine carried a crew of 40 and was in service for 48 years, until 2001.

An interactive tour on board explores the sections of the vessel – the torpedo compartments with bunk beds and lockers, the engine room, the command center, ammunition storage, and radio

Isla El Frontón, a former penal colony, off the coast of Callao

room. Visitors can operate the periscope and drive the 5-inch gun on the deck.

A light and sound show enabling visitors to experience underwater submarine combat marks the end of the tour.

5
Callao's Islands

🚍 **Plaza Grau**

Several islands lie off the coast of Callao, with Isla San Lorenzo being the largest in Peru. Due to a lack of fresh water, the island was not colonized, but over 3,000 pre-Hispanic tombs reveal its ritual significance. The island also contains graves of pirates, and a naval cemetery from the War of the Pacific. Today, it serves as a naval base and is off-limits to tourists, but tour boats skirt along the coastline, offering glimpses of the resident Humboldt penguins.

In the shadow of San Lorenzo is Isla El Frontón. Nicknamed the Island of Death, it once served as a penal colony for criminals and political prisoners. It was shut down after a series of riots in 1986, which left 118 inmates (mainly members of the Shining Path; *p200*) dead. Today, the crumbling prison ruins can be visited on guided tours.

Further from the mainland, the rocky Palomino Islets are home to an array of seabirds, including Inca terns, pelicans, gulls, boobies, and cormorants. The star attraction is the 8,000-strong colony of sea lions, who will playfully swim around tour boats – wetsuits are also provided for those keen to get in the water.

Boat trips to the islands depart from Callao's jetty at Plaza Grau in the mid-morning hours, returning to the jetty in the afternoon.

6
Museo Nacional de Arqueología, Antropología e Historia del Perú

📍 **Plaza Bolivar, cnr of San Martín & Vivanco, Pueblo Libre** 🕒 **For renovation** 🌐 **mnaahp.cultura.pe**

This comprehensive collection of Peruvian artifacts charts the country's history from the pre-Hispanic Paracas, Nazca, Wari, and Inca periods, to colonial and republican times. It showcases around 70,000 ceramics and contains Peru's most important collection of ancient human remains. It also features a series of portraits of the viceroys from the 18th and 19th centuries.

The museum is home to the Quinta del Virrey Pezuela, an old mansion used by liberators such as José de San Martín (1821–22) and Símon Bolívar (1823–26) during the Peruvian War of Independence.

Both the museum and mansion are closed for renovation until at least 2029.

> **In the shadow of Isla San Lorenzo is Isla El Frontón. Nicknamed the Island of Death, it once served as a penal colony for criminals and political prisoners.**

BEACHES IN AND AROUND LIMA

With more than 1,156 miles (1,860 km) of shoreline, Peruvians have long revered the Pacific Ocean, as testified by friezes found at 2,000-year-old archaeological complexes along the coast. Come December, when Lima's grey haze finally lifts, Limeños head south on weekends. By January, most city-dwellers move for the summer to one of the string of beaches stretching down the coast. Here, golden sands, headlands, and coves are plentiful, providing ample opportunity for surfing and swimming.

The beaches near the bustling resort town of Punta Hermosa offer consistent waves, making this Lima's top surfing destination. Punta Rocas, with its world-class exposed reef break, is also a draw; this bay hosts international surfing competitions. San Bartolo is a popular beach, with clear water and some excellent seafood restaurants, but for sun-seeking Limeños, the pick of the seaside towns is the traditional fishing village of Pucusana. Rent a boat here for a chance to see a colony of basking sea lions.

7 Museo de Oro del Perú

Alonso de Molina 1100, Monterrico-Surco
10:30am–6pm daily
Jan 1, May 1, Jul 28 & Dec 25   museoperu.com.pe

Miguel Mujica Gallo's massive private Gold Museum displays numerous ceremonial knives and vases studded with turquoise. Ornate funerary masks, crowns, helmets, figurines, earrings, necklaces, an impressive gold ceremonial bag, and a tunic appliquéd with gold are also on view.

Labeling on the exhibits, unfortunately, is poor, with inadequate explanation in Spanish and almost none in English, making an audio guide essential.

The building's upper floor is set aside for Armas del Mundo (Arms of the World), a vast collection of ancient firearms and military paraphernalia. On view is an 1812 sword of Russian Tsar Alexander I, and the pistol that belonged to Chilean President Salvador Allende.

In 2001, the museum was rocked by scandal, with the National Institute of Culture and the Tourism Protection Bureau declaring that almost all its estimated 7,000 pieces were replicas. However, the owners claim to have only genuine gold pieces on display now.

← A gold funerary mask adorned with pendants at the Museo de Oro del Perú

8 Pantanos de Villa

Av Hernando LaValle s/n, Chorillos   From Lima
6:30am–6:30pm daily
pantanosdevilla.pe

This wetland area, located 11 miles (18 km) south of Lima, is one of the main coastal refuges for more than 210 bird species, including the majestic great egret. With its *totora* reed-lined pools and seven beautiful lagoons, Pantanos de Villa is Lima's last remaining natural reserve. There are signposted trails and lookout towers for bird-lovers here.

Outside the birding hours of dawn and dusk, the area is open to visitors who fancy kayaking round the reed beds.

9

Pachacámac

📍 **Pan-American Hwy South, KM31.5, Lurín** 🕐 **9am–5pm Tue–Sat, 9am–4pm Sun** 🌐 **pachacamac.cultura.pe**

Dating from 200 CE, this complex of adobe pyramids rising out of the Lurín Valley was a key pilgrimage center on Peru's central coast, and home to a much-venerated oracle. It flourished through the centuries and pilgrims traveled great distances to pay homage to the god Pachacámac (He who Enlivens the Universe and Everything).

Pachacámac was expanded by the Wari and their designs can be seen on the ceramics and textiles found here. However, most of the compounds and pyramids date from after their downfall.

When the last Inca king, Atahualpa, was imprisoned by Pizarro, he complained that the oracle had falsely predicted his victory. His account of gold at the site led soldiers there but they were disappointed by the "ugly" idol they found instead.

The Incas built five separate complexes, including the Templo del Sol (Temple of the Sun) and the Palacio de Las Mamaconas (House of the Chosen Women), which has stonework on its entrance gate, a rarity on the coast.

The on-site museum houses a collection of pre-Hispanic relics, including Paracas textiles, ceramics, and a two-faced image of Pachacámac.

10

Museo del Automóvil Colección Nicolini

📍 **Av La Molina** 🕐 **10am–7pm daily** 🌐 **museodeautosnicolini.com**

Packed into a warehouse on the eastern outskirts of the city, this museum takes visitors on a virtual road trip through the 20th century with its collection of 120 beautifully polished vintage cars. Lovingly restored by the owner, Jorge Nicolini, the cars now comprise the largest collection of antique vehicles in Peru.

A Lincoln 1925, which was discovered being used as a taxi, was the first vehicle acquired by Nicolini in 1962. The oldest in the collection is a 1901 French-made Boyer, while other notable cars include a 1966 Corvette Stingray, number 214 of only 525 ever manufactured, and a 1903 Clement.

> **Did You Know?**
>
> Some say the women of Pachacámac hid some of the Inca gold so cleverly that it is still to be discovered.

← Exterior of the on-site museum at Pachacámac

EXPERIENCE PERU

Traditional dancing in Cusco town

| The Southern Coast 136

| Arequipa, Canyons, and
Lake Titicaca 150

| Cusco and the Sacred Valley 170

| Central Sierra 196

| Cordillera Blanca 206

| The Northern Desert 222

| The Northern Highlands 236

| The Amazon Basin 248

Sand dunes stretching into the distance

THE SOUTHERN COAST

Remains uncovered in this dry tract reveal a fascinating blend of cultures, dating back at least 5,000 years. The Paracas civilization fashioned textiles in 300 BCE with an artistry that still resonates today. The Nazca people created their mysterious giant drawings in the desert some 2,000 years ago, and the purpose of these enormous geoglyphs puzzles experts to this day. The aqueducts they built remain in use, and the ceramics they produced are among the finest of the pre-Columbian era. Despite the aridity of the land, agriculture thrives here thanks to the centuries-old systems of irrigation that use underground water supplies. The Spanish first introduced grape stocks in the 1550s and such was the success that the district around Ica is now Peru's wine basin and home to the national drink, pisco. The region also played an instrumental trading role in the 19th century due to its island deposits of *guano* (bird droppings), then a sought-after fertilizer.

THE SOUTHERN COAST

Must Sees
1. Nazca Lines
2. Reserva Nacional de Paracas

Experience More
3. Islas Ballestas
4. El Chaco (Paracas)
5. Ica
6. Tambo Colorado
7. Nazca
8. Cahuachi
9. Cementerio de Chauchilla
10. Baños Termales de Putina
11. Tarata
12. Petroglifos de Miculla
13. Tacna

NAZCA LINES

◨ E6 ◷ 12 miles (20 km) N of Nazca, Pan-American Hwy South, KM420 ✈ In Nazca ℹ Nazca Municipalidad (Town Hall); 056 522 418

Dispersed over the high desert plateau between the towns of Nazca and Palpa, this collection of geoglyphs comprises more than 70 human figures and stylized animals, and 10,000 lines. First noticed from the air in 1927, these enigmatic ancient lines remain one of the world's greatest archaeological mysteries.

It almost never rains on the Peruvian coast, which is why the remarkable Nazca Lines have survived so many centuries, preserving the secrets of an ancient culture. Etched into the plains between 500 BCE and 500 CE, they were declared a UNESCO World Heritage Site in 1994. German mathematician and astronomer Maria Reiche began studying the Nazca Lines in the 1940s and devoted her life to uncovering their mysteries. She believed the lines were created by tying a chord to an axis, just as a compass is used to draw a circle. Debate continues about their original purpose, with theories including a giant astronomical calendar, ceremonial center, or alien landing strip.

> **HIDDEN GEM**
> **Palpa Lines**
>
> Etched on the desert by the Paracas culture 1,000 years before the Nazca Lines, these lines are just as puzzling. Found around a 30-minute drive from Nazca, they can be viewed from the platforms at Palpa.

Must See

Highlights

Whale
△ The first geoglyph to be discovered, it probably depicts a killer whale (or orca). The Nazca were a coastal culture, and here they favor the largest creature of the ocean.

Spider
△ The spider is identified as being both a symbol of rain and fertility, and a representation of the soothsayers, who used these creatures to predict the future.

Monkey
△ Regarded as a divine being, the monkey also appears on Nazca ceramics. The geoglyph has only nine fingers and Reiche suggested it may have been made to mark the equinoxes.

Hummingbird
△ Measuring 315 ft by 217 ft (96 m by 66 m), this is one of the best-known geoglyphs. The Nazca believed hummingbirds were messengers between men and condors, which they considered to be gods.

VIEWING THE LINES

You can admire the lines from the viewing platform at KM420 *(pictured)*, or visit one of the cheaper viewing platforms, where on-site guides provide brief details in Spanish. Another way to see the lines is from one of the three- to nine-seater planes flying out of Nazca airport. Prices start from around US$90 for a 35-minute flight, but it will be US$240 if you want to include the Palpa Lines. Aero Nasca *(aeronasca.com)* is a reputable air carrier.

↑ The geometric patterns of the enigmatic Nazca Lines, as seen from above

RESERVA NACIONAL DE PARACAS

D6 **177 miles (285 km) S of Lima** **From Pisco** **956 750 765** **9am–4pm daily**

The desert meets the sea at Peru's largest stretch of protected coastline, where towering cliffs border beaches swarming with wildlife. A cycle circuit is the best way to take in the reserve's key sites, including the impressive El Candelabro geoglyph and the Paracas Necropolis burial ground.

The country's first designated national reserve provides a habitat for more than 1,800 species of plants and animals. Birdlife is particularly rich, and here visitors can find flamingos, Humboldt penguins, pelicans, and terns. Occasionally, condors can be seen overhead, along with red-headed turkey vultures.

The Islas San Gallán and La Vieja, lying just off the coast, are the only places for the endangered *potoyunco* (Peruvian diving petrel) to reproduce in Peru.

Touring the Reserve

A morning boat trip to the nearby Islas Ballestas (p144), part of the neighboring marine reserve, is normally combined with an afternoon in the reserve, although renting a bike, e-bike, or quad grants greater freedom for exploring the latter. At the reserve, an 18-mile (30-km) biking circuit starts at a viewpoint for the rock formation La Catedral and continues south to Playa Roja, a curiously red-sand beach formed from particles of granodiorite rock. Nearby, the restaurants of Lagunillas serve up fresh seafood. Heading north, the Museo de Sitio Julio C. Tello displays textiles, ceramics, and skulls from the Paracas culture (700 BCE). Not far from here is El Candelabro, a 595-ft (180-m) geoglyph stamped into the hillside. In the surrounding waters, also a part of the reserve, marine mammals abound, including sea lions, dolphins, and the endangered marine otter.

Must See

Did You Know?

Flamingos found here inspired the colors of the Peruvian flag after Liberator San Martín visited the bay.

TOP 3 PLACES TO SPOT WILDLIFE

Punta Arquillo
9 miles (15 km) SW of park entrance
This cliff lookout is perfect for spotting fur seals and the rarer marine otter.

Bahía de Paracas
Behind the Museo de Sitio Julio C. Tello
The shoreline behind the museum is great for spying birds like flamingos, gulls, and heron from June to November.

Lagunillas
5.5 miles (9 km) SW of park entrance
Keep an eye out for South American sea lions and fur seals in the waves in the bay.

← Hikers exploring the vast golden stretch of the Reserva Nacional de Paracas

1 Exterior of the Museo de Sitio Julio C. Tello, which displays artifacts from the Paracas culture.

2 The three-pronged El Candelabro is thought to have been a navigational aid or a Nazca ritual symbol. It is best appreciated from the water.

3 Beautiful brown pelicans and guanay cormorants regularly inhabit the rocks at the reserve.

EXPERIENCE MORE

3
Islas Ballestas

D6 ◻162 miles (261 km) S of Lima ◻From El Chaco

The Ballestas Islands are among the most popular draws on the southern coast. The arches and caves of these islets shelter more than 160 species of marine birds, including Humboldt penguins, boobies, and pelicans, as well as immense numbers of sea lions. Dolphins, whales, and sea turtles sometimes appear in the surrounding waters, too. Old, rusted factory remains on the islands are a throwback to the 19th century when *guano* (mineral-rich bird droppings) was an important fertilizer and provided a vital source of revenue for the country.

It is possible to take a boat tour around the islands, but visitors are not allowed to disembark. On the way, look out for El Candelabro de Paracas *(p142)*, a 595-ft (180-m) geoglyph within the Reserva Nacional de Paracas *(p142)*, that is only fully visible on the way to and from the islands. Some claim it is a pirate's sign.

> **INSIDER TIP**
> **Watch the Birdie**
>
> Boats to the Islas Ballestas are uncovered, so take a hat with a visor or wide brim. *Guano* harvesting may have ceased here, but no one has told the avian inhabitants, and "bird-bombings" have disrupted many a perfectly aligned photo.

4
El Chaco (Paracas)

D6 ◻158 miles (254 km) S of Lima ◻From Lima ℹ iPerú Av los Libertadores; 980 894 433; 8am-12:30pm & 1:30-5pm Wed-Sun

A former seaside getaway for Lima's well-heeled, El Chaco, also known as Paracas, is still a favorite among vacationing Peruvians. Exclusive harborside hotels with tempting swimming pools line the shores of the pelican-studded harbor, and a stroll along the promenade at sunset is an excellent way of soaking up the town's mellow atmosphere.

It's a nicer place to stay than neighboring Pisco, although pollution from nearby fishmeal factories means swimming in the bay is not recommended. However, kayaking and windsurfing are popular water activities, as are the boat trips to the Islas Ballestas, which generally leave at 9am and 10am.

5
Ica

D6 ◻192 miles (310 km) S of Lima ✈Charter services from Lima ◻From Lima ℹ Dircetur Av Grau; 056 238 710 (ext 29); 8am-12:30pm & 2-4:30pm Mon-Fri

The Paracas and Chincha cultures inhabited this area long before the Inca settled

> **Did You Know?**
>
> El Chaco is where General San Martín's army made landfall in 1820 to liberate Peru from the Spanish.

Adobe walls of Tambo Colorado, once colored with bright pigments

here in the 14th century. Later in 1563, the Spanish arrived and established their own settlement here, naming it Villa de Valverde. The village was then renamed in 1640, and is now Peru's premier wine center, with vineyards dating back to the 16th century. Its Vendimia (grape harvest festival) takes place in the first two weeks of March, and pisco-soaked raisins sometimes feature in *tejas*, Ica's delicious traditional confectionery.

Known as the "city of eternal sun" due to its dry weather, Ica was badly affected by the 2007 earthquake, Peru's worst since 1974. A chapel in the Neo-Classical Sanctuario del Señor del Luren collapsed during evening Mass, killing several people and injuring dozens. While over 2,800 pre-Hispanic artifacts in museums across the Ica region also suffered extensive damage, Ica's Museo Regional Adolfo Bermúdez Jenkins escaped virtually unscathed. It houses an interesting collection of Paracas, Nazca, Ica, Wari, and Inca artifacts, including mummies and skulls that show evidence of ancient surgical techniques.

The oasis of Huacachina, a green lagoon attractively situated amid towering dunes, is just 3 miles (5 km) from Ica. The water is not clean enough for swimming (although you can rent a paddleboat). However, most visitors come to sandboard or ride the dunes.

↑ Boats bobbing in El Chaco harbor, where trips depart for Islas Ballestas

Tambo Colorado

D6 Los Libertadores Hwy, opposite Pan-American Hwy South, KM229 To Humay from Pisco via Los Libertadores; stop at KM39 10am–5pm daily

Formerly a significant administrative center of the Inca, Tambo Colorado sits at the base of steep foothills in the Pisco river valley, and was home to soldiers and the upper echelons of the Inca Empire. It was a connecting point on the Inca road joining Ayacucho with the coast. It is thought that the site was the summer residence of Pachacútec, the ninth Inca. Tambo Colorado is one of the best-preserved adobe ruins in Peru. Niches in the outer walls bear traces of the red and yellow pigment used to decorate them, and alcoves are adorned with carvings of human figures.

STAY

DM Hotel Nazca
Rooms match the colonial ambience of this hotel. A sunny garden with a large pool is perfect for lazy days, and there's also a brilliant planetarium.

E6 Jirón Bolognesi 147, Nazca
056 522 293

Hotel Viñas Queirolo
Utter luxury in the Queirolo vineyard with stylish balcony suites, a magnificent pool, tennis courts, and a gourmet restaurant.

D6 Carretera San José de los Molinos Km 11, Ica hotelvinas queirolo.com

---

Paracas Sunset Hotel
An affordable choice with a pool ringed by sun loungers and flowering plants.

D6 Av Los Libertadores, Paracas paracassunset.com

EAT

Tambo de Tacama
A spellbinding setting – the pink hacienda of the Tacama vineyard – for gourmet Peruvian dishes. Grab a spot on the patio for traditional dance performances on weekends.

🅐 D6 🅐 Calle Nicanor León 140. Urb. Sr. de Luren, Ica
🅦 tambodetacama.com

⑤⑤⑤

La Olla de Juanita
Enjoy rustic criollo specialties, such as *papa a la huancaina* (potatoes with a spicy sauce) and *chicharrón de cerdo* (pork crackling with sweet potato and salad), on a vine-lined terrace within the Tres Esquinas pisco *bodega*.

🅐 D6 🅐 Fundo Tres Esquinas, Ica
🅦 laolladejuanita.com

⑤⑤⑤

Los Angeles
A no-frills, great-value restaurant offering tasty criollo-style food and a wide variety of vegetarian dishes. The owner is fluent in English and French.

🅐 E6 🅐 Bolognesi 266, Nazca 📞 51 956 345 151

⑤⑤⑤

La Casa Rustika
Friendly, with a good range of international and Peruvian dishes, including a renowned beef lasagna.

🅐 E6 🅐 Bolognesi 372, Nazca 📞 998 996 754

⑤⑤⑤

⑦
Nazca

🅐 E6 🅐 285 miles (460 km) S of Lima 🚌 For Nazca Lines 🚌 From Lima or Ica

The discovery of the Nazca Lines *(p140)* put the town of Nazca on the map, and that is the main reason most people visit the area. The **Museo Antonini**, however, also makes a worthwhile stop. It displays many of the finds from the nearby Cahuachi site. The collection gives an insight into all aspects of Nazca society, and includes mummies and distorted heads – the Nazca wrapped the heads of their newborns in leather or wood bands.

On the other side of town, the Planetarium inside the DM Hotel Nazca *(p145)* has intriguing evening talks on the theories behind how and why the Nazca Lines were carved into the desert.

Another important archaeological site is the Acueducto de Cantalloc. The 35 spiraling aqueducts form part of a sophisticated system of irrigation, originally built by the Nazca, but still used by local farmers today.

Some 56 miles (90 km) east on the road to Cusco, the altiplano grasslands of the **Reserva Nacional Pampa Galeras Barbara D'Achille** is home to herds of vicuñas, the rarer relative of the llama.

Did You Know?
The world's tallest sand dune, Cerro Blanco, lies near Nazca. Even sandboarding down it takes four minutes.

→ Adobe pyramid at Cahuachi, a huge ceremonial center of the Nazca culture

Museo Antonini
🅐 Av de la Cultura 600
🕘 9am-7pm daily 🅦 museo antonini.org

Reserva Nacional Pampa Galeras Barbara D'Achille
🅐 Nazca-Cusco Rd KM 89
🚌 From Nazca 📞 056 522770
🕘 8am-5pm daily

⑧
Cahuachi

🅐 E6 🅐 11 miles (17 km) NE of Nazca 🕘 8am-5pm daily

Cahuachi, an enormous Nazca ceremonial center, reached its zenith more than 2,000 years ago. It is dominated by a 100-ft- (30-m-) high central pyramid and plaza. Forty other pyramids were sculpted from the landscape with massive mud-brick adobe walls applied over them. Some 5,000 tombs have been identified but, sadly, Cahuachi has suffered from looting.

Italian archaeologist Giuseppe Orefici has been excavating the site for decades and has concluded it was home to priests who conducted public ceremonies

Repositioned skulls within the excavated graves at the Cementerio de Chauchilla

and rituals to thank the gods for water. Many of the site's treasures can be seen at the Museo Antonini in Nazca.

Cementerio de Chauchilla

E6 18 miles (29 km) S of Nazca 7am–5pm daily

Chauchilla Cemetery, naturally enough, is full of graves dating back to the Chincha period (1000–1400 CE). At one stage mummies were scattered across the site, courtesy of tomb-raiders who fleeced the bodies of valuables and discarded textile scraps, bones, and carcasses in the desert. From an archaeologist's point of view, they effectively robbed the dead of their identities and thus hindered researchers' ability to piece together the history of the people found here.

There are thousands of graves but only 12 have been restored; they show shrouded mummies in squatting positions with bleached skulls and long matted hair. There is also a children-only grave.

Normally the mummies would have been well preserved by the arid sands, rich in salt and nitrates, but their exposure to the elements destroyed the mummified skin and faded the bones.

TOP 4 SOUTHERN BEACHES

Puerto Inca
Pre-Columbian ruins make for a great hike before a swim at the crescent-shaped beach.

Chala
Have super-fresh seafood at this tumble-down fishing village.

Punta San Juan de Marcona
View sea lions, pelicans, and Humboldt penguins from the cliffs.

Punta San Fernando
A rich supply of marine life and Andean condors are often visible here.

Pool fed by natural hot springs at the Baños Termales de Putina

10

Baños Termales de Putina

F7 🚗 63 miles (100 km) N of Tacna 🚌 From Tacna
⏰ 4am–8:30pm Tue–Sun

North of Tacna the highway climbs up into the mountains, beginning its journey to Puno (p164), and these thermal baths make for a pleasant break on the route. Reached by paved Inca road, the thermal springs originate in the nearby Yucamani volcano. Rich in sodium chloride, magnesium, and zinc, the water is believed to have medicinal properties and is heated to 102–113° F (39–45° C). Two outdoor pools and a handful of smaller and hotter private indoor tubs are available. There are changing facilities, and families are welcome, although some of the rock-cut stairways are steep. The best time for a quiet dip is early morning.

11

Tarata

F7 🚗 55 miles (89 km) N of Tacna 🚌 From Tacna

The attractive town of Tarata sits 10,144 ft (3,000 m) above sea level, ringed by verdant Andean countryside and spectacular agricultural terracing. Its chief attraction is its elegant Iglesia San Benedicto de Abad, with delicate religious carvings on its facade. Construction began in 1611, but was completed 130 years later.

Tarata connects to neighboring Ticaco via the Cápac Ñan (p69), the royal Inca road. Visitors can walk past pre-Inca archaeological sites, likely belonging to the Aymara and Tihuanaco cultures.

12

Petroglifos de Miculla

F7 🚗 14 miles (23 km) NE of Tacna 🚌 From Tacna
⏰ 9am–5pm Tue–Sun

The Petroglifos de Miculla, one of South America's largest

collections of its kind, features 1,500 shapes etched into low boulders. The carvings prominently depict humans engaged in daily activities like agriculture, hunting, dancing, and conflict. Other drawings evidence rituals associated with cults of water, earth, and the cosmos, thought to have been carved between 500 and 1500 CE. There's a huge area to explore here, including two rope bridges across dry ravines.

13

Tacna

F7 **766 miles (1,233 km) S of Lima** **From Lima or Arequipa**

The town of Tacna marks Peru's frontier with Chile. A 10,000-strong population lived here under the Aymara dynasty when the Spanish claimed the area for themselves in 1535 and began a brutal period of oppression and enslavement. Later, Tacna became the focus of Peru's fight for independence when revolutionary Francisco Antonio de Zela unsuccessfully attempted to overthrow Spanish rule in 1811. Casa de Zela, his former home, is now a museum charting his life.

In 1880, Tacna fell under Chilean control after Peru's defeat in the War of the Pacific. This history is narrated in the Museo Histórico Regional de Tacna, while northwest of the town, eight sculptures line Cerro Intiorko in tribute to those who died during the war. The Treaty of Lima, signed in 1929, finally saw Tacna become Peruvian territory once again. This is celebrated every July 28 by the Procesión de la Bandera, when a military and civilian parade carries a Peruvian flag through the town's streets.

Unusually, Tacna has no central plaza; instead, the Paseo Cívico is the town's focal point. Its Neo-Classical fountain was designed by Gustave Eiffel – better known for the Eiffel Tower. A few blocks north, the **Museo Ferroviario** contains steam locomotives retired from use on the Tacna–Arica rail line.

↑ Paseo Cívico, Tacna, with its ornamental fountain

Museo Ferroviario
Calle Gregorio Albarracín and Av 2 de Mayo 8:30am–4pm Tue–Sat museoferroviario.regiontacna.gob.pe

← Petroglifos de Miculla, home to ancient art and carvings *(inset)*

CROSSING TO CHILE

Peru's only international railroad is between Tacna and Arica, Chile. Built in 1856, it reopened to passengers in 2016. The cheerful yellow one-carriage train makes the 38-mile (62-km) trip twice a day, although a $70 million (USD) modernization plan is in the pipeline. Immigration and customs formalities are dealt with at the stations at either end, usually quite swiftly, making this a relatively painless way to cross the border. Just south of Tacna station, the old railroad yards now house the Museo Ferroviario, the National Rail Museum of Peru, with steam engines, wagons, carriages, and some delightful vintage cars converted to run on rails.

Birds soaring above Arequipa's cathedral

AREQUIPA, CANYONS, AND LAKE TITICACA

The colonial city of Arequipa sits in stark contrast to its untamed surrounds. Rock art found in this region is testimony to a civilization dating back more than 8,000 years, while lush 2,000-year-old agricultural terraces recall the ingenuity of the Collagua people.

In the 14th century, Inca leader Mayta Cápac sealed his victory over the Collagua by marrying the daughter of a local chief and building her a house made of copper. This same mineral wealth – gold, silver, lead, copper, quartz – drew the Spanish conquistadores in the 16th century. Such heritage is on full display in the Baroque churches that dominate villages such as Chucuito, though the forced Indigenous labor needed to complete such works is less widely advertised.

Farther east lies the sapphire expanse of Lake Titicaca, hailed in Inca mythology as the birthplace of their civilization. Ancient settlements of weavers, fishers, and farmers of Aymara or Quechua descent still ply their trade around the shore and on near and far islands, including the famous floating isles made entirely from reeds – home of the area's oldest inhabitants, the Uros.

AREQUIPA, CANYONS, AND LAKE TITICACA

Must Sees
1. Arequipa
2. Lake Titicaca
3. Cañón del Colca

Experience More
4. Cañón de Cotahuasi
5. Sillustani Burial Towers
6. Lampa

Arequipa's cathedral and the Plaza de Armas, one of Peru's finest squares

AREQUIPA

F7 ◨627 miles (1,009 km) SE of Lima ☒ From Cusco ☒ From Puno ☒ From Puno and Lima ⓘ iPerú; Plaza de Armas; 054 223 265; 9am-6pm daily

Nicknamed "the white city," Arequipa is built almost entirely from sillar, a white volcanic rock. It is Peru's second-largest city and has a long history as a hub for sheep and alpaca wool exports, which still thrive today.

① La Catedral

◨ Plaza de Armas ◷ 5-6pm daily; museum: 10am-5pm Mon-Sat ⓦ museocatedral arequipa.org.pe

Originally constructed in 1621, the cathedral was damaged during a series of earthquakes and fire and rebuilt by architect Lucas Poblete in 1868. The cathedral is regarded as the most important Neo-Classical religious building in the country. Flanked by two arches, it is the only cathedral in Peru that stretches the entire length of a plaza. The main altar is made of Carrara marble, as are the 12 columns representing the 12 apostles.

GREAT VIEW
Yanahuara

The Yanahuara district, just 10 minutes from Arequipa's city center, offers a picturesque view of the city and countryside with the majestic Misti volcano in the background.

② Casona Iriberry

◨ Cnr of Santa Catalina & San Agustín ℂ 054 204 482 ◷ 9am-1pm & 4-8pm daily

Built in 1793, the volcanic rock walls of the Casona Iriberry, also known as Casa Arróspide, are thought to be the thickest in Arequipa. Formerly a private home, it is now the Complejo Cultural UNSA, and part of the Universidad de San Agustín. Rooms, where art and photography exhibitions and film nights are held, open on to a series of charming stone patios. The top terrace has great views of the beautiful nearby cathedral.

③ Casa del Moral

◨ Calle Moral 318 ℂ 054 210 084 ◷ 8:30am-5:30pm Mon-Sat ☒ From noon on public hols

This 18th-century home is named after an ancient *mora* (mulberry) tree that, although dead, is still standing in its central patio; a new mulberry has been planted beside it. Intricate carvings, in sillar, of puma heads with snakes emerging from their mouths adorn the stone gateway, along with a crown suspended above a coat of arms held up by two angels. Inside, there are displays of furniture from colonial and republican times, Cusco School (*p179*) oil paintings, and 16th-century maps. The rooftop looks out over the towering volcanoes that surround the city.

④ Museo Histórico Municipal

- Plaza San Francisco 407
- 054 204 801
- 8am–3pm Mon-Fri

The history of Arequipa is the focus here, with photographs of the old city, maps, historical documents, and a number of archaeological pieces on show. Also highlighted are Arequipa's famous residents. A series of satirical caricatures and works by famous artist Jorge Vinatea Reynoso (1900–31) are very insightful.

⑤ Convento de la Recoleta

- Jirón Recoleta 117
- 054 270 966
- 9am–1:30pm & 3–5pm Tue-Sun

Situated in the Antiquilla neighborhood, a 10-minute walk from the main plaza, this convent was founded by the Franciscans in 1648. Its enchanting four cloisters, featuring tranquil gardens and sillar columns, are an example of Arequipa's old colonial style.

Also of interest are the exhibition rooms on pre-Columbian artifacts, including ceramics and textiles, and a room dedicated to Amazonian cultures. There is also a library housing over 23,000 books from the 16th and 17 centuries.

⑥ Iglesia San Francisco

- Calle Zela
- 054 223 058
- Hours vary, call ahead

Despite being battered by earthquakes, the 16th-century San Francisco church is still standing. The church features an unusual brick entrance-way, and the convent contains paintings from the Cusco School (p179).

Must See

EAT

Crepísimo
Savory and sweet crepes, a bar, and a sun-plastered terrace.

- Calle Santa Catalina 208, Cercado
- crepisimo.com

S/ S/ S/

Chicha
Restaurant of acclaimed chef Gastón Acurio. Sophisticated dining rooms offering regional foods, many with Arequipa's famous freshwater shrimp.

- Santa Catalina 210, Cercado
- chicha.com.pe

S/ S/ S/

EXPERIENCE Arequipa, Canyons, and Lake Titicaca

STAY

Costa del Sol Wyndham
A luxury resort 15 minutes away from the city.

📍 Plaza Bolívar s/n, Selva Alegre 🌐 costadelsolperu.com

Ⓢ Ⓢ Ⓢ

La Plaza Arequipa
A boutique hotel with balconies overlooking the city's main square.

📍 Portal de San Agustín 🌐 laplazaarequipahotel.pe

Ⓢ Ⓢ Ⓢ

La Casa de Melgar
An 18th-century house with several gardens.

📍 Calle Melgar 108 🌐 lacasademelgar.com

Ⓢ Ⓢ Ⓢ

---

⑦

Mundo Alpaca

📍 Juan de la Torre 101, San Lázaro ⏰ 8:30am–6:30pm daily 🌐 mundoalpaca.com.pe

This museum includes traditional Andean weaving demos, an area with live camelids, and the first weaving machinery used by the Michell y Cia textile firm, which was founded in 1931. There is also an art and textile gallery that includes works of highly sophisticated weavers from the coast, highlands, and jungle, as well as a collection of pre-Columbian textiles. Also on show here are the prize-winning watercolor and oil paintings from the museum's annual competition, the oldest in the country. The shop offers alpaca wool goods.

⑧

Casa Tristán del Pozo

📍 Calle San Francisco 108 ⏰ 9am–3pm & 4–6pm Mon–Fri (to 1pm Sat) 🌐 fundacionbbva.pe/casonas-y-museos/casa-tristan-del-pozo/

This colonial home takes its name from General Domingo Tristán del Pozo, who commissioned it in 1738. Built of white volcanic stone, its facade features intricately carved Baroque details above the windows and entrance. Inside, there are arched roofs and expansive patios. Today, it is home to a bank, a small museum, and an art gallery.

---

⑨

Iglesia de la Compañía

📍 Cnr of Calle General Morán & Álvarez Thomas ☎ 054 212 141 ⏰ 9am–1pm & 3–6pm daily

The Jesuit church of La Compañía is one of the city's oldest. Originally designed by Gaspar Baez in 1573, the first structure was flattened by an earthquake in 1584. Profuse mestizo ornamentation incorporating flowers, faces, and spirals is engraved into the volcanic rock facade.

> 💬 **INSIDER TIP**
> **Best Nightlife Spot**
>
> Spend a leisurely evening at the rooftop bar and restaurant Déjà Vu *(Calle San Francisco 319B)* grooving to catchy music. The terrace is perfect for a pisco sundowner.

Inside, the main altar is carved in the Churrigueresque style – Spanish Baroque with a Latin twist, involving gold leaf and cherubs with Inca faces. The cloisters now house shops.

---

⑩

Casa-Museo Mario Vargas Llosa

📍 Av Palma 101 ☎ (054) 283 574 ⏰ 8:30am–3pm Mon–Fri

This high-tech interactive museum is located in the home where the Nobel laureate Mario Vargas Llosa

→ Iglesia de la Compañía's embellished interior, and *(inset)* its grand facade was born. A guided tour in Spanish takes you through 17 rooms, organized chronologically, with holograms and 3D videos in spaces that recreate Vargas Llosa's world, including a fantastic bar that figures prominently in one of his novels.

Museo Santuarios Andinos de la Universidad Católica de Santa María

La Merced 110 9am-6pm Mon-Sat (to 2pm Sun) ucsm.edu.pe/museo-santuarios-andinos/

The museum's most famous exhibit is Juanita, la Dama de Ampato (the Lady of Ampato) – the Andes' first frozen female mummy, and considered one of the world's best-preserved. Along with Juanita, there are several other mummies that were discovered in Ampato. All children, they were found with textiles, gold and silver figurines, dolls, and ceramics in their mountain tombs.

Museo de Arte Virreinal de Santa Teresa

Calle Melgar 303 10am-3pm Mon-Sat museosantateresa.org

Founded in 1710 as a monastery for the Barefoot Carmelite nuns of Santa Teresa and San José, the convent only opened to the public in 2005. Over a period of 300 years, the nuns have gathered a unique collection of colonial paintings, sculptures, and decorative objects, exhibited in 13 rooms. The museum

Must See

closes briefly at noon, when the nuns sing the Angelus. Although they are in a private section, their singing can be heard in the museum area. The shop sells soaps, apple cider vinegar, and cakes and cookies, all made by the nuns.

Iglesia La Merced

Calle Merced 110 054 213 233 8:30am-3:45pm Mon-Fri

Construction of this sillar stone church began in 1551 and was completed in 1607. The side entrance features an image of the Virgin Mary with two "saints of mercy." A series of paintings portraying the Virgen de la Merced are on display. The attached convent has a library, too.

MONASTERIO DE SANTA CATALINA

Calle Santa Catalina 301 ⏰ **9am–6pm daily (to 7:30pm Tue)**
🌐 **santacatalina.org.pe**

Covering an entire city block, the Monastery of Santa Catalina was founded in 1579 by Doña María de Guzmán, a wealthy widow who became a nun. This site resembles a small town, featuring 100 rooms, three cloisters, a church, and a gallery of superb paintings.

In its heyday the monastery housed 450 people, a third of them nuns and the rest servants. The first to join the Order of St. Catherine of Siena were poor Creole women and women from upper-class families. The monastery underwent reform in the 1870s when Sister Josef Cadena replaced the hedonistic lifestyle with religious austerity. As a result, the servants were freed in 1871 and many of them joined the order.

The convent was opened to the public in August 1970, since tourism was thought to be the best option to raise the funds required to install electricity and running water. Today, around 15 nuns live here in an area that is off-limits to visitors. Multilingual guides are available for guided tours.

Did You Know?

The monastery's nuns would meet in the Plaza Zocodover on Sundays to exchange handmade items.

Must See

Timeline

1715–1723
▼ Claustro Mayor, the Main Cloister, is the largest in the monastery and was worked on between 1715 and 1723. It is decorated with 32 frescoes, 26 of them depicting Mary's life and 9 showing the public life of Jesus.

1748
The bell tower, Torre del Campanario, was built. The steeple has four bells facing the streets around the monastery. The oldest bell is toward the south, facing Calle Ugarte Street, and bears the inscription "Santa Catalina Ora Pronobis 1749."

1660
▲ The white sillar Iglesia de Santa Catalina was constructed. It has a semi-circular dome, a long nave, and an elaborate main altar.

1770
Lavandería, the communal laundry, was established. Water ran through a central channel into 20 earthenware jars which served as washing troughs.

CLAUSTRO DE LOS NARANJOS

The Orange Tree Cloister, an open space situated in the west of the complex, takes its name from the orange trees planted there. It is painted a striking cobalt blue and features a series of beautiful arches and columns, which are adorned with a splendid series of mural paintings. The three crosses stationed here, however, are the most important feature. Representing eternal life, they are used by nuns in the monastery to reenact the Passion of Christ (the final days of Jesus' life) on Good Friday every year. Unfortunately, the public cannot view this ancient tradition, since the monastery is closed on that day, recalling the period when the order was completely cloistered from the world.

← With its terra-cotta walls, Calle Sevilla is one of the monastery's prettiest streets

EXPLORING MONASTERIO DE SANTA CATALINA

Claustro Mayor
The Main Cloister is bordered by five confessionals on the left side, ensuring the nuns retain a degree of privacy during their declarations. Thirty-two beautiful frescoes decorate the cloister walls. The majority of them show biblical scenes depicting the life of the Virgin Mary, while the remainder portray the life of Jesus.

Calle Córdoba
Córdoba Street, as the name implies, is inspired by the architecture of Andalusia. Terra-cotta pots filled with geraniums line the gleaming white walls, which trap the sun all year round.

The 18th-century wall on the right of this street is made of volcanic stones from Arequipa. These sillar blocks each measure 18 inches by 16 inches (45 cm by 40 cm). The 20th-century building on the left side of the street is out-of-bounds for visitors. The area forms part of the complex in which the nuns live today.

Cocina
The kitchen was probably designed as a chapel, given its high roof. The walls are blackened with soot from the coal- and wood-burning stove. The original utensils now sit unused. The Plaza Zocodover, close by, marks the center of the complex.

Lavandería
The communal laundry was built at a time when Arequipa's only water source was a series of small canals. The 20 huge earthenware jars, earlier used to hold grain or store wine, doubled up as wash basins. The water for washing was channeled through a central canal, with offshoots leading into individual jars. At the bottom of each jar was a plug which was removed once the washing was finished. This helped in draining all the dirty water down to an underground canal which was connected to the river. The laundry is located at the end of a long boulevard called Calle Toledo.

↑ Three crosses and orange trees in the blue Claustro de los Naranjos

> **SOR ANA DE LOS ÁNGELES MONTEAGUDO**
>
> Santa Catalina was also home to Sister Ana of the Angels (1602–86), who was beatified by Pope John Paul II in 1985. She was educated in the monastery until she was about 11 years old, joined the order, and was eventually elected Mother Superior. It is said that an ill painter, who made the only known portrait of her *(right)*, was completely cured of all his ailments by the time he finished the painting.

Iglesia de Santa Catalina
Dating back to 1660, the Church of Santa Catalina has been reconstructed several times after a number of earthquakes in the region caused serious damage to the structure. However, the original design of the chapel has been retained.

It is made of white sillar (local volcanic stone). The long aisle leads to the main silver altar, which is heavily embossed with religious motifs. This altar is positioned

Must See

← Plaza Zocodover, found directly at the center of the complex

> **HIDDEN GEM**
> **Sister Ana's Cell**
>
> Sister Ana, known as a miracle-worker, was buried in the monastery. Her humble cell and the utensils she used more than 300 years ago are on display in her rooms, and are well worth a visit.

as the most important examples of religious art on the continent. These works are displayed in the Religious Art Gallery, which is housed in two large rooms in the shape of a cross with exposed block walls made of sillar. This space was once used as a shelter for homeless widows and single mothers. There are numerous paintings from the admired Cusco School *(p179)*, including the *Divine Shepherdess*, believed to be the work of artist Marcos Zapata. There is a depiction of St. Michael, dressed in Spanish armor, complete with a feathery helmet, as well as a portrait of St. Catherine, or Santa Catalina, with a description of the scene written on a panel that is held by an angel.

under an impressive dome. There is also an altar dedicated to Sister Ana of the Angels. A grand European organ takes pride of place in the high choir.

Pinacoteca

When restoration began on the monastery before it was opened to the public in 1970, workers uncovered a cache of religious paintings dating back to the Peruvian Viceroyalty *(p71)*. Experts restored the 400 artworks, many of which were hailed

↑ Superb collection of paintings on display in the Pinacoteca

LAKE TITICACA

G6 ✈ From Lima & Arequipa 🚌🚆 From Cusco & Arequipa 🚢 From Puno; 7:30am tour recommended ℹ️ In Puno

At an elevation of 12,500 ft (3,800 m), Lake Titicaca is the highest navigable lake in the world. South America's second-largest lake, it covers 3,210 sq miles (8,300 sq km) of Peru and Bolivia, and is 120 miles (194 km) long and 50 miles (80 km) wide at its broadest point. Islands are sprinkled across the lake, and the inhabitants live traditionally, with life centered around fishing, farming, and weaving, increasingly supplemented by tourism.

① Isla del Sol

📍 9 miles (14 km) from Copacabana, Bolivia 🚢 To Copacabana 🚌 From Copacabana

Famed as the birthplace of the Incas, the Island of the Sun is actually in the Bolivian waters of the lake. Close to the Chinkana maze ruins is a sacred rock carved into the shape of a puma. Farther along are two large footprints, supposedly made when the sun came down to earth to give birth to the first Incas. A stairway leads up from the water's edge at Yumani to what is known as a fountain of youth.

> **Did You Know?**
>
> Ruins of an ancient temple, dating back 1,500 years, were discovered in the lake's waters in 2000.

② Iglesia Santiago Apóstol de Pomata

📍 Pomata, 67 miles (108 km) SE of Puno 🚌 From Puno ⏰ 8am–4pm daily

This Dominican church surveys both town and lake from its hilltop position. Built in pink granite, it is known for its intricate sandstone facade, which fuses Indigenous symbols with Baroque. It is one of southern Peru's most beautiful churches. Inside are windows made from *huamanga* stone, a towering gold-leaf altar adorned with coiled columns, and Cusco School paintings *(p179)*.

③ Isla de la Luna

📍 4 miles (7 km) from Isla del Sol 🚢

The *aqllawasi* (monastery) is the most important archaeological site on the Island of the Moon. In Inca times, the island housed the "chosen women," who took part in special ceremonies dedicated to the sun. The main palace, which was rebuilt in the 1960s, has some 30 rooms centered around a courtyard.

④ Islas Uros

📍 4 miles (6 km) from Puno 🚢 ℹ️ 977 946 569

The Uros developed their unique floating islands

↑ Soaking up the views on the edge of Lake Titicaca

centuries ago to escape hostile cultures on the mainland. They consider themselves to be "the oldest people on earth." Legend says they existed even before the sun. Following invasions by Aymara and Inca populations, the Uros ended up at the bottom of the pre-Columbian hierarchy. They speak Aymara today and many of them live on the mainland.

The largest of the floating islands, Huacavacani, is estimated to be 160 years old, housing a meeting hall and a school. The islanders use the ubiquitous *totora* (a reed-like papyrus) for food and firewood – fires are carefully built on a layer of stone – as well as to make their boats, houses, and handicrafts. Most islanders earn a living from fishing and tourism.

⑤
Isla Suasi

🏠 43 miles (70 km) NE of Puno 📞 997 971 417

The only building on this small, privately owned island is a luxury eco lodge which mimics traditional architecture with its thatched roof and stone walls. There are also protected areas for birds and where alpacas, llamas, and vicuñas roam freely.

Must See

ISLAND HOMESTAYS

As there are no hotels on the lake, villagers on the islands of Taquile, Amantaní, and Anapia happily share their homes with visitors. Guests help in everyday tasks – like harvesting, fishing, and building houses. Homestays *(turismo vivencial)* need to be booked in Puno, either by visiting the community tour operators, whose offices are down at the main jetty, or the iPerú office, which can put you in touch with the communities.

↑ One of the rustic arches dotted around Isla Taquile

⑥ Isla Taquile

22 miles (36 km) E of Puno
917 940 190

Some 350 Quechua-speaking families still live here, following the Inca creed of *Ama suwa, Ama quella, Ama llullav* (do not steal, do not be idle, do not lie). There is no police force – a reflection of their belief in honesty – and problems are solved by elected community leaders at the Sunday meetings. The people wear colorful clothes, which are only allowed to be knitted by men. Red knitted caps distinguish married men from bachelors, who don red and white. Señoritas wear multi-colored pompoms, while married women wear bright red ones on their heavy, layered skirts. With no cars, donkeys, or llamas, residents carry supplies on their backs up 545 steep steps from the jetty to the hilltop village.

> ### EAT
>
> **Restaurante Mojsa**
> Great view over Puno's main square and regional food with a sophisticated twist, including grilled alpaca.
>
> Calle Lima 365, Puno
> mojsarestaurant.com
>
> ⓈⓈⓈ
>
> ---
>
> **Café Bar de la Casa del Corregidor**
> A relaxed atmosphere in a 17th-century colonial house. Simple, delicious dishes.
>
> Jirón Deustua 576, Puno 994937576
>
> ⓈⓈⓈ

⑦ Isla Amantaní

25 miles (40 km) from Puno Comité Central de la Isla de Amantaní: 987 451 284

The lake's largest island has religious centers dating back to the Tiahuanacos (500 BCE–900 CE). Amantaní islanders are famous for their baskets, woven from *ichu* (a native grass), and their granite carvings. Sacred Inca sites crown the island's peaks. Local shamans read the future in coca tea leaves, so be sure to have a translator on hand.

⑧ Juli

49 miles (79 km) SE of Puno From Puno

Evidence of human occupation around Juli goes back 10,000 years, long before the Dominicans arrived in 1534 and turned the existing Indigenous settlement into their most important religious hub, a center for training missionaries for Bolivia and Paraguay.

The presence of four colonial churches, constructed to convert the local population, has earned the town the nickname of "Little Rome." San Juan Bautista de Letrán dates from 1570 and has dozens of Cusco School paintings depicting the life of John the Baptist and St. Teresa.

Iglesia de San Pedro Mártir, which was completed in 1560 and remodeled in the 20th century, combines a lovely Renaissance facade with a Baroque altarpiece and paintings by Bernardo Bitti (1548–1610).

⑨ Puno

27 miles (44 km) SE of Juliaca From Lima & Arequipa From Cusco & Arequipa Plaza de Armas; 997 971 417

Puno was a modest Indigenous settlement until Viceroy Conde de Lemos founded San Carlos de Puno as the capital of Paucarcolla province in 1668.

The Baroque-style **Catedral de Puno** on Plaza de Armas was designed by the 18th-century Peruvian architect Símon de Asto. The **Iglesia de San Juan Bautista** on Parque Pino is the sanctuary of Mamita Candelaria, Puno's patron saint.

Museo Carlos Dreyer houses pre-Hispanic and colonial artworks collected by the German artist Carlos Dreyer, including Moche ceramics, Inca silverwork, and Paracas textiles.

The historic steamship **Yavari**, built in England in 1862, is moored on Lake Titicaca as a museum. This former gunboat took six years to reach the lake: its 1,300 pieces were transported 350 miles (560 km) by mule.

The **Museo de la Coca y Costumbres** is a small but interesting museum exhibiting the history, traditions, and uses of coca. It also offers coca leaf readings. An additional exhibition room houses a sample of the hand-embroidered costumes used in the dances for the Virgen de la Candelaria (Virgin of the Candles) festivities *(p41)*.

The Mirador de Kuntur Wasi (House of the Condor) viewing platform offers a great view over Puno and Lake Titicaca, but be sure to check with a reliable guide before taking the road up to the platform as it is in bad shape and has become quite dangerous.

Catedral de Puno
Plaza de Armas ⏰ 8am–noon & 3–6pm Mon-Fri, 8am-1pm & 3-7pm Sat

> ### PERU'S FOLKLORIC CAPITAL
> Puno melds the two ancient Andean civilizations of the Aymara from the south and the Quechua from the north with colonial influences. The result is a rich diversity of high-spirited folkloric festivals, often hailed as the best in all of Peru. The most important event is the Festival de la Virgen de la Candelaria in honor of Mamita Candelaria, Puno's patron saint.

Iglesia de San Juan Bautista
Parque Pino, Av Independencia ⏰ 8:30am-1pm & 3:30-6pm Mon-Fri, 9am-noon Sat

Museo Carlos Dreyer
Calle Conde de Lemos 289 ☎ 951 141 485 ⏰ 9am-6pm Mon-Sat

Yavari
Moored in the Bay of Puno, Lake Titicaca ⏰ 9am-5pm daily 🌐 yavari.org

Museo de la Coca y Costumbres
Calle Llave 581 ☎ 51 981 908 686 ⏰ 9am-7pm Mon-Sat

Must See

⑩

Chucuito
11 miles (18 km) SE of Puno 🚌 From Puno

This once important colonial town is now best known for its Templo de la Fertilidad, an archaeological site with 86 stone phalluses in rows in an open-air walled-off area. There are two colonial churches, Santo Domingo and Nuestra Señora de la Asunción, with murals painted by Italian artist Bernardo Bitti. A 15-minute drive south of Chucuito takes you to the local farmers' market at Acora, where barter is still the main form of trade.

↓ Scenic view over Puno from the Mirador de Kuntur Wasi

CAÑÓN DEL COLCA

F6 ◉ 28 miles (42 km) W of Chivay village ◉ From Cusco or Arequipa to Chivay or Cabanaconde ◉ Can be hired for 2-3 days from Chivay

Nearly twice the depth of the Grand Canyon in the US, the Colca Canyon is home to 2,000-year-old pre-Inca agricultural terraces, traditional Andean villages, and trails zigzagging down its steep valleys. The region also ranks as *the* place for spotting the national bird: the Andean condor.

Reaching a depth of 11,155 ft (3,400 m), the 62-mile (100-km) Colca and neighboring Cañón de Cotahuasi (p168) are among the deepest on the planet. For the most adventurous, hiking down into the canyon or up into nearby snow-tufted peaks are unmissable activities. The gushing waters of the Río Colca also offer a white-water rafting route with 300 rapids along a 25-mile (40-km) course. Along the canyon's southern edge, roadside viewpoints grant panoramic vistas of its unfathomable depths.

Along the Canyon's Southern Rim

A line of 14 villages trace the southern rim of the canyon, inhabited by the original Indigenous Cabana and Collagua people. In each, a main plaza is crowned by an attractive church. Chivay bookends the canyon to the east, in walking distance of the mineral-rich La Calera hot springs, believed to treat rheumatism and arthritis. Continuing west, Yanque is where villagers perform the Waititi dance in the square early every morning. Some 21 miles (34 km) farther on, the Mirador Cruz del Cóndor has sweeping views into and across the canyon, while just after dawn, Andean condors glide in the thermal air currents above. The westernmost village is Cabanaconde, where the two- and three-day trails begin their descent into the canyon.

↑ Collagua terraces, carved out for cultivation by the Collagua and Cabana people 2,000 years ago

> **CONDORS**
>
> Considered sacred by the Inca, the Andean condor *(Vultur gryphus)* is the world's largest flying bird, measuring 4 ft (1.2 m) long with a wingspan of 10 ft (3 m). Despite weighing around 27 lbs (12 kg), it can fly for hours without using its wings, simply gliding on thermal currents and hunting carrion using its heightened sense of smell and remarkable eyesight. Once a common sight in the Andes, it is now listed as "vulnerable" by the World Conservation Union due to centuries of hunting.

Must See

↑ Cruz Del Condor offering spectacular views of the valley of Colca Canyon

↑ Relaxing at one of the five pools at La Calera hot springs

Hiking into the Canyon

From Cabanaconde, a steep path descends into the canyon, arriving at the lush, hummingbird-filled Sangalle Valley, dotted with rustic lodgings and a refreshing swimming pool – the perfect antidote to the hike down. An alternative, lesser-known route leaves from Cabanaconde toward the bubbling geysers at Chuirca. It follows the path of the Colca river to reach the hamlet of Llahuar, where hikers can stay overnight and spend an evening soothing their tired muscles in hot springs beneath a ceiling of stars. Tours can be arranged from agencies in Arequipa, although guides are cheaper hired directly from Cabanaconde; mules are an optional extra.

STAY

Colca Lodge & Spa
Serene riverside setting and thermal hot pools.

⌂ Urb Selva Alegre, Cercado, Yanque
🌐 colca-lodge.com

S/ S/ S/

La Casa de Santiago
Cozy guesthouse whose hammock-slung garden overlooks the canyon. Staff organize treks into the canyon.

⌂ Grau, Cabanaconde
🌐 lacasadesantiago.com

S/ S/ S/

Admiring a forest of large cacti at the Cañón de Cotahuasi

EXPERIENCE MORE

STAY

Hotel Valle Hermoso
This rustic guesthouse exudes charm. Rooms overlook a garden filled with fruit trees and grazed by llamas. Fresh organic produce is served for breakfast on the patio.

Calle Tacna 106, Cotahuasi
054 581 057

$)$$)$$)

④ Cañón de Cotahuasi

E6 124 miles (200 km) NW of Arequipa From Arequipa

At 11,560 ft (3,535 m), Cotahuasi is reportedly the deepest canyon in the world and twice as deep as the USA's Grand Canyon. The impressive landscape of the canyon combines sheer, shadowy cliffs rising out of riverbanks, towering snowcapped mountains, terraced citrus groves, fields of maize, stands of eucalyptus, spectacular *Puya raimondii* (p211) – the world's largest species of bromeliad – and hot springs.

In Quechua, *cota* translates as "union" and *huasi* as "house," thus Cotahuasi means "united house" or in this case, "united community." The canyon was an important route in Inca times, connecting the Pacific coast with Cusco. Remnants of these roads still link many of the traditional, adobe villages here. The unmistakable imprint of the Spanish conquistadores is also clear. Every settlement has a chapel and belfry, and sometimes even a bullring.

Villages in the canyon have their own attractions. Liucho has soothing hot springs, while Pucya is a 1-mile (2-km) hike from the stone ruins of Maukallacta, built by the Wari but later used as an administrative hub by the Inca. Other sights include the Mirador Bañadero del Cóndor, where in the rainy season (Dec–Apr), condors can be spied bathing in the waters below. A 200-ft- (60-m-) high waterfall, the Cataratas de Sipia, near the village of the same name, is another treasure.

⑤ Sillustani Burial Towers

F6 21 miles (34 km) NW of Puno 8:30am–5pm daily

Standing on the shores of the pristine Laguna Umayo, Sillustani is famous for its *chullpas* (circular burial towers), some of which are more than 40 ft (12 m) high.

The Collas, who dominated the area before the Incas, buried their leaders in towers

Lampa's Iglesia de Santiago Apóstol, with its eerie display of skeletons *(inset)*

that are wider at the top than at the base. The Lagarto and Intiwatana *chullpas* are the best examples, and whole groups are buried in one *chulpa*. The opening to the towers is always on the east side.

The insides of the tombs are said to be shaped like a woman's womb, with the corpses mummified in a fetal position. Some tombs have carvings of lizards, a symbol of life due to their ability to regrow their tails.

Blocks and ramps used to hoist the towers, demonstrate the difficulty of constructing them.

6
Lampa

F6 · 50 miles (80 km) N of Puno, 22 miles (35 km) N of Juliaca · From Juliaca

Known as La Ciudad Rosada, meaning "the pink city," the dusty salmon- and maroon-tinted roofs and walls of Lampa add a welcome splash of color to the surrounding golden grass plains.

The city's other main attraction is the Iglesia de Santiago Apóstol. The church is made from river stones and lime mortar and dates back to the 1650s. Local luminary and mining engineer Enrique Torres Belón, who was responsible for the restoration of the church in the 1950s, added a marble-covered chapel and crowned it with a replica of Michelangelo's statue *La Pietà*. The Vatican provided a plaster mold of the famous statue, which, instead of being destroyed after casting as agreed, is now on display in the Town Hall.

Torres Belón, who was also the president of Peru's Congress in 1957, was buried in the chapel along with his wife and his mother.

The church also has a fine collection of colonial paintings from the famous Quito and Cusco schools *(p179)* and an elaborate carved pulpit. In a rather macabre display, hundreds of bones removed from the catacombs during restoration of the building can be seen hanging on the walls around them.

TOP 3 BARS AND CLUBS

Kamizaraky
G7 · Jirón Grau 158, Puno
Live rock, reggae, and jazz on weekends and 1970s and 80s classics on week nights.

Museo del Pisco
F7 · Calle Moral 229, Arequipa · museodelpisco.org
Hip bar in a historic stone building with a cocktail menu as extensive as its name might suggest.

La Casona Forum
F7 · San Francisco 317, Arequipa
A collection of bars and clubs all under one roof. Expect music like salsa, reggaeton, and techno.

Exquisite stonework at Machu Picchu

CUSCO AND THE SACRED VALLEY

For two centuries, Cusco and its environs were the homeland of the Incas. Although the area was occupied by other cultures for several centuries before the Incas arrived, including the Wari in the 8th and 9th centuries CE, it was under Inca control that Cusco reached its peak as an administrative, religious, and military hub. According to 16th-century writings, 13 Inca emperors ruled over the valley from the 12th to the 15th century. From here, they built the Inca Empire in less than a century.

In 1533, Francisco Pizarro and the Spanish arrived in Cusco and, following the crushing defeat of the Incas, founded their own city, turning pre-Hispanic structures into colonial mansions. Gradually, Cusco and its surrounds became a symbol of *mestizaje*, a blend of Spanish and Andean elements, both architecturally and culturally.

Yet disputes between the Spanish and Indigenous people remained, reaching its peak during the uprising of 1780, which was spearheaded by Indigenous leader Tupac Amaru II. Cusco also became a key site of conflicts in the push for Peruvian independence, notably during the 1814–15 rebellion. After almost a century of fluctuating fortunes, Cusco then hit the global headlines in 1911 when American explorer Hiram Bingham brought the ruins of Machu Picchu to international attention.

CUSCO AND THE SACRED VALLEY

Must Sees

1. Cusco
2. Inca Trail
3. Machu Picchu

Experience More

4. Vinicunca (Rainbow Mountain)
5. San Pedro de Andahuaylillas
6. Pikillacta and Rumicolca
7. Tipón
8. Raqchi
9. Pisac
10. Calca
11. Moray
12. Chinchero
13. Ollantaytambo

THE AMAZON BASIN
p248

CUSCO AND THE SACRED VALLEY

7 TIPÓN
6 PIKILLACTA AND RUMICOLCA
5 SAN PEDRO DE ANDAHUAYLILLAS
4 VINICUNCA (RAINBOW MOUNTAIN)
8 RAQCHI

AREQUIPA, CANYONS, AND LAKE TITICACA
p150

↑ The Spanish arches and cobbled streets of the Plaza de Armas

CUSCO

F6 • 685 miles (1,102 km) SE of Lima • COSITUC, Boleto Turístico, Av Sol 103; 8am-5:30pm Mon-Fri, 8:30am-12:30pm Sat

Founded by the Incas and later filled with Spanish arches and squares and narrow cobbled streets, the historic town of Cusco was declared a UNESCO World Heritage Site in 1983. Despite high tourist traffic as one of the best places to stop before undertaking the Inca Trail, it still retains a traditional Andean atmosphere. *Soroche*, or altitude sickness, is not uncommon here, so taking it easy for the first 24 hours is recommended.

① Plaza de Armas

In Inca times, this square was mainly used for ceremonial purposes. The stone arches of the plaza reflect a Spanish influence, along with the cathedral and the Jesuit Iglesia de La Compañía. The latter is often mistaken for La Catedral (*p178*) due to its elaborate facade.

Two flags fly in the plaza, the red-and-white Peruvian national flag and a rainbow-colored flag said to be the banner of the ancient Inca Empire, Tahuantinsuyu.

② Museo Inka

Cuesta del Almirante 103
084 237 380 • 9:15am-4pm Mon-Fri, 8:45am-1:45pm Sat

Built on the top of Inca foundations, the museum is also known as the Palacio del Almirante (Admiral's Palace), named after Admiral Francisco Aldrete Maldonado, who once owned the building.

The exhibition is a must for Inca enthusiasts. It comprises mummies, ceramics, textiles, jewelry, metalwork, and gold objects. Of particular interest is the assortment – allegedly the world's largest – of *keros* (Inca wooden drinking cups).

③ Museo de Arte Precolombino

Plaza Nazarenas 231
8am-10pm daily
mapcusco.pe

The former Inca ceremonial court, Kancha Inca, was transformed into a mansion for the Spanish conquistador Alonso Díaz in 1580. In 2003 it was converted into the Museum of Pre-Columbian Art (MAP).

The 11 rooms are now filled with 450 masterpieces dating from 1250 BCE to 1532 CE. The Mochica gallery contains standout ceramic pieces. The museum also has an impressive collection of funerary ornaments.

> The exhibition is a must for Inca enthusiasts. It comprises mummies, ceramics, textiles, jewelry, metalwork, and gold objects.

> **INSIDER TIP**
> **Tourist Tickets**
>
> The Boleto Turístico *(cosituc.gob.pe)* grants you entry to 16 sites and museums in Cusco and the Sacred Valley, and costs S/130. Partial tickets for fewer sites are also available.

④ Sacsayhuamán

- 1 mile (2 km) NE of Cusco
- 084 240 006
- From Cusco, or walk
- 7am–5:30pm daily

This impressive example of Inca military architecture is made up of three large terraces which overlap in a zigzag formation. The stones are so perfectly aligned that it was said that not even a fine knife could penetrate the joints. While designing Cusco, the Incas imagined it in the shape of a puma, with this site representing the head and its serrated walls as the teeth.

The Temple of Hanan Qospo is housed here and is dedicated to the cult of the Sun (Inti), Moon (Quilla), and other deities of the Incas.

⑤ Iglesia de la Compañía

- Plaza de Armas
- 9–11:45am & 1–5:45pm Mon–Fri, 1–5:45pm Sat & Sun

Constructed in 1571 on the palace of Huayna Cápac, the 11th Inca, La Compañía had to be rebuilt after the earthquake of 1650. Regarded as one of the best examples of colonial Baroque architecture in Peru, it features a great carved stone facade and a 69 ft (21 m) high cedar altar covered in gold leaf.

Must See

STAY

Tierra Viva Cuzco Plaza

Just off the Plaza Mayor, this small hotel in a colonial residence has a 17th-century courtyard of stone pillars and flagstone floor.

- Calle Suecia 345
- tierravivahoteles.com

S/ S/ S/

Hotel Rumi Punku

A charming hotel mixing Inca walls and a colonial structure with modern additions.

- Calle Choquechaca 339
- rumipunku.com

S/ S/ S/

Art for sale in one of the courtyards in the San Blas district

6
San Blas District

Iglesia de San Blas
8:30am–6pm Mon-Sat

Dotted with colonial houses featuring Inca stone walls, San Blas is also known as the artisans' district. Once the domain of Quechua nobility, its network of narrow streets is now home to the workshops of Cusqueño artists who practice metalwork, and stone- and woodcarving.

Iglesia de San Blas, built in 1560, is Cusco's oldest parish church. Its ornate pulpit features some fine Baroque woodcarving. The fascinating Museo de Coca, dedicated to the history of the controversial coca leaf (p75), is also worth a visit. There is a gift shop here; be aware that coca tea is legal in Peru but not in most other countries outside South America.

7
Koricancha and Santo Domingo

Plaza Intipampa, cnr Av El Sol & Calle Santo Domingo 084 254 234
8:30am–5:30pm Mon-Sat

Koricancha, meaning the "golden enclosure," was built to honor Inti or the Sun god. It was the richest Inca temple and had gold-plated walls flecked with precious stones. The garden featured life-sized gold and silver statues of animals, local trees, and maize stalks. Mummified bodies of noble Incas were kept here for ceremonies. Unfortunately, the temple was drained of all its treasures soon after the arrival of the conquistadors.

The Iglesia and Convento de Santo Domingo were built on top of the Inca shrine. The building brings the two cultures together. It is difficult to imagine how the temple must have looked as so little remains of it now. However, the imposing trapezoidal architecture, pebbled floor, wall niches, and holes that are thought to be either drains or speaking tubes, hint at its past glory.

8
ChocoMuseo

Calle Garcilaso 210
9am–7:30pm daily
chocomuseo.com

This museum is an ideal place for chocolate-lovers. It houses a cafeteria and a shop offering cacao from different parts of Peru. The museum has several sections on the history of cacao from the time of the Mayans, including their processing techniques, plus a section especially for children. There are different activities that can be suited to the time frame of visitors. It also holds a 2-hour chocolate factory workshop where visitors can make their own

> **HIDDEN GEM**
> **Centro de Textiles Tradicionales**
>
> A 10-minute stroll from the ChocoMuseo, this exhibition showcases traditional textiles. The shop (textilescusco.org) sells top-class work by local weavers.

Must See

chocolate bars or truffles, starting from Peruvian cacao beans. Register online for the workshops.

⑨
Museo Machu Picchu

- Casa Concha, Calle Santa Catalina Ancha 320
- 9am-5pm Mon-Sat
- museomachupicchu.com

This museum, set within an 18th-century mansion, focuses on the Inca citadel that is Machu Picchu. It houses the 360 artifacts that American explorer Hiram Bingham – considered the first person to make public the existence of Machu Picchu – took back to Yale to study in 1912 and which were returned to Peru 99 years later, in 2011. These include early photographs. The two floors also display the San Antonio Abad University collection from later excavations and objects found during restoration of this museum.

⑩
Calle Hatunrumiyoc

This street is named after the famous 12-angled stone which is perfectly fitted into the right-hand side of the wall (visible while walking uphill). The stone was taken from the wall of the palace of Inca Roca, the sixth Inca emperor. It is now a part of the Archbishop's Palace. The wall is a brilliant example of the Inca's skill in polygonal polished stone-masonry, which they used to construct support walls.

⑪
Museo y Convento de Santa Catalina

- Calle Santa Catalina Angosta 401
- 51 984 999 753
- 8:30am-5:30pm Mon-Sat

Built over the Inca ruins of the Acllawasi (House of the Chosen Women), this convent opened in 1610. The interior includes beautifully painted arches and Baroque frescoes.

The museum, which opened in 1975, is dedicated to colonial and religious art.

⑫
Museo de Arte Religioso

- Cnr Calles Hatunrumiyoc & Herrajes
- 084 221 386
- 8am-6pm daily

Housed in the Palacio Arzobispal (Archbishop's Palace), the museum displays religious paintings from the 17th and 18th centuries, including works by Diego Quispe Tito, regarded as the master of the renowned Cusco School of painters *(p179)*.

The palace features carved cedar ceilings, stained-glass windows, and a room displaying life-size models of Cusco's archbishops.

The house, which once belonged to the Marquis de San Juan de Buenavista, was built with stones plundered from Inca Roca's palace, whose remains lie below.

EAT & DRINK

MAP Café
An elegant space in the Museo de Arte Precolombino offering exquisite food and fine wine to match.

- Plazoleta Nazarenas 231
- mapcusco.pe

S/ S/ S/

Calle del Medio
This restaurant and bar with a balcony overlooking the main square is great for enjoying a pisco sour with colorful Peruvian fusion dishes.

- Calle del Medio 113, Plaza de Armas
- 084 248 340

S/ S/ S/

Café D'Wasi
A cozy spot serving top-notch coffee, delicious breakfasts, and light bites.

- Calle Santa Catalina Angosta 175
- cafedwasi.peru.com

S/ S/ S/

← The acclaimed 12-sided Inca stone on Calle Hatunrumiyoc

⑬ LA CATEDRAL

Plaza de Armas **084 222 781** **10am–6pm daily**

Dominating Cusco's main square, La Catedral is the superb setting for over 400 works of art from the Cusco School, hailed as one of the most important painting movements in the Americas. The splendid Renaissance facade of the cathedral contrasts with the Baroque interior, which is lavishly adorned with gold and silver.

Construction of the cathedral began in 1560 but took almost 100 years to complete. It was built on top of the palace of the eighth Inca, Viracocha, using red granite slabs from the fortress at Sacsayhuamán. Two auxiliary chapels sit on either side of the main church. To the right is El Triunfo, Cusco's first church, built on top of the main Inca armory to symbolize Spain's victory over the Incas. It has an elaborately carved altar and a crypt that contains the ashes of historian Garcilaso de la Vega. The 18th-century Jesús, María y José chapel is on the left, and, as the name suggests, features images of Jesus, Mary, and Joseph.

Did You Know?

A massive earthquake struck Cusco in 1650, depicted on a large canvas in the cathedral.

The facade and altar of the Iglesia Jesús, Maria y José chapel includes images of the sacred family.

Fashioned from Bolivian silver, the Neo-Classical main altar weighs more than 885 lbs (400 kg). It was constructed between 1792 and 1803.

The chapel was built between 1733 and 1735.

One of the towers, according to legend, has an Inca prince enclosed within and when it falls, he will emerge to claim his birthright.

The magnificently carved 17th-century cedar choir stalls by Giménez de Villarreal feature images of saints and popes.

Must See

↑ La Catedral's grand facade towering over Plaza de Armas

↑ One of the stunning Baroque-style gold altarpieces

Painted by Marcos Zapata, the Last Supper is on display here. It has an Andean touch, with Christ and his disciples enjoying a meal of roasted guinea pig, and drinking chicha (maize beer).

The first Spanish church to be built in Cusco, its name, El Triunfo, is a constant reminder of the Spanish "triumph" over the Incas.

Finely carved granite altar

↑ The impressive cathedral complex, with its churches and chapels

THE CUSCO SCHOOL

The Escuela Cusqueña was a Roman Catholic art tradition initiated by the Spanish conquerors, which used paintings, such as the *Adoration Of The Magi (below)*, to convert the locals to Catholicism. However, the movement was eventually used as a subtle form of cultural resistance by the Indigenous and *mestizo* artists against the colonizers.

179

INCA TRAIL

F6

The Incas developed an extensive network of roads partly based on pre-Inca routes, covering about 19,000 miles (30,000 km), to connect their wide-ranging empire. These paths range from the Cápac Ñan (p69) to the Q'eswachaka Rope Bridge (p37). The famous Inca Trail, linking Machu Picchu with the Sacred Valley, is the best preserved of these roads. The Incas used to run along this trail, which they used to send messages across the empire. The present-day trail covers diverse landscapes and passes more than 30 Inca sites. Broken up into sections, it takes four days to complete.

The 24-mile (39-km) route starts at Piskacucho, near Chilca (KM82), and reaches its highest poin at Abra de Warmiwañusca, a mountain pass that leaves many a hiker panting for breath. All hikers must go as part of a group with an agency, led by a licensed guide. Reservations must be made at least six months in advance as there is a limit of 500 people a day, including both trekking staff and hikers. December to April are the wettest months; the trail can be muddy. The trail is closed in February for maintenance work.

① Patallacta

4 miles (6 km) from KM82

Crop terraces, houses, and other edifices show Patallacta's (also known as Llactapata) significance in the region. At 9,843 ft (3,000 m) above sea level, it supplied Machu Picchu with maize, their staple crop.

The stone houses were believed to be occupied by the nobility and religious authorities, while the rest of the people lived in humble mud and cane homes. Pulpituyuj, the large circular tower built on a huge rock, may have served as an altar or prison. Around 15 families still farm the surrounding land.

② Huayllabamba

8 miles (13 km) from KM82

Huayllabamba is the largest and last Andean community found on this trail. At 10,040 ft (3,060 m), the village, located at the foot of a mountain, is set amid terraces where maize and potato are cultivated. On clear days, you can see the snow-covered peak of Wakaywilka (Mount Veronika) (18,640 ft/5,682 m) in the Cordillera Urubamba in the distance. Many hiking

> **INSIDER TIP**
> **Camino Sagrado de los Incas**
>
> This one-day version of the trail, from KM104, gives a flavor of the Inca Trail and offers magnificent mountain views en route to Machu Picchu. There are 250 permits available per day.

↑ Hiking up one of the passes along the Inca Trail

groups camp here on the first night. This is also the last place to buy supplies such as snacks and bottled drinks.

③
Abra de Warmiwañusca

🚩 14 miles (23 km) from KM82

This mountain pass is 13,780 ft (4,200 m) above sea level and is the hardest to climb due to the lack of oxygen at this altitude. According to Inca mythology, the Andes were formed by giants turned into stones. This pass was thought to be a reclining woman. The Incas believed they had to climb over her to get to the other side. Warmiwañusca translates as "dead woman" in Quechua, hence the name Dead Woman's Pass.

The landscape changes here to barren and cold high plains, with the wind whistling through the pass. Hikers often place a stone on an *apacheta* (mound of rocks of spiritual significance) located at the highest points on the trail as an offering to Pachamama (Mother Earth).

④
Runkurakay

🚩 17 miles (28 km) from KM82

The ruins at Runkurakay have only a single north-facing entrance and exit. Some believe that Runkurakay was used as a marker by travelers going to and from Machu Picchu to determine how much traveling time they had left. Others suggest that it was simply a post used to guard the road. Its position on the edge of the pass offers superb views across the valley.

> **Did You Know?**
> You can get up to four stamps in your passport along the Inca Trail to Machu Picchu.

Must See

↑ The circular Runkurakay ruins, overlooking the valley

⑤ Sayakmarca

📍 22 miles (35 km) from KM82

Perched high on a ridge at a height of 11,810 ft (3,600 m) above sea level, Sayakmarca can only be reached by a narrow stairway cut into the mountain. It is carefully adapted to blend in with the natural mountain forms. The complex is thought to have been a sacred ceremonial center devoted to astronomy. Although Sayakmarca means the "inaccessible town" in Quechua, it did have a permanent supply of water and food storehouses, which indicate its importance.

Hiram Bingham named the site Cedrobamba in 1915 after discovering a cedar wood forest nearby. It was renamed in 1941 by anthropologist Paul Fejos to reflect the site more accurately.

⑥ Phuyupatamarca

📍 25 miles (41 km) from KM82

One of the best-preserved towns on the trail, it is called the "town above the clouds" because at night the clouds settle in the ravines and the complex rises majestically above them. However, at sunrise the clouds disappear.

Hiram Bingham unearthed the ruins in 1915 and christened them Qorihuayrachina. As at Sayakmarca, Paul Fejos renamed them in 1941.

The curved walls and geometric terraces superbly blend with the shape of the mountains, illustrating the deep respect the Incas had for their natural environment. The ceremonial baths reflect the Inca's mastery at controlling a natural force, spring water.

⑦ Wiñay Wayna

📍 27 miles (44 km) from KM82

This impressive Inca complex is situated at 8,860 ft (2,700 m) above sea level. The ruins were unearthed in 1941 by

↓ Wiñay Wayna terraces, and its stonework *(left)*

Must See

→ Train arriving in Machu Picchu Pueblo (Aguas Calientes)

Paul Fejos, but it was Peruvian archaeologist J. C. Tello who named it Wiñay Wayna in 1942. Meaning "forever young," Wiñay Wayna is also the name of a local orchid that blooms perennially.

Its location near a major access road and the striking architecture suggest that Wiñay Wayna was an important township for the Incas. The town is divided into four distinct sectors. There is the agricultural area with terraces, the religious or ritual area, the tower area, which features some of the best architecture, and the urban sector. This last one is made of rectangular single- and double-story buildings with trapezoidal windows, doors, and wall niches, as well as stairways and a series of ten fountains that run from the top of the slope to the bottom. Significant sections of the complex illustrate the high-quality cut stone assembly of the Incas. This is the last ruin before Machu Picchu, which is just 4 miles (6 km) from here. It offers fantastic views of the beautiful valley and the surrounding mountains.

Machu Picchu Pueblo (Aguas Calientes)

📍 5 miles (8 km) from Machu Picchu 🚆 To Ollantaytambo & Cusco 🚌 To Machu Picchu ℹ️ In Town Hall

Machu Picchu Pueblo is the last town for visitors going to the ruins and the end of the line for travelers arriving by train from Cusco *(p174)*. It's also known as Aguas Calientes, meaning "hot springs" in Spanish, and is popular among visitors for its natural pools.

The town's economy revolves around tourism so there are many hotels, restaurants, and countless souvenir and handicrafts stalls. Even the railroad track changes into an open market once a train leaves the station.

For hikers with aching muscles, there are **thermal baths** just out of town, including one filled with icy mountain water.

Thermal baths
📍 End of Av Pachacutec 🕐 5am–8pm daily

> **GREAT VIEW**
> **Intipunku**
>
> Signs along the Inca Trail direct hikers to the Intipunku (Sun Gate), the final section of the trail. It offers a stunning 180-degree view of Machu Picchu, especially at sunrise.

MACHU PICCHU

F5 ◆ **69 miles (110 km) NW of Cusco** ◆ **To Machu Picchu Pueblo (Aguas Calientes), then bus or walk to Machu Picchu** ◆ **6am–5pm daily (last entry: 4pm) (reserve at least four months ahead)** ◆ **Av El Sol 103, Galerías Turísticas, Cusco; open 8:30am–4:30pm Mon–Sat; machupicchu.gob.pe**

The lost city of the Incas is arguably the most famous sight in all of South America. Visitors from around the world come to admire its dramatic mountaintop setting and remarkably well-preserved ruins.

The citadel is built of rock at an altitude of 7,710 ft (2,350 m), on the saddle of a mountain flanked by sheer drops to the Urubamba Valley below. Machu Picchu was never sacked by the Spanish as they failed to find it, but instead was simply abandoned and left to nature to reclaim. Comprising an upper and lower section with houses, temples, fountains, plazas, and agricultural terraces, the Inca city is linked by scores of stairways and paths, and watered by natural springs. No other civilization has managed to assemble so many colossal stone blocks so seamlessly. However, the city's function remains baffling. Experts speculate that it served as a place of worship, a sight for tracking stars, and the ninth Inca emperor Pachacútec's country estate.

> **INSIDER TIP**
> **Machu Picchu on a Budget**
>
> Take a minibus from Cusco to the hydro-electric station and walk for 2–3 hours beside the railroad tracks to Machu Picchu Pueblo. You can also take a 2–3-hour walk up to the ruins, although the bus ride is US$24 return and takes a mere 20 minutes.

↑ Exquisite Inca stonework; blocks connected flawlessly like pieces in a jigsaw, without mortar *(inset)*

> **VISITING MACHU PICCHU**
>
> Trains to Machu Picchu leave regularly from the station at Poroy, a 20-minute drive outside the city of Cusco, and from Ollantaytambo, halfway along the railroad route. Incarail and Perurail offer several budget options for the scenic trip through the Urubamba Valley to Machu Picchu Pueblo (Aguas Calientes) *(p183)*. A local bus zigzags up the mountain to the historic Inca site. You can reserve online at incarail.com or perurail.com. For the best views, opt for the 24-mile (39-km) hike on the Inca Trail *(p180)*, which takes four days.

Must See

Spectacular view of the ruins, terraces, and stairways, with Huayna Picchu forming the backdrop

EXPLORING MACHU PICCHU

① Fountains

The Incas harnessed a natural spring located on a steep slope to the north of Machu Picchu, building a 2,457-ft- (749-m-) long canal to bring the water down to the city. They channeled the water through a series of 16 fountains, often referred to as the "stairway of fountains." The water collects in the cut stone base of the fountain before going into a circular drain that delivers it to a channel leading to the next fountain.

② Caretaker's Hut

Perfectly positioned to allow the caretaker to observe the access points to the city's south, this has been restored with a thatched roof, similar to how it would have looked when the site was inhabited.

③ Royal Sector

The buildings here feature characteristic Inca rock lintels and abnormally spacious rooms, and lie in close proximity to the Temple of the Sun, leading experts to surmise that this is where Pachacútec, the ninth Inca emperor, lodged when he was in Machu Picchu. The entrance and exit to the Royal Palace via a single portal also signifies a high level of security. Hiram Bingham, the explorer who disclosed Machu Picchu to the world in 1911, believed that the room at the front of the inner patio was the Inca ruler's bedroom. It features ten trapezoidal niches that would have housed significant ornaments.

Intihuatana, used by the Incas to plan agricultural cycles

↖ ⑦ 250 yd (230 m)

Agricultural terraces were cut into the mountainside

The Temple of the Sun, Machu Picchu's only round building

↘ ② 130 yd (120 m)

↑ The Machu Picchu complex, including the various temples, terraces, and ruins

↓ ④ 109 yd (100 m)

Must See

↑ Terraces covering Machu Picchu, once used by farmers

④
Funerary Rock
Researchers believe that this rock may have been used as a sacrificial altar. Hiram Bingham, however, suggested it was a mortuary slab on which deceased Inca nobles were laid out in all weathers to mummify. Just above the rock lies the upper cemetery, where Bingham uncovered a significant number of tombs.

⑤
Sacred Plaza
The Principal Temple, the Sacristy, the House of the High Priest, the Temple of the Three Windows, and the Intihuatana make up the Sacred Plaza. The Principal Temple features fine architecture, while the Sacristy is famed for the two rocks lining the entrance: one of them is said to contain 32 angles. A stairway behind the building leads up to the Intihuatana.

⑥
Intihuatana
This stone indicates the precise dates of the solstices, equinoxes, and other astronomical periods. The June (winter) solstice was said to be the most important day of the year, when the sun is said to cast its longest shadow from the pillar. At this moment the sun is said to be "hitched" to the rock, hence its name, "hitching post to the sun." From this day onward the days become longer, meaning more time to work the land and produce food. Interestingly, the Intihuatana tilts 13 degrees to the north, which is the ancient city's latitude.

STAY

El MaPi
This contemporary, rustic-chic hotel is a few steps from Machu Picchu Pueblo's town center.

📍 Av Pachacútec 109   🌐 inkaterra.com

⑤⑤⑤

Casa del Sol
Stylish boutique hotel; home to a spa and offering local, organic food.

📍 Av Imperio de los Incas 608   🌐 casadelsol hotels.com

⑤⑤⑤

Panorama B&B
Just outside of town, this bed and breakfast has pleasant rooms and great views of the river.

📍 Av Hermanos Ayar 305   📞 51 952 335 044

⑤⑤⑤

← Funerary Rock, located near the hut, with its curious engraved shapes

↑ Fascinating condor-shaped rock at the Temple of the Condor

7
Sacred Rock

The enigmatic carved rock, which mimics the shape of a mountain, is believed to have been used as an altar to worship the Apus, the gods of the Mountain, Water, and Fertility. Anthropologists believe that the rock mirrors the Pumasillo (Puma's Claw), a prominent mountain peak in the Cordillera Vilcabamba, which is still revered by Andeans today. The Sacred Rock appeals to the gods whose form it re-creates. It may also have been used as a sacrificial altar to appease the gods.

8
Temple of the Three Windows

Located on the eastern side of the Sacred Plaza, the rectangular temple features three walls, with the open side facing the plaza. The wall opposite has three trapezoidal windows, elegantly flanked by two niches. During the winter solstice, the first rays of sunlight would stream through these windows, illuminating the interior and creating a breathtaking spectacle. The windows also afford sweeping views of the surrounding ruins below and across the valley.

9
Temple of the Condor

The temple earned its name from the two slabs that create the stylized representation of a bird's outspread wings, with the head defined by the intricately carved rock on the ground. Modern-day historians believe that the niches within the temple served as altars where mummies were placed during sacred ceremonies devoted to the condor, which was revered as one of the most important deities in Inca mythology.

10
Temple of the Sun

Machu Picchu's only round building has two tower windows precisely aligned with the points where the sun rises on both the summer and winter solstices. The temple is regarded by many as having the most sublime stonework in all of Machu Picchu, and its entrance is considered the finest in the city. Built over a large, polished rock, the walls

> **Did You Know?**
>
> In Quechua, "Machu Picchu" means "Old Mountain."

→ Stunning view of the mountains surrounding the Temple of the Sun of the temple sinuously mimic its natural curve, causing the entire perimeter wall to bend inward. Additionally, the structure includes compartments designed to hold offerings or idols. Archaeologists believe that this remarkable temple served as an astral observatory, with Inca astronomers gleaning information about their crop cycles from the position of the constellations and the solstices.

---

⑪

Common District

The Common District, also known as Secular District or Industrial Quarter, is located above the Temple of the Condor. Historians believe the area housed storage buildings and residences for the workers of the realm because the construction is inferior to that of the upper section. The two circular rocks protruding from the floor may have played a role in a ritual, being filled with offerings of *chicha* or blood, or in an astrological ceremony as the sun, moon, and some stars are reflected when the mortars are filled with water. Their real purpose, however, remains a mystery to archaeologists.

→ Solstice Window at the Temple of the Sun

Must See

CLIMBING

If you plan to climb either Huayna Picchu or Montaña Machu Picchu, make sure you reserve an early morning entry slot and buy a ticket for a circuit that allows you to visit the ruins and do a climb. The mountains, however, are not for the faint-hearted – Huayna Picchu is more vertical, but Montaña Machu Picchu is higher, with very steep steps. The recent addition to the climbing menu, Huchuy Picchu (Small Mountain), is a more modest goal.

INCA CULTURE AND RELIGION

At its height in the 15th and 16th centuries, the Inca Empire encompassed thousands of square miles, stretching almost the entire length of the Andes and assimilating customs from the cultures they dominated. The Incas were audacious engineers, constructing spectacular mountaintop citadels and monumental buildings. They developed elaborate farming terraces, sustaining their crops by canal and drainage systems. Their social structure was extremely rigid, with the emperor being revered as a living god. The Incas worshipped the sun, moon, earth, and mountains. Animals, such as the condor and puma, were also considered sacred.

SOCIAL HIERARCHY

Inca society was strongly hierarchical, with the Sapa Inca, the emperor, holding absolute power. Beneath him were high priests of noble blood, who led all religious ceremonies, and then regional leaders known as *curacas* whose role was largely administrative. They imposed the Inca's strict taxation system on the population.

RELIGION

The Incas revered Inti, the Sun god, who nourished the earth and controlled the harvests. The Sapa Inca, believed to be the son of the Sun god, made offerings to the sun during religious ceremonies. Festivals and ceremonies linked with the Cult of the Sun and worship of Inti were significant in the Inca calendar.

↑ Inca Emperor Atahualpa, in 1532, during the Spanish conquest

FARMING

The Incas carved up mountains into vast terraced farmlands supporting the banks of the terraces with stone walls. They cultivated maize and potatoes, and raised llama and alpaca for food and as pack animals. Canal systems were used to divert water from rivers, sometimes many miles away, to the fields.

CULT OF THE SUN

Festivals Inti Raymi (Festival of the Sun, *p66*) was celebrated annually on June 21, the winter solstice in the Southern Hemisphere.

Ceremonies/Rituals Divination played a large part in religious life. Everything, from treating illness to determining the correct sacrifices, was performed by the high priest. Infusions of ayahuasca and coca leaves were integral to all ceremonies.

Ancestors The Inca treated their mummified dead as though they were still alive, parading them through the streets during festivals.

Keros These drinking vessels were used during ceremonies to drink *chicha* (maize beer).

Sacrifice Animal and human sacrifice was practiced periodically.

1 Inca priest at the Inti Raymi festival celebrated in Cusco.

2 Coca leaves in a field.

3 Illustration of 16th-century Inca life.

4 Wooden *keros* (Inca Cup) depicting a face.

Did You Know?

The Incas used *quipus*, strings with a complex system of knots, as a record-keeping device.

↑ Crop terraces at Moray, where the Incas experimented with plants

The extraordinary Vinicunca (Rainbow Mountain) →

EXPERIENCE MORE

4
Vinicunca (Rainbow Mountain)

F6 From Cusco Apr–Aug

Surrounded by the towering peaks of the Andes, turquoise lagoons, and skies that are home to the majestic condor, Vinicunca, or Rainbow Mountain, is considered sacred by the locals. Just a 3-hour drive from Cusco, it is typically visited as a long day trip, although acclimatization in Cusco is essential before starting the hike. The superfit can club it with the classic Ausangate Trek (p43). A far less strenuous and shorter hike at Palccoyo offers similar breathtaking views. It's advisable to reserve a tour in advance, as several firms in Cusco offer excursions, most of which include a basic meal or refreshments. Bring your own water as there are no shops nearby. Public transport to Checacupe is another option, and travelers can hire a local guide. During peak season, the mountain can be as busy as Machu Picchu.

5
San Pedro de Andahuaylillas

F6 22 miles (36 km) S of Cusco From Cusco 8:30am–noon & 2–5pm Mon–Sat, 8:30–10am & 3–5pm Sun

The simple mud-brick facade of this 17th-century church – built on top of a pre-Hispanic *huaca* (ceremonial site) – gives no hint of the lavish treasures within that earned it the nickname the Sistine Chapel of the Americas.

These include a gold-leaf ceiling, a Baroque cedar and gold-leaf altar, and two restored 17th-century pipe organs, which are the oldest parish organs in the Americas.

6
Pikillacta and Rumicolca

F6 19 miles (30 km) S of Cusco From Cusco 7am–6pm daily

Pikillacta, meaning the City of Fleas, was one of the pre-Inca cities built at the peak of the Wari culture. It had numerous 13-ft (4-m) enclosures forming a protective garrison, along with hundreds of two-story buildings made of mud and stone.

Pikillacta has an almost perfect geometrical design, divided into big rectangular blocks with straight streets. Its walls were originally coated with mud and whitened with gypsum.

Nearby, the remains of two Inca gates, known as Rumicolca, were built on Wari foundations and served as a checkpoint for travelers heading to Cusco. The Boleto Turístico (p175), the tourist ticket sold in Cusco, is valid here.

> **Did You Know?**
> The people of Pikillacta appear to have accessed the second floor of their houses by ladder, not stairs.

7

Tipón

F6　16 miles (25 km) N of Cusco　From Cusco　7am–6pm daily

The striking stone canals, terraces, and stairways that make up Tipón are said to be part of a royal estate built by the eighth Inca ruler, Wiracocha. According to experts, it was once a place of agricultural research and worship. Water is chaneled through traditional stone structures, underground aqueducts – some of which are still used today – and decorative waterfalls, showcasing the Incas' impressive grasp of hydraulics. The Boleto Turístico tourist ticket is also valid here.

8

Raqchi

F6　73 miles (118 km) SE of Cusco　From Cusco　7am–6pm daily

Located on the Cusco–Puno road, this remarkable 15th-century stone-and-mud temple of the supreme god Wiracocha still has some walls standing 39 ft (12 m) high. The complex includes housing for the nobility and circular silos that stored food.

↑ Ruins of Tipón, once a series of terraces irrigated by elaborate waterworks

EAT

El Albergue Restaurant
Tenderloin steaks of locally reared alpaca make for a Peruvian dining experience in the Sacred Valley.

F6　Estación de Tren, Ollantaytambo　6–9:30am, noon–3:30pm, 6–8:30pm daily　elalbergue.com/food-beverages

S/ S/ S/

El Huacatay
Enjoy Peruvian food with Mediterranean influences on its splendid patio.

F6　Jirón Arica 620, Urubamba　elhuacatay.com

S/ S/ S/

Tres Keros
This atmospheric restaurant serves Peruvian classics of trout ceviche and lomo saltado.

F6　Av Torrechayoc s/n, Urubamba　084 201 701

S/ S/ S/

193

Colorful handicrafts and textiles on display at the crafts market in Pisac

9
Pisac

F6 **20 miles (32 km) N of Cusco** **From Cusco**

A favorite day trip from Cusco, the town of Pisac is renowned for its crafts market and the **Pisac Ruins,** one of the most significant Inca sites.

Inhabited since the 10th or 11th century, this became an important regional capital once the Incas arrived. It is thought the town began as a military post, then grew into a ceremonial and residential center. Agricultural terraces and steep paths lead to the hilltop fort, which has walls of polished stone. Highlights are the Templo del Sol, or Temple of the Sun; the Templo de la Luna, or Temple of the Moon, and the Intihuatana, designed to track the sun's movements. The Boleto Turístico (p75) is valid here.

Pisac Ruins
7am–6pm daily

> **INSIDER TIP**
> **Market Savvy**
>
> Visit Pisac on a Sunday, when, in addition to the town's famous artisans' market, farmers from the surrounding area set up stalls selling fresh produce.

10
Calca

F6 **31 miles (50 km) N of Cusco** **From Cusco**

Nestled in the shadow of the Pitusiray and Sawasiray mountains, Calca was once an important Inca administrative center. Today, all that remains are the maize fields and the archaeological ruins of Huchu'y Qosqo (Little Cusco), just outside town. Despite its name, the adobe ruins seem to bear little resemblance to the real Cusco's streets.

Of special interest are the hot sulfur springs of Machacancha and the cold waters of Minasmoqo.

11
Moray

F6 **31 miles (50 km) NW of Cusco** **From Cusco to Urubamba, then** *colectivo* **from the turnoff to Moray** **7:30am–5pm daily**

At first glimpse Moray looks like a Greek amphitheater, but researchers believe it may have been an Inca crop laboratory designed to find the best conditions for particular crop varieties to thrive. There are four overlapping *muyus* (slightly elliptical terraces), each tier experiencing varying levels of sun, shade, and elevation. Built on retaining walls filled with soil, and watered by a complex irrigation system, the terraces show traces of about 250 cereals and vegetables. The Boleto Turístico (p75) can be used at this site.

The nearby **Salinas de Maras** (salt pans), dating back to pre-Columbian times, are in stark contrast. The natural salty water is channeled into 3,000 artificial pans and left to evaporate in the sun. Hundreds of people work on the site even now, using ancient techniques.

Salinas de Maras
10 miles (16 km) NE of Moray *Combis* (minibuses) from Urubamba 7am–5pm daily

12
Chinchero

F6 **18 miles (28 km) NW of Cusco**

Dubbed the birthplace of the rainbow, Chinchero is perched about 12,375 ft (3,772 m) above

Paddyfield-like salt pans on hillside terraces at Salinas de Maras sea level on the Anta plain, surveying the Sacred Valley. The tenth Inca, Túpac Yupanqui, reportedly built his palaces here. In the mid-16th century, Manco Inca, a puppet emperor appointed by the Spanish conquistador Pizarro, who rebelled against the colonizers, burned down the village, thereby cutting off his Spanish pursuers' supply lines. Viceroy Toledo established a plantation here (exploiting Indigenous labor to work it) and built an adobe church above the main plaza over Inca foundations.

A massive stone wall in the main plaza, featuring ten trapezoidal niches, recalls the Inca, as do extensive agricultural terraces, seats, and stairways carved into rocks just outside the village.

Quechua-speaking locals preserve the Inca customs: wearing traditional dresses, farming the terraces, and weaving. A colorful handicrafts market takes place in the main plaza three days a week. Every Sunday, residents from the surrounding villages gather at the main plaza and exchange their agricultural products and handicrafts using a barter system. Much of this is likely to change since construction work is ongoing on a new international airport. The Boleto Turístico *(p175)* is valid here.

13

Ollantaytambo

F6 **60 miles (97 km) NW of Cusco** **From Cusco** **Ruins: 7am–6pm daily**

Spectacular Ollantaytambo is described as a living Inca town. The residents still strive to maintain ancient traditions such as tilling their fields with foot plows. The place takes its name from Ollanta, the Inca general who fell in love with Pachacútec's daughter. Significant for the greatest Inca victory over the Spanish in Peru, the town was reconquered by the Spaniards in 1537.

Originally named Qosqo Ayllu, this Inca town is divided into individual *canchas* (courtyards). Each courtyard has one entrance. A series of carved stone terraces, built to protect the valley from invaders, leads up the hillside to the fortress, Araqama Ayllu. The fort comprises the Temple of the Sun, the Royal Hall, or Mañacaray, the Princess's Baths, or Baños de la Princesa, and the Intihuatana, used to trace the sun's path.

Although unfinished, the Temple of the Sun is one of the finest examples of Inca stonework. Six pink monoliths, designed to glow as the rays of the rising sun hit the structure, fit perfectly together. The T-joints, filled with molten bronze, hold the wall in place, and traces of puma symbols can still be seen on the surface.

SHOP

Awamaki
Stocking beautifully woven, high-quality knitwear, bags, and purses, this tiny fair-trade store supports Indigenous weaving cooperatives in nearby Andean communities.

F6 **Calle Principal s/n, Ollantaytambo** **awamaki.org**

Traditional and lively Negritos folk parade in Huánuco

CENTRAL SIERRA

Around 12,000 years ago, hunter-gatherers occupied the caves of the scenic Ayacucho valley, at the heart of the Central Sierra. The Wari Empire (600–1100 CE) later dominated the region, with the area around present-day Ayacucho becoming the center of their empire. Their sophisticated agricultural terracing and systems of governance influenced the Incas, whose grip on the mountainous region occurred some few hundred years after the Wari culture disintegrated. In the late 16th century, the Spanish took control of the Central Sierra, building cities such as Huamango and Huánuco.

A bloody and decisive battle took place just outside Ayacucho in 1824, an event that helped ensure Peruvian independence. In the 1980s and 90s, the region bore the brunt of the atrocities committed by Sendero Luminoso (Shining Path), a communist guerrilla group, and the retaliatory government-backed military; thousands of civilians were killed, tortured, raped, or disappeared and many more were forced to flee to the coast. After the capture of their ringleaders in 1992, Shining Path went into decline and has now all but disappeared. Today, visitors are drawn to the area's spectacular mountainous scenery and lively traditional festivals, along with the vibrant and varied crafts scene.

CENTRAL SIERRA

Must See
1. Ayacucho

Experience More
2. Huancayo
3. Huánuco
4. Huaytapallana
5. Concepción
6. Mantaro Valley
7. Huancavelica
8. Quinua
9. Cueva de Pikimachay
10. Palcamayo
11. Complejo Wari

↑ La Catedral, overlooking the leafy Plaza de Armas

❶ AYACUCHO

🅰 E5 🚗 357 miles (575 km) SE of Lima ✈🚌 ℹ iPerú tourist office: Jirón Cusco 108; 06 631 8305; 9am-1pm & 2-6pm daily (to 1pm Sun)

This area was initially settled by the Wari, before the Spanish founded Ayachucho here in 1539. The city is famed for its rich tradition of arts and crafts and its Holy Week celebrations. A pleasant climate, leafy plazas, and colonial architecture make strolling around it a pleasure.

①
Iglesia de Santo Domingo

🏠 Cnr of Bellido & 9 de Diciembre ⏰ 9am-noon & 4-7pm Mon-Fri

This church has a Renaissance facade which was later embellished with columns and a balcony. The Spanish Inquisition used this balcony to hang its victims. Inside, there is a fusion of Andean and Catholic influences, as seen in the portrait of an Inca face on the gold-leaf altar, and a hummingbird motif used for decoration. The bells were rung to declare independence from the Spanish after Peru's victory at the Battle of Ayacucho in 1824.

②
Museo de la Memoria

🏠 Prolongación Libertad 1229, Cuadra 14 ⏰ 9am-1pm & 3-5pm Mon-Fri, 9am-1pm Sat 🌐 anfasep.org/museo-de-la-memoria

This museum tells the story of violence by Shining Path (Sendero Luminoso) rebels and the brutal response by the military in the 1980–2000 internal conflict, most harshly felt in Ayacucho. Photographs, documents, and clothing are on display; all texts are in Spanish. The work of the museum's association, founded by women seeking justice for those who disappeared or were detained, is ongoing as mass graves continue to be found.

③
Casa-Museo Joaquin López Antay

🏠 Jirón Cusco 424 📞 940 336 214 ⏰ 3-6pm Mon-Sat

The home of Ayacucho's acclaimed *retablo* artisan Joaquín López Antay (1897–1987), this fascinating museum showcases many of his spectacular works. Originally carried by Spanish evangelizing priests, his portable wooden altars were adopted and adapted by Andean artists, who filled them with a decorative fusion of Andean and religious

---

THE SHINING PATH

This guerrilla group was founded in the 1960s (p73). After assassinating unpopular government officials, they turned to the brutal murder of peasants. The military response was equally harsh, and the torture and murder of often innocent people was greatest in Ayacucho. Memories of the conflict are still vivid here.

scenes. López Antay's workshop illustrates the intricate process of *retablo* making and the museum provides insights into his life. There is also a gift shop.

④
La Catedral

🏛 **Plaza de Armas** 🕙 **10am-noon & 4-6pm Tue-Sun**

Located beside the university, on the elegant Plaza de Armas, Ayacucho's 17th-century cathedral has an inauspicious pink and grey facade. The interior is more impressive, with a gilded altar and ornately carved pulpit, which is best viewed when it is illuminated during the evening service. The cathedral is the center of the famous candlelit Holy Week procession *(p41)*, when a crowd gathers here to follow an effigy of Christ around the city. There is also a Museum of Religious Art inside the church that exhibits works brought to Peru from Rome during the colonial period.

⑤
Iglesia San Francisco de Paula

🏛 **Cnr of Garcilaso de la Vega & Cusco** 🕙 **10am-noon & 4-6:30pm Mon-Fri & some weekends**

This church rivals Cusco's San Blas *(p176)* as the site of Peru's finest carved pulpit. The altar here is one of the few in the city not covered in gold leaf, but is instead made from Nicaraguan cedarwood carved with dozens of angels. The church, built in 1713, also holds a range of Flemish paintings.

⑥
Compañía de Jesús

🏛 **28 de Julio, Arequipa & San Martín**

This Jesuit church, built in different architectural styles, has a facade of flowers sculpted in stone. Inside, the gilded altar, carved wood interior, and a good collection of colonial religious paintings and sculptures are worth seeing. Next door is the Jesuit school where Indigenous children were forced to learn Latin and classical painting, before the Jesuits were eventually expelled from South America in 1767.

⑦
Casa Boza y Solís-Prefecture

🏛 **Portal Constitución, Plaza de Armas** 🕙 **8am-1pm & 3-5pm Mon-Fri**

This two-story mansion, built in 1748, has been turned into government offices. The interior courtyard has an original stone fountain and the upper floor is decorated with glazed Sevillian tiles. Visitors are allowed to see the cell of María Parado de Bellido, an Indigenous revolutionary figure who was incarcerated here before being executed by the Spanish in 1822.

SHOP

Santa Ana
Browse the workshops and galleries of artisans working with silver, cloth, alabaster, wood, and ceramic.

🏛 **Barrio Santa Ana, 0.6 miles (1 km) south of the Plaza de Armas**

Mercado Artesanal Shosaku Nagase
Five blocks north of the Plaza Mayor, this market sells ceramic churches, textiles, and *retablos*.

🏛 **Av Maravillas 101, Plazoleta María Parado de Bellido**

EXPERIENCE MORE

② Huancayo

E5 ❖ 224 miles (360 km) E of Lima ❖ From Lima
ⓘ iPerú: Pasaje Mariscal Castilla 131, by Parque Tupac; 01 574 8000; 9am–6pm Mon–Fri

Situated at a height of 10,696 ft (3,260 m) in the Mantaro Valley, Huancayo is a busy, modern commercial center. It is also the trade hub for the nearby villages. For a good view of the city, head to the Cerrito de la Libertad, a hill a short distance from the center. Beyond the hill stand the dramatic sandstone towers of Torre Torre.

The Huancayo region is both culturally and agriculturally one of the richest in the Andes. Every Sunday, a huge market draws villagers from nearby communities to sell agricultural produce and local handicrafts. Huancayo is also a good base for visiting these rural areas, each with its own traditional dress and dance. Additionally, this region also offers local culinary specialties, such as *pachamanca* (marinated meat, potatoes, spices, and vegetables cooked in a hole dug in the ground, covered by hot stones).

Home to the Wari culture from around 600 CE, Huancayo was absorbed into the Inca Empire in 1460. The Calle Real, part of the Cápac Ñan *(p69)* from Cusco to Cajamarca, runs through the city. Developed by the Spanish in 1572, Huancayo still features a few colonial buildings, notably La Merced. It was in this church that the Peruvian constitution was approved in 1839.

THE ANDES BY TRAIN

The 80-mile (128-km) "Tren Macho" (male train) weaves its way across the Andes between Huancayo and Huancavelica. It's so-called because its lack of maintenance gave rise to the saying: "it leaves when it wants to and arrives when it can." Locals hope that this will no longer be the case, however, as a major US$565 million upgrade is underway to repair the 38 tunnels and 15 viaducts and modernize the train.

③ Huánuco

D4 ❖ 280 miles (450 km) NE of Lima ❖ From Lima
ⓘ Dircetur, 2 de Mayo 1305; visithuanuco.com

The capital of its department, the busy Andean city of Huánuco is situated on the banks of the Río Huallaga at an altitude of 6,214 ft (1,894 m). Once an important Inca trading center on the Cápac Ñan, an ancient road network connecting Cusco and Quito in Ecuador, Huánuco was settled by the Spanish in 1539. Several colonial-era buildings remain, including the city's cathedral.

Just outside Huánuco is the **Templo de Kotosh**, one of Peru's oldest sites, dating back to 2000–1500 BCE. Rediscovered in 1935, it wasn't excavated until 1960, and much about the ancient Kotosh culture remains unknown. Significant findings include two mud moldings depicting crossed arms, believed to be between 4,000 and 5,000 years old. The site features three stone enclosures and replicas of the mud moldings in the temple. Local guides are available to take visitors around for a small tip.

Templo de Kotosh

3 miles (5 km) W of Huánuco 062 512 507 9am-5pm daily

④ Huaytapallana

E5 22 miles (36 km) NE of Huancayo

Huaytapallana, meaning "a place to collect wild flowers" in Quechua, is the highest summit in the cordillera of the same name. Local shamans and the Indigenous followers flock to the mountain to perform rituals and give offerings to the *apu* (mountain spirit) at a designated amphitheater near the car park, to avoid contaminating the reserve.

While climbing the mountain is forbidden, a challenging 5.6-mile (9-km) circular route takes travelers close to the glacier. The trail starts with a steep ascent to a viewpoint at above 15,700 ft (4,800 m), requiring acclimatization. It winds around six stunning, electric-blue glacial lakes, with a severe climb back to the car park.

Day trips from Huancayo are available during the dry season (May–Sep/Oct). Visitors should bring warm clothes, waterproof gear, snacks, and plenty of water.

⑤ Concepción

E5 14 miles (22 km) NW of Huancayo From Huancayo

A quiet village, Concepción lies in the Mantaro Valley. Nearby is the 18th-century Franciscan **Convento de Santa Rosa de Ocopa**, established as a training base for missionaries heading to the Amazon. The convent museum exhibits Indigenous artifacts, taxidermied wildlife, old maps, and photographs. Its library houses a collection of over 25,000 volumes, including some hundreds of years old, along with colonial religious art,

> **HIDDEN GEM**
> **Reserva Paisajistica Nor Yauyos Cochas**
>
> This protected nature reserve, 42 miles (70 km) west of Huancayo, is well worth a day trip. It is renowned for its spectacular, virtually pristine scenery, including the dramatic rock formations of the Cañón de Shucto.

↑ Drystone walls above the cloud line near Huánuco

↑ Beautiful, ornate chapel of the Convento de Santa Rosa de Ocopa

and works by contemporary Huancayo-born artist Josué Sánchez (b.1945).

The beautiful convent features cloisters, stone fountains, and a garden. Guided tours (in Spanish) are included in the entry fee.

Convento de Santa Rosa de Ocopa

4 miles (6 km) from Concepción 51 901 34 807 9am-noon & 3-6pm Wed-Mon

⑥ Mantaro Valley

E5 From Huancayo

The Mantaro Valley is a fertile agricultural region producing maize, potatoes, artichokes, and carrots. A busy highway runs parallel to the river, with turn-offs to villages known for their unique crafts, music, and dance, and hosting lively festivals year-round. All the villages are accessible from Huancayo.

Traditional techniques used in local crafts are centuries old. Look for woven blankets and ponchos in Hualhas, *mates burilados* (intricately carved gourds) in Cochas Grande and Chico, and silver filigree jewelry in San Jerónimo (which has a market on Wednesdays).

7 🍴 💻 🏨

Huancavelica

⛰ E5 🚗 92 miles (147 km) S of Huancayo 🚌 From Huancayo & Lima

This attractive town, the capital of the department of the same name, is located in a high, remote area known for mining and agriculture. At one time a strategic Inca center, the Spanish town was founded in 1571 after the discovery of vast deposits of mercury nearby. The Spanish exploited the area's mineral wealth, bringing in enslaved people to mine for silver and mercury. Due to the gradual depletion of resources, the mines were closed in the mid-1970s.

At 12,140 ft (3,700 m), and hemmed in by steep mountains, the town enjoys a dramatic setting and still retains some fine examples of Spanish colonial architecture. The churches are renowned for their intricate silver altars. Each Sunday a lively market attracts villagers from the surrounding rural communities, who come in their traditional dress.

December and early January are festival periods for Huancavelica and its surrounding villages, with the iconic *Supaypa Wasin Tusuq* (Scissors Dance) being performed during this time *(p53)*.

---

8 🍴 🏨

Quinua

⛰ E5 🚗 23 miles (37 km) NE of Ayacucho 🚌 From Ayacucho

In the rolling hills 23 miles (37 km) northeast of Ayacucho *(p200)* lies Quinua, at almost 10,827 ft (3,300 m) above sea level. This touristy village has an attractive cobbled plaza and is famous for its ceramic crafts. The roofs of the houses in the region are adorned with small ceramic churches, decorated with painted flowers and maize. These churches are believed to be good luck charms by the locals, and are used to ward off evil spirits.

Local artisans also produce handmade guitars, *retablos*, and comical alabaster figurines of bands of musicians or groups of chatting women. The ceramics, made from the rich, red local clay, are on display at workshops and are also sold at the small market held every Sunday.

Just outside the village lies the site of the Battle of Ayacucho, where, on December 9, 1824, after years of struggle, pro-independence forces led by Antonio José de Sucre defeated Spanish royalist troops. This bloody battle brought an end to colonial rule in the country, setting the seal on independence for Peru. The battlefield is a ten-minute walk from the town, and a 132-ft- (40-m-) high white obelisk commemorates the event. There is an annual week-long festival held every December to celebrate the victory. Locals in Quinua and people all over Peru celebrate with festivities that include feasting, folk music, and dance.

> **Did You Know?**
>
> The manufacture of ceramics provides jobs for over 70 per cent of Quinua's working population.

Exploring the ruins at Wari, capital of the empire-building Wari culture

⑨
Cueva de Pikimachay

▲E5 ◈15 miles (24 km) W of Ayacucho

Situated close to Ayacucho, this cave is hewn out of limestone and is thought to date back to 20,000 BCE. It holds evidence of long-term human occupation – the earliest in all of South America. These ancient inhabitants are thought to have been nomadic hunters and gatherers. Remains of chopping implements, basalt, and blades have been found, along with bones of a giant sloth. It was not until 4,000 BCE that agriculture was introduced, and people started cultivating crops such as beans, squash, and chilies.

Beyond the Cueva de Pikimachay is the Huatuscalle, a remote viewpoint that looks over the confluence of ríos Urubamba, Cachi, and Mantaro. Dramatic mountain scenery provides a stunning backdrop.

Tour operators based in Ayacucho can arrange personalized tours for visitors that take in Quinua, Cueva de Pikimachay, and the Huatuscalle.

---

⑩
Palcamayo

▲D5 ◈82 miles (132 km) N of Huancayo ▭From Tarma

Palcamayo is a small town situated in a green valley. The area's main attraction is the **Gruta de Huagapo**, an enormous limestone cave considered one of the deepest in South America. Although speleologists have explored 9,006 ft (2,745 m) of the cave, its exact depth is still unknown.

The entrance to Huagapo, which means "cave that cries" in Quechua, is through a huge hole in the mountainside from which an underground river flows. The entrance leads into a giant chamber that is 99 ft (30 m) high and 66 ft (20 m) wide. Exploring the first 984 ft (300 m) of the cave is fairly straightforward, but professional equipment, including scuba gear, is needed to go farther. The light fades and temperature drops as visitors venture deeper into the cave. Local boys act as guides, providing ropes and torches for a fee.

Gruta de Huagapo
◈2 miles (4 km) from Palcamayo
◷8am–5pm daily

---

⑪
Complejo Wari

▲E5 ◈14 miles (22 km) N of Ayacucho ◷8am–5:30pm Tue–Sun

The road from Ayacucho on the way to Quinua passes the Complejo Wari. Built on a hill, at 8,100 ft (2,470 m), Wari was the capital of the first known expansionist empire in the Andes, and covers an area of approximately 4 sq miles (10 sq km). Divided into five main sections, it comprises rectangular buildings set out on a grid system, with a complex of streets, squares, tombs, paths, and irrigation channels. Some restoration work has been carried out, making this an interesting guided excursion from Ayacucho (usually combined with a visit to Quinua). The site museum provides a useful introduction and displays some of the artifacts from the ruins.

← Grand facade of Huancavelica's Iglesia Santo Domingo

STAY

Hotel Presidente
Comfortable and clean, this popular hotel is in a great central location in Huancavelica. The bedrooms are large, and heaters keep guests cozy at night. There's also a delightful pool area.

▲E5 ◈Plaza de Armas, Huancavelica
🌐huancavelica.hotelpresidente.com.pe

S/ S/ S/

Stunning lake at the Paso Punta Unión on the Santa Cruz Trek, Huaraz

CORDILLERA BLANCA

This mountainous region – named Cordillera Blanca (White Mountain Range) after its perennially snow-covered peaks – was inhabited by hunter-gatherers some 10,000 years ago; their paintings still adorn caves in the area. Between 1500 and 500 BCE, the Chavín culture flourished in the region's fertile valley of the Callejón de Huaylas. This agro-pastoralist group dominated northern Peru, constructing the impressive ceremonial center at Chavín de Huántar around 1200 BCE; it attracted pilgrims from as far away as the Amazon. The Inca Empire spread into the area over 2,000 years later, building temples, fortresses, and roads.

In 1574, Huaraz was founded by the Spanish, who enslaved the local Indigenous population to exploit the area's mineral and agricultural wealth. Almost 300 years after this, the city was almost destroyed by the Great Peruvian Earthquake in 1970, which killed around 70,000 people in the region. Since then, improved road links with Lima – which were part of the reconstruction work – have helped Huaraz's growing reputation as the epicenter of climbing and trekking in Peru. Its sparkling snowy mountains, stunning glacial lakes, and villages rich in traditional Andean culture now attract over 200,000 visitors a year.

CORDILLERA BLANCA

Must Sees
1. Parque Nacional Huascarán
2. Chavín de Huántar
3. Caral

Experience More
4. Caraz
5. Carhuaz
6. Campo Santo, Yungay
7. Huaraz
8. Chacas
9. Baños Termales de Monterrey
10. Cordillera Huayhuash
11. Sechín

PARQUE NACIONAL HUASCARÁN

🅐D4 🏠13 miles (40 km) N of Huaraz 🚌🚖From Huaraz ℹ️SERNANP, Federico Sal y Rosas 555, Huaraz; sernanp.gob.pe

Situated in the Ancash region, the Huascarán National Park encompasses almost the entire Cordillera Blanca. Gleaming mountain peaks, jeweled turquoise lakes, and unusual fauna make this park an essential part of any visit to Peru.

Declared a UNESCO Biosphere Reserve in 1977, and a World Heritage Site in 1985, the park aims to protect the region's flora and fauna, its geological formations, and archaeological remains. Locals participate in the growing adventure tourism industry, meaning that revenue is channeled to their communities.

A Climber's Paradise

With 50 towering snowcapped peaks over 18,700 ft (5,700 m), the area is attractive for hikers, climbers, and naturalists alike and is easily accessible from Huaraz (p220) or Caraz (p218). Both these lofty towns have good hotels, equipment rental shops, and mountain guides, and Huaraz has a lively pre- and post-trek scene. Regular minibuses run between major villages, and the main road is in good condition. Short trips can be organized to the surrounding mountains and lakes, such as Laguna 69 and snowcapped Chacraraju, or longer hikes, particularly the Santa Cruz Trek, for the more adventurous hikers.

> **Did You Know?**
>
> Ten mammal species, including the spectacled bear, can be found here, plus 112 species of birds.

Must See

PUYA RAIMONDII

Named after the Italian scientist Antonio Raimondi, this is the world's largest bromeliad and is found in just a few isolated Andean areas, such as the Parque Nacional Huascarán and the Cañón de Cotahuasi *(p168)*. One of the most ancient plant species in the world, it has a rosette of pliable, cactus-like leaves, and blooms once in its 100-year lifetime. The elongated cluster of flowers grows from a single main stem, which can reach 40 ft (12 m) in height.

This area is home to the highest mountain in Peru, Huascarán, at 22,205 ft (6,770 m). Freezing temperatures, glaciers, and avalanches make it a challenging climb. Alpamayo, once voted the most beautiful mountain in the world, is also found here, as is Artesonraju, believed to be the mountain in the latest Paramount Pictures logo.

Activities in the Park

High-altitude hiking is the most favored activity here, with mountain biking and paragliding gaining in popularity. For those not as bold, Chinancocha, a splendid lake, has rowboats on rent. Day tours from Huaraz also take you to groves of *Puya raimondii* in the park's southern end, which bloom between May and August.

← Laguna 69, with Chacraraju mountain behind; walking through the national park *(inset)*

TOP 4 SPECTACULAR DAY HIKES

Punta Olímpica
Anticipate a beautiful valley, lakes, and broad views of Huascarán.

Laguna 69
A difficult 9-mile (14-km) hike starting at Yurac Corral. It takes around six hours there and back, but splendid views of the crystalline lake are ample reward.

Laguna Wilcacocha
A short but rough ascent into the Cordillera Negra, above Huaraz, with spectacular sunsets.

Quebrada Rajucolta
Prepare for a rough road leading to a valley south of Huaraz, but expect an exceptional canyon, cascades, and forests. Allow four hours to get there and back.

→ Magnificent glacier-fed Lagunas Llanganuco and surrounding mountains

SANTA CRUZ TREK

This four-day trek is one of the most popular in the Cordillera Blanca. The high-altitude trail snaking through panoramic mountain scenery passes beneath a dozen towering peaks which are over 18,700 ft (5,700 m) high.

The trail can begin from Lagunas Llanganuco. The path is well defined, and there are many long and moderate to difficult ascents along switchback trails, as well as more level walking alongside rivers and across verdant meadows.

The highest pass is Punta Unión at 15,590 ft (4,750 m). Here the cordillera opens up in front of trekkers to reveal a breathtaking 360-degree panorama of snowy peaks and glistening glacial lakes.

↑ Stopping by Taullicocha on the Santa Cruz Trek

Camping at this altitude is a chilly but spectacular affair. To wake up surrounded by towering ice-capped peaks is a once-in-a-lifetime experience. It is a suitable trek for amateur hikers, providing they are fit, properly acclimatized, and have the right equipment and clothing.

> **Here the cordillera opens up in front of trekkers to reveal a breathtaking 360-degree panorama of snowy peaks.**

Must See

400
The number of stunning lakes within the park.

LAGUNAS LLANGANUCO

> **INSIDER TIP**
> **Altitude Sickness**
>
> Due to the high altitude in this region, make sure you bring warm clothing and drink plenty of water. It is also wise to spend up to three days acclimatizing in Huaraz before visiting the park. As a general rule, do not embark on any treks if you experience any signs of altitude sickness (p275).

Situated 18 miles (28 km) east of Yungay, these two lakes sit in an awesome glacial valley 12,630 ft (3,850 m) above sea level. The peaks of Huascarán and Huandoy loom above them, covered by glaciers all year round. Surrounded by the rare Polylepis trees, the dazzling turquoise waters glow in the midday sun.

At 4,747 ft (1,450 m) long, the first lake, Chinancocha, is the most popular with visitors. You can rent a rowboat or explore the lake's spectacular surroundings on horseback. The second lake, Orconcocha, is the smallest at the end of the valley, at 2,986 ft (910 m) in length. It offers a wide variety of flora and wildlife.

It is best to arrive in the morning as the lakes get shady later in the day and the afternoons often bring clouds and an icy wind. Pick-ups and minibuses from Yungay run throughout the day in the tourist high season, which lasts from May through to September. The lakes are also accessible from Huaraz or Cashapampa, which is just beyond Caraz.

CHAVÍN DE HUÁNTAR

D4 **19 miles (30 km) SE of Wari; 0.6 miles (1 km) from Chavín village**
From Huaraz **From Huaraz** **9am–4pm Tue–Sun**

Comprising a series of underground tunnels, temple structures, and superb wall carvings, this intricate complex is a phenomenal construction. Built and used by the oldest major culture of Peru, the Chavín de Huántar is one of the most significant prehistoric sights in the country.

Located in the Ancash region, Chavín de Huántar lies at 10,335 ft (3,150 m) above sea level on the Río Mosna. Declared a World Heritage Site by UNESCO in 1985, this was the major ceremonial center for the Chavín people who inhabited the area between the 15th and 5th centuries BCE. The complex, which displays a pattern of additions and renovation, has two distinct parts: an original temple with underground passageways and carved stelae, and a much larger and later extension, which comprises a pyramid-like building leading down to the main plaza. The original temple buildings sit to the right of El Castillo, the most important building in the complex. In 2022, a team of archaeologists unearthed an even older network of 35 tunnels, hidden beneath the main complex.

Did You Know?

Trading *ch'arki* (llama jerky) was the main source of commerce for the Chavín culture.

El Castillo, in the extension of the original temple's right wing, is believed to date from 500–200 BCE.

Underground tunnels, connected by ramps and stairs, are extremely well-ventilated despite there being just one doorway.

The black-and-white portal, Porch of Falcons, on El Castillo comprises a large carved lintel spanning the cylindrical columns.

THE CULT OF CHAVÍN (1300–400 BCE)

The Chavín dominated northern Peru more than 2,000 years before the Incas. Thanks to abundant agricultural production, they had more free time to pursue artistic and religious practices. Their principal deities (anthropomorphic feline characters) were represented in stone stelae, such as this jaguar carving.

Must See

↑ Exploring the sacred ceremonial center

The Lanzón de Chavín, in an underground passageway, is a 13-ft- (4-m-) tall granite monolith. It has a carving of the Chavín's principal deity.

← The grand Chavín de Huántar complex

The large Sunken Plaza is believed to be where thousands of pilgrims gathered during important festivals.

Low platforms flank each side of the Sunken Plaza

↑ Incredible underground passageways and chambers

CARAL

3

◫ D5 ◧ 110 miles (176 km) N of Lima, off Pan-American Hwy North, KM 182
◷ 9am–4pm daily ◪ caralperu.gob.pe

Located on an arid strip of desert above the verdant Supe Valley, the UNESCO World Heritage pyramids of Caral are one of the cradles of civilization. At around 5,000 years old, this fascinating archaeological site is the oldest urban center in the Americas.

Despite being discovered in 1905, Caral wasn't excavated until 1994, as archaeologists wrongly believed the site to be a more recent construction. The site encompasses an impressive range of temples, houses, and plazas that date to 2,627 BCE, around the same time as when the Great Pyramid of Giza in Egypt was being built. Radiocarbon dating has proven that the advanced, preceramic civilization of Caral flourished in the Americas 1,000 years earlier than believed.

The site is exceptionally well preserved due to its lack of silver and gold artifacts, which made it of little interest to looters. Research by Peruvian archaeologist Ruth Shady has shown that the site was divided into two, the Sector Alto (Upper Zone) and the Sector Bajo (Lower Zone). The former contains most of Caral's 20 stone structures, which include six pyramids with ceremonial plazas, surrounded by residential buildings.

The complexity of the buildings and their vast size suggest a culture capable of large-scale planning and decision-making processes. Archaeologists believe that thousands of workers, managed by artisans and supervisors, would have been required to provide the necessary labor to construct the city. *Shicras*, woven reed bags filled with rocks, found at the site were possibly used to build the primitive but earthquake-proof foundations for buildings.

The sunken circular plaza of the Great Pyramid

A central stairway leads up from the circular plaza to the atrium.

The atrium was the ceremonial courtyard, with tiered seating.

Rectangular altar with underground ventilation

Did You Know?

A *quipu* (knot system used to record information) found here is one of the oldest of its kind in the world.

Must See

ARCHAEOLOGICAL DIGS

Digs led by archaeologist Ruth Shady since 1994 have uncovered fascinating artifacts that offer an insight into life on the site. These include seed and plant fragments from species endemic to the Amazon and the Andes, indicating Caral's role as an important trade center, connecting inland and coastal communities. Rectangular religious offerings made from cotton, known as *Ojos de Dios* (God's Eyes), also indicate that cotton was the city's main crop, cultivated here and used to exchange for shellfish with fishers on the coast.

Site Highlights

Pyramid of the Circular Altar

Made of stones bonded with mortar, this pyramid was plastered and painted white, yellow, and red.

Amphitheater

▷ The sunken amphitheater was one of the main buildings of the city and was used for religious and political functions. Celebrations were held here, with 32 flutes made of condor and pelican bones, and 27 cornets fashioned from deer and llama bones, found during excavations.

Pyramid of the Gallery

▷ Containing an underground passageway painted white and with seven niches, this was thought to have been used for individual worship. Residential buildings with ceremonial altars next door were inhabited by priests.

The east wing had seven superimposed terraces with stairways and rooms.

Great Pyramid

◁ This pyramid covers an area the size of four soccer fields. A 30-ft- (9-m-) wide staircase climbs from its foot to an atrium, three floors above, complete with a ceremonial fireplace. The leaders could survey the city from this impressive building.

Pyramid of the Huanca

▽ This three-tier structure has a staircase leading up to a ceremonial area with a view of a large obelisk. It is thought to have had an astronomical purpose.

↑ Overlooking Caral's Great Pyramid complex, with its circular plaza at the forefront

EXPERIENCE MORE

4
Caraz

D4 ◆ **42 miles (67 km) N of Huaraz, Callejón de Huaylas** ◆ **Frequent** *colectivos* **from Huaraz & Yungay** ◆ **Municipalidad, Plaza de Armas**

A small town at the end of the Callejón de Huaylas, Caraz has avoided total devastation from the earthquakes and avalanches that have destroyed so much of the valley. A flower-lined road leads into town, which has a leafy Plaza de Armas.

At 7,450 ft (2,270 m), Caraz is lower than nearby Huaraz *(p220)* and has a milder, much more agreeable climate. The tourism industry is developing slowly here to accommodate trekkers and climbers – it is the starting point for the panoramic Santa Cruz Trek *(p212)* and also for ascents of Alpamayo.

There are a number of good places in the area in which to stay and eat as well.

Not far from Caraz are the ancient ruins of Tunshukaiko – a platform structure thought to date back to the Huaraz culture, around 2000 BCE. The setting, in a lush valley with the cordilleras Blanca and Negra on either side, is spectacular, although there is little to see at the site.

A road runs 20 miles (32 km) east from Caraz through an impressive canyon bordered by 3,200-ft (1,000-m) high granite walls, leading to Laguna Parón. This lake is surrounded by snowy peaks, including Mount Pirámide, at a height of 19,310 ft (5,885 m). Parón is less visited but just as spectacular as the Lagunas Llanganuco.

5
Carhuaz

D4 ◆ **20 miles (32 km) N of Huaraz, Callejón de Huaylas** ◆ **Frequent** *colectivos* **from Huaraz**

This quiet little town in the northern Callejón de Huaylas has a limited tourist infrastructure, although it is a stopping point for trekkers in the Cordillera Blanca. The town lies at 8,655 ft (2,638 m) and has an attractive main square; a bustling market is held every Sunday morning with displays of agricultural produce and crafts from all over the region. Each September, for ten days, Carhuaz comes alive with dancing, drinking, music, and firework displays at the annual celebration of the Virgen de la Merced festival, thought to be the most raucous in the valley.

A number of good walks from Carhuaz have remained relatively unexplored as visitors favor the longer treks into the Cordillera Blanca. A pretty 5-mile (8-km) walk east from Carhuaz leads to the Baños de Pariacaca, the bubbling hot thermal waters of the natural rock pools beside a chilly river. For the brave, these are a fun place to swim.

The trail continues to the Lakes Hike, a rugged trek that passes between Laguna

> **A bustling market is held every Sunday morning in Carhuaz, with displays of agricultural produce and crafts from all over the region.**

> **INSIDER TIP**
> **Canyon Blast**
>
> With a pot-holed gravel surface, sheer rock-cut walls, and 35 pitch-black one-lane tunnels, the road that barrels along the Cañón del Pato (Duck Canyon) north of Caraz is considered one of the world's most dangerous. It's the ultimate pedaling challenge for adventurous mountain bikers.

Remains of the 1970 earthquake's destruction at Yungay

Rajupaquinan, Laguna 513, and Lagunas Auquiscocha. The longest and most spectacular hike is to a small village called Yanama. This three-day trip into the Quebrada Ulta (13,780 ft/4,200 m) features fantastic views of the towering peaks of the Parque Nacional Huascarán *(p210)*. Other major treks in Quebrada Ulta can be accessed from Chacas via a paved road through Ulta. Information on these is available at local hostels and trekking shops.

Campo Santo, Yungay

D4 7 miles (12 km) S of Caraz *Colectivos* from Caraz & Huaraz
8am–6pm daily

The Callejón de Huaylas suffered immense tragedy in the last century due to a number of devastating *aluviónes*. When the high-altitude lakes of the cordillera breach as a result of earthquakes or excessive snowmelt, they send deadly cascades of water, ice, mud, and debris on to the villages below. In 1970 an enormous earthquake (measuring 7.7 on the Richter scale) rocked central Peru and the resulting *aluvión* wiped out the village of Yungay, burying around 18,000 people.

An enormous mass of ice and granite was dislodged from the west face of Huascarán's north peak by the earthquake and it hurtled down toward Yungay at over 190 mph (300 kmph), burying the entire village and sparing only 400 lives. The site, known as Campo Santo or holy ground, is an expansion of where the original cemetery stood. It is open to visitors, and the thick layer of soil that covers the former village is adorned with paths and flowers. It is a poignant and evocative sight; the tip of the cathedral's spire and the tops of four palm trees are all that remain of the Plaza de Armas, and there are a number of monuments marking the sites of former homes. A large statue of Christ on a nearby hillside looks over the ruined village. It was to this point that 243 residents managed to climb and escape. Other catastrophic mudslides in 1941 and 1962 claimed around 9,000 lives.

←
The snowcapped Mount Pirámide at Laguna Parón, near Caraz

STAY

O'Pal Sierra Resort
A lovely spot, with comfortable bungalows set in a large garden. There's a pool, and a restaurant and bar. Excellent value.

D4 Carretera Pativilca Km 266, Caraz
51 994 583 473

Ⓢ Ⓢ Ⓢ

The Lazy Dog Inn
In idyllic countryside outside Huaraz, this family-friendly eco-lodge offers suites, cabins, and rustic tipis, plus home-cooked meals.

D4 Km 3.3 Cachipampa Alto, Huaraz Wthelazydoginn.com

Ⓢ Ⓢ Ⓢ

Andino
This Swiss-run hotel featuring suites with Jacuzzis and fireplaces offers cordillera views from the upper floors. Good restaurant with a long wine list.

D4 Jirón Pedro Cochachin, Huaraz Whotelandino.com

Ⓢ Ⓢ Ⓢ

← A local trader walking past fruit stalls at Huaraz market

Museo Arqueológico de Ancash

📍 Plaza de Armas 📞 043 421 551 🕘 9am-5pm Tue-Sun

8
Chacas

📍 D4 🚗 73 miles (118 km) NE of Huaraz 🚌 From Huaraz

The bus journey to the rural town of Chacas starts from Huaraz and passes through a tunnel beneath the pass at Punta Olímpica (16,044 ft/ 4,890 m). The town, which has retained its original Andean-Spanish architecture, is home to the famous Don Bosco School. This cooperative, established in 1976, teaches disadvantaged children the art of woodcarving and carpentry, and the profits are used to fund medical and agricultural projects in the area. Beautiful carvings created by the children can be seen decorating many gates and balconies in the town. The Mozo Danza, a

---

EAT & DRINK

Café Andino
A relaxed place with a roaring fire and cozy corners for playing board games. Great coffee and waffles.

📍 D4 📍 Jirón Lucar y Torre 530, Huaraz 🌐 cafeandino.com

$ $ $

Trivio
European dishes at this taproom-restaurant serving local Sierra Andina craft beer, with occasional live music.

📍 D4 📍 Parque del Periodista, Av Luzuriaga, Huaraz 🌐 triviorestobar.com

$ $ $

Creperie Patrick
Savory and sweet crepes, onion soup, and fondues are the stars of this restaurant with its resident French chef. It has a full bar.

📍 D4 📍 Av Luzuriaga 422, Huaraz 📞 921 176 340

$ $ $

7
Huaraz

📍 D4 🚗 250 miles (402 km) N of Lima 🚌 From Lima
ℹ️ iPerú, Plaza de Armas; (043) 428 812

Huaraz makes a good base for visitors to explore the incredible Parque Nacional Huascarán *(p210)* and the Callejón de Huaylas. The town is situated at an altitude of 10,142 ft (3,091 m), with the colossal peaks of the Cordillera Blanca and Negra mountain ranges rising on either side. The busy main street, Avenida Luzuriaga, teems with cafés, bars, and hiking shops. People from nearby communities come into town to sell local products such as cheese, honey, and sweets, as well as handicrafts.

The informative **Museo Arqueológico de Ancash**, on the main square, is definitely worth a visit. Spread over three floors, it takes visitors through the region's history from around 10,500 BCE to 700 CE. Displays include ceramics, trepanned skulls, carved stones, and assorted artifacts. The delightful garden at the back includes over 120 monoliths, heads, and other pieces of carved stone from the Recuay culture.

→ Trekking up the beautiful Peruvian Andes, accompanied by a horse ritual warrior dance, is performed in the streets during the feast of the Virgen de la Asunción, in August.

9 Baños Termales de Monterrey

D4 **3 miles (5 km) N of Huaraz** **Colectivo from Huaraz** **927 965 283** **7am–5pm daily**

The hot springs of Monterrey are famous for their curative properties. The spring water's high temperature is believed to be good for digestive and other health-related problems.

> **INSIDER TIP**
> **Bathing Basics**
>
> Don't expect a tourist-style spa experience at Peru's rural thermal springs. These are local baths for the community (who often run them too); travelers are welcome, but facilities will be basic and you may have to wait in line for cubicles.

Monterrey is located at a height of 8,868 ft (2,703 m) in the Callejón de Huaylas, the beautiful valley between the Cordillera Blanca and Negra mountain ranges. About 22 miles (35 km) farther up the valley is Chancos, located at the foot of Mount Copa. It has bathing pools fed by springs and natural sauna caves, which have been adapted into private cubicles.

10 Cordillera Huayhuash

D4 **From Huaraz or Huánuco**

Just 19 miles (30 km) long, this remote and pristine range incorporates dramatic mountain scenery, turquoise lakes, and rolling grasslands. There are seven peaks over 19,600 ft (6,000 m), including Yerupaja, which at around 21,765 ft (6,634 m) is the second-highest mountain in Peru, and Siula Grande, at 20,853 ft (6,356 m). There are seven other peaks over 18,000 ft (5,500 m) high.

Although barely 31 miles (50 km) away, Huayhuash is different from its more famous neighbor, the Cordillera Blanca. There are no broad valleys, mountain passes are more treacherous, and access is limited. At one time, the only trekking here was a 12-day loop of the range from Chiquián. Today, buses carry hikers on the dirt road from Huaraz to Huallanca, where shorter, five-day trips are possible. Guides and mule handlers can be hired at either starting point. A period of prior acclimatization is essential.

11 Sechín

C4 **3 miles (5 km) SE of Casma** **From Casma** **9am–5pm daily**

Thought to be dated between 3,500 and 1,200 BCE, the ruins at Sechín were first excavated in 1937 by Peruvian archaeologist J.C. Tello. The stone frieze on the outside wall of the main temple depicts a gruesome battle scene: warriors dressed in loincloths and carrying staves or clubs stand over their victims, who are shown with severed heads and limbs. It is thought that the temples were intended to commemorate an important battle, but it is still unknown which culture constructed this ancient complex. Inside the temple, earlier mud structures are being excavated even today.

"Reed horse" sea rafts on Huanchaco beach near Trujillo

THE NORTHERN DESERT

This region was the cradle of the Moche, Sicán, and Chimú kingdoms that emerged just under two thousand years ago. All depended on fishing and agriculture, using advanced irrigation techniques to make the most of the scarce water resources along this arid coastal strip. The Moche (100-800 CE) constructed fine adobe temples, and produced splendid ceramics and artifacts of copper and gold, such as the treasures found in the Lord of Sipán's burial chamber. Between 750 and 1375 CE, the Sicán (or Lambayeque), thought to be descendants of the Moche, established trade routes with Ecuador and Colombia, and produced more elaborate gold, silver, and copper work. The Chimú culture built their own sophisticated cities, in particular Chan Chan (c. 850 CE), the largest adobe city in the world. The region's more recent past can be seen in Trujillo, which was founded by the Spanish in 1534. After surviving a major siege by Inca forces in 1536, the city developed into an important port for the Spanish fleet. In 1820, Trujillo's place in national history was assured when it became the first Peruvian city to declare independence from Spain. These days, the region's richly flavored culinary delights and the coastal beach resort of Máncora attract as many visitors as its historical sites.

THE NORTHERN DESERT

Must Sees
1. Trujillo
2. Museo Tumbas Reales de Sipán

Experience More
3. Huaca del Sol y de la Luna
4. Chan Chan
5. Huanchaco
6. Chiclayo
7. Complejo Arqueológico El Brujo
8. Máncora
9. Batán Grande
10. Tumbes
11. Zorritos
12. Túcume

TRUJILLO

C4 348 miles (560 km) N of Lima 6 miles (10 km) NW From Lima iPerú: Plaza de Armas, Jirón Diego de Almagro 420; 044 294 561; 9am-1pm & 2-6pm Mon-Sat

Ranked as Peru's fourth-largest city, Trujillo's pleasant climate has earned it the title of "the city of eternal spring." Founded in 1534, Trujillo became the northern coast's most important settlement in the 16th century. Today, it is an oasis of greenery with brilliant Moche and Chimú archaeological sites nearby.

① Plaza de Armas

Trujillo's main square is said to be the largest in Peru. At the center of Plaza de Armas is a giant marble and bronze monument dedicated to the figures of the Wars of Independence, designed by the German artist Edmund Moeller (1885–1957) and inaugurated in 1927.

Every Sunday, a flag-raising ceremony accompanied by a parade is held. At certain times, enchanting *marinera (p52)* dancers perform. The famous Peruvian Paso horses can also be seen striding through the plaza.

← Flag-raising ceremony and parade at the Plaza de Armas

② La Catedral

Cnr of Independencia & Orbegoso 976 909 049 9am-1pm & 4-7pm Mon-Fri, 9am-1pm Sat (for guided visits only)

On one side of the Plaza de Armas is the cathedral, also known as the Basilica Menor. First erected in the early 17th century, it was destroyed by a series of earthquakes and later rebuilt between 1647 and 1666. It features colorful Baroque sculptures and paintings from the Escuela Quiteña, a style of painting which originated in 17th-century Quito.

The cathedral also has a museum featuring a number of beautiful 18th- and 19th-century religious paintings and sculptures.

③ Casa Urquiaga

Pizarro 446 981 064 315 9:30am-3:30pm Mon-Fri

This magnificently restored mansion, also known as Casa Calonge, originally belonged to Bernardino Calonge, who

Bright facade of Trujillo's cathedral, overlooking the Plaza de Armas

founded the city's first bank. Painted royal blue with white window grills, it was bought from the Urquiaga family in 1972 and is now owned by the Banco Central de Reserva del Perú. The 18th-century mahogany desk of Simón Bolívar, who lived here after proclaiming Peru's independence in 1821, is preserved.

The building features three interior courtyards. Several Moche and Nazca ceramics, along with many Chavín and Chimú gold ornaments, are also on display in the house.

④
Iglesia la Merced

Pizarro 550 **8am-noon & 4-8pm daily**

This church, originally built in 1536, was destroyed in an earthquake. It was designed and rebuilt around 1636 by Portuguese artist Alonso de Las Nieves. During the 1970 earthquake it suffered severe damage. The building, with its restored dome, features beautiful and picturesque molded figures representing scenes from the life of St. Peter Nolasco, the French founder of the Mercedarian congregation. Other features include unusual altarpieces painted on the walls, dating from the time before free-standing altars were used, as well as a priceless Rococo pipe organ.

⑤
Museo del Juguete

Independencia 705 **044 208 181** **9am-4:30pm Wed-Sat**

This museum exhibits an unusual collection of toys put together by one of the most distinguished Peruvian artists, Trujillo-born painter Gerardo Chávez. Highlights of the nearly 1,000 permanent exhibits include a unique 2,500-year-old Vicus whistle, pre-Columbian Chancay rag dolls, genuine 18th-century French bisque porcelain dolls, post-war metal cars, and battalions of tin soldiers. The museum aims to become the biggest private toy collection in Latin America. It is sponsored by Espacio Cultural Angelmira, headed by Chávez, and is located on the first floor. Below, a smartly decorated café-bar offers drinks and snacks.

⑥
Mural de la Humanidad

Universidad de Trujillo, Juan Pablo II and Jesús de Nazareth

Covering two walls of the Universidad de Trujillo, this spectacular mosaic mural is the longest on the continent. Known as the Mural of Humanity, it contains over 30 million tiny mosaics, depicting ancient Peruvian cultures and historical events alongside landscapes, wildlife, and more contemporary scenes. Designed by renowned Peruvian artist Rafael Hastings, and created by Carlos del Mar and a team of other artists, the mural took 16 years to complete.

A SHORT WALK
TRUJILLO'S CENTRO HISTÓRICO

Distance 1 mile (1.5 km)   **Time** 30 minutes

Packed with stately public buildings, ornate churches, and brightly colored Republican-era mansions, Trujillo's historic center is a visual treat. Most of these attractions lie in and around the resplendent Plaza de Armas, where on 29 December, 1820, the city became the first in Peru to declare its independence from Spain. This momentous event is commemorated by the imposing monument to liberty in the center of the plaza, and with an annual regional public holiday involving celebrations and civic parades. Many of the mansions here are closed to the public, but their impressive exteriors can still be admired from the street.

The standout feature of the 16th-century Franciscan church **Iglesia de San Francisco**, is the gleaming, gilded baroque altarpiece.

Casa Garci Holguín, the city's oldest surviving mansion, was built in the mid-16th century to house the lieutenant governor.

First built in the early 17th century, the striking mustard-colored **La Catedral** (p226) was destroyed over two earthquakes, then rebuilt between 1647 and 1666.

↑ Monumento a la Libertad in Plaza De Armas, Trujillo

Dedicated to regional history and cultural events, **Casa de la Identidad Regional** was once home to Don Manuel Cavero, former mayor of Trujillo.

A marble and bronze monument, **Monumento a la Libertad** commemorates the country's independence and is topped by a symbol of youth and freedom.

This immaculately restored house, **Casa Urquiaga** (p226), has an impressive Neo-Classical facade and three charming interior courtyards.

Museo del Juguete (p227) houses a fascinating museum of antique toys, which houses over 5,000 exhibits. The lilac exterior has carved wooden balconies.

Established in 1674 to house an order of Spanish Franciscan nuns, **Iglesia y Convento de Santa Clara** hit the headlines in 1674 when 26 nuns declared that they had been possessed by the devil.

Locator Map
For more detail see p224

Also known as the **Casa de los Leones** ("House of Lions"), which sit atop the ornate Rococo portal, this is arguably the city's best-preserved colonial mansion.

An early 19th-century mansion, **Palacio Iturregui** was home to General José Manuel de Iturregui, the father of Peruvian independence. It is now occupied by the exclusive Club Central.

Casa de la Emancipación is where Trujillo's independence from Spain was plotted. It features traditional Trujillo wrought-iron window casings.

Built during the 16th and 17th centuries, **Iglesia de San Agustín** has an ornately carved wooden pulpit and extravagant gold-leaf altarpiece.

→ Luxurious furnishings of a colonial-style room in the Palacio Iturregui

Casa Orbegoso's portal bears the coat of arms of the noble Spanish Orbegoso family. It was the residence of Mariscal Luis José de Orbegoso, an early president of Peru (1833–35).

MUSEO TUMBAS REALES DE SIPÁN

C3　Av JP Vizcardo y Guzmán s/n, Lambayeque　From Chiclayo　074 283 977　9am–5pm Tue–Sun

This museum is one of Latin America's biggest, with three floors and ten themed sectors. The exhibits include 1,400 objects of gold, silver, copper, bronze, precious stones, and ceramics of extraordinary beauty.

The pyramid-shaped Museum of the Royal Tombs of Sipán was inaugurated in 2002. Designed by architect Celso Prado Pastor, it is inspired by Huaca Rajada, a Moche mausoleum where the Lord of Sipán was buried 1,700 years ago. The pre-Columbian sovereign's tomb was uncovered in 1987 by archaeologist Walter Alva and is arguably the richest tomb in the Americas.

Exploring Museo Tumbas Reales de Sipán

The visit, unusually, begins on the third floor with a video presentation of the Huaca Rajada excavations and Moche culture. Entering through the third floor enables visitors to experience seeing a tomb the way an archaeologist does: working down from the top, beginning with the most recent features, digging down to ever older, more specific findings, and ending at the dream find – a royal tomb laden with riches.

↑ A selection of the museum's vast collection of pottery

Mochica ceremonial jewelry

Human-sized mannequin

← The high priest, who watched over religious worship and rituals

Did You Know?

Peanuts were an important Mochica food staple and appear on many of their pots and jewelry.

← Unique museum facade, designed by Celso Prado Pastor

Must See

Collection Highlights

Third floor

▼ The entrance features a dark-glass antechamber, which blocks UV rays and allows the eyes to adjust to the muted, sepulchral lighting. Highlights on this floor include a fabulous collection of ceramics depicting various aspects of Moche life such as hunting, fishing, fighting, and sexual encounters. Gods and religious ceremonies were also popular subjects, such as Ai Apaec *(right)*, the main deity of the Moche people.

Second floor

▶ Much of this floor is dedicated to the Lord of Sipán Sector, where some of the most dazzling finds of the tomb are displayed. There are splendid adornments for the face and body of the Lord of Sipán, who archaeologists believe was a warrior-priest of high rank, including ear ornaments and a gold peanut necklace, made from large, peanut-shaped beads *(right)*. Constructed principally of gold, silver, copper, and turquoise, this veritable treasure trove has been exhibited around the world.

First floor

▼ Finally, at the base of the museum, a precise reproduction of the Lord of Sipán's tomb is displayed in all its splendor. The Lord was flanked by two warriors, one of whom was buried with his dog. The bodies of two young females were interred at his head and feet, and a small boy was found in a niche above the burial. One of the men and the women were missing their left feet – the reason for the amputation remains a mystery.

231

EXPERIENCE MORE

3
Huaca del Sol y de la Luna

C4 ◨ 5 miles (8 km) SE of Trujillo on the Pan-American Hwy, then unpaved road ◨ 9am-4pm Tue-Sun
w huacasdemoche.pe

This archaeological site includes two pyramids. The imposing Huaca del Sol (Temple of the Sun) used to be 1,132 ft (345 m) long and 535 ft (160 m) wide, before it was ransacked by treasure hunters in the 17th century. Though only a third of the temple remains, it is still the largest pre-Columbian adobe structure in the Americas, believed to have been built by almost 200,000 workers, in around 500 CE. The interior is closed to the public.

Close by is the six-level Huaca de la Luna (Temple of the Moon). It has interconnected rooms and patios with friezes of anthropomorphic figures. The on-site museum (accessible with a separate ticket) is worth visiting before a guided tour of the temple.

4
Chan Chan

C4 ◨ 4 miles (7 km) W of Trujillo ◨ From Lima ◨ 9am-6pm Mon-Sat
w museochanchan.pe

On the UNESCO World Heritage List since 1986, this site is considered the largest adobe city in the world and is one of Trujillo's major attractions. Chan Chan was built between 1100 and 1300 CE as the capital of the Chimú Empire and residence of the Tacaynamu dynasty. It once had a population of 100,000, many of whom were skilled artisans and military personnel. The Chimú sovereigns ceded to the Incas after a siege in around 1470.

The complex is made up of nine sectors or citadels. The best preserved and most visited is Ciudadela Tschudi. A marked route leads through large sunken plazas, chambers, restored corridors, temple cloisters, residential areas, and military barracks. Most have friezes depicting sea creatures. Over the years, some of the structures have been damaged by floods, as well as by invaders and *huaqueros* (tomb-raiders).

Huaca El Dragón is the best-restored structure of the Chan Chan complex. It is also called Huaca Arco Iris (rainbow) after the motifs found on its inner walls dating back to the Nazca, Wari, or Tiahuanaco cultures. There is a museum on site, too.

Exploring the Chan Chan complex; detail of the well-preserved remains *(inset)*

> **THE PERUVIAN HAIRLESS DOG**
>
> Known as *perros sin pelo*, this ancient breed can be traced back to pre-Columbian times. Ceramic hairless dogs from the Vicus, Moche, Chimú, and Chancay cultures have been excavated along the north and central coast, offering evidence of their Peruvian origins. The Inca kept them as pets to please the Sun god and Moon goddess. The Spanish conquest nearly caused the breed's extinction, but fortunately these alert, intelligent animals survived in rural areas, where people believed in their magical forces.

The "reed horse" sea rafts of Huanchaco along the coast

5 Huanchaco

C4 ◘ 7 miles (12 km) NW of Trujillo ▣▣ From Lima

The best beach resort near Trujillo retains some of its fishing village ambience and is renowned for its ceviche. Although the water is too cold for swimming, it is perfect for surfers all year round. The town's 16th-century past is visible in the Baroque-style church of La Virgen del Perpetuo Socorro. The major attractions, however, are the sea rafts or *caballitos de totora*, which translates as "little reed horses." Locals, who still use them, are the only ones who can build these vessels, first used by the Moche some 2,500 years ago.

6 Chiclayo

C3 ◘ 124 miles (200 km) N of Trujillo ▣ From Lima ▣ From Lima & Trujillo

Chiclayo has a long and ancient history of Moche, then later Lambayeque, settlement. Today, it is a commercial hub and northern Peru's second-largest city after Trujillo. Major attractions here are the Neo-Classical-style cathedral, built in 1869, and the Mercado Modelo (Central Market). The market is particularly interesting for its herbs and healing charms, used by local *curanderos* and *brujos* (witchdoctors and healers). Chiclayo serves as the most convenient base for visiting all major archaeological and historical sights in the area.

About 6 miles (10 km) north of Chiclayo lies the 17th-century town of Lambayeque. Little remains of its colonial-era architecture but Casa de la Logia o Montjoy on Calle 2 de Mayo still has a 210-ft (64-m) wooden balcony, said to be the longest in colonial America. The main attractions here are the museums. The state-of-the-art Museo Tumbas Reales de Sipán exhibits the discovery of the Lord of Sipán's tomb *(p230)*. The **Museo Arqueológico Nacional Brüning** has a collection of Sicán, Moche, Chimú, and Lambayeque archaeological artifacts curated by German engineer Hans Heinrich Brüning (1848–1928).

Another museum worth a visit is **Museo Nacional de Sicán**, a 5-mile (8-km) bus ride away in Ferreñafe. On display here are golden artifacts, ceramics, and utensils; found in the tombs at Batán Grande, they rival the Sipán finds.

West of Chiclayo is El Pimentel, a town known for its lovely beach and an old pier. The latter is the longest in Peru and once held the weight of a train which was used to unload cargo from the arriving steam ships.

Museo Arqueológico Nacional Brüning

◘ Av Huamachuco, Cuadra 8, Lambayeque ☎ 074 282110 ◕ 9am–5pm daily

Museo Nacional de Sicán

◘ Av Batán Grande, Cuadra 9, Ferreñafe ☎ 074 286 469 ◕ 9am–5pm Tue–Sun

7 Complejo Arqueológico El Brujo

C4 ◘ 28 miles (45 km) NW of Trujillo, off the Pan-American Hwy toward Magdalena de Cao ◕ 9am–4pm daily ⊕ elbrujo.pe

In 2006, archaeologists announced the discovery of a well-preserved and tattooed 1,500-year-old mummy of a young woman. She was found in a mud-brick pyramid called Huaca Cao Viejo, part of the El Brujo Moche complex. In the tomb with La Señora de Cao (The Lady of Cao) were funerary objects such as gold sewing needles and metal jewelry, which are now on display.

↑ Distinctive Moche jar at the Complejo Arqueológico El Brujo

⑧ Máncora

B2 · 14 miles (23 km) S of Punta Sal · From Tumbes · vivamancora.com

Máncora is without doubt the trendiest beach town in Peru. Young surfers, Western backpackers, and well-to-do Limeños all head to this town for its pretty beaches, mainly Las Pocitas, 3 miles (5 km) to the south. It is also renowned for its lively bars and clubs.

About 7 miles (11 km) to the east are the Baños de Barro, natural hot springs with sulfurous waters believed to have curative properties.

⑨ Batán Grande

C3 · 24 miles (38 km) NE of Chiclayo on the road to Ferreñafe · *Colectivo* from Chiclayo

Blending nature and history, Batán Grande consists of around 20 adobe pyramids situated in the heart of the Santuario Histórico Bosque de Pomac, an ancient forest of *algarrobo* (mesquite) trees rich in birdlife. Between 1978 and 2001, Japanese archaeologist Izumi Shimada unveiled many tombs from the middle Sicán period (900–1100 CE). Some of the best gold artifacts found here are displayed at the Museo Nacional de Sicán *(p233)*. The Sicán culture (in Muchik language, *Sicán* means "Temple of the Moon") arose after the Moche fell, but the site was abandoned in the 12th century.

⑩ Tumbes

B2 · 90 miles (140 km) N of Talara · From Lima

Just south of the border with Ecuador, Tumbes was originally inhabited by the Tallanes, who are related to the coastal communities of Ecuador. It was also the point of dispute in a border war with Ecuador between 1940 and 1941 that was finally won by Peru. The city is a key access point to the Parque Nacional Cerros de Amotape, a tropical dry forest home to jaguars, among other animals. It's also the gateway to Peru's main mangrove reserve (Santuario Nacional Los Manglares de Tumbes), which contains five types of mangrove and over 140 bird species. It is best accessed from Puerto 25, 15 miles (25 km) northeast of the city.

⑪ Zorritos

B2 · 16 miles (28 km) SW of Tumbes · *Colectivo* from Tumbes

The area's biggest fishing village, Zorritos has great beaches. It's also home to many migratory birds, making it a favorite with bird-watchers.

About 6 miles (9 km) south of Zorritos, at KM1232 of the Pan-American Highway, is Bocapán, the main access road to the Parque Nacional Cerros de Amotape. Created in 1975, this national park conserves a large dry equatorial forest and protects endangered animals, including the Tumbes crocodile and South American river otter. Visitors need to get permission from the Tumbes office

> **Young surfers, Western backpackers, and well-to-do Limeños all head to Máncora for its enchanting beaches, mainly Las Pocitas, 3 miles (5 km) to the south.**

Playa Vichayito at Máncora, one of Peru's best sandy beaches

Túcume consists of 26 major adobe pyramids about 131 ft (40 m) high and other lesser buildings constructed around Cerro Purgatorio, a 646-ft (197-m) promontory lookout also known as Cerro La Raya, after a stingray that, as legend has it, lives within it.

Túcume is thought to have been a center of pilgrimage where there were high priests with a great understanding of agro-astrology. Significant studies were conducted here by Thor Heyerdahl, an ethnographer and explorer. Heyerdahl found evidence of a pre-Columbian maritime culture, confirming theories that inspired his journey across the Pacific Ocean from Peru to Polynesia in 1947.

Evidence of the Chimú and Inca occupations of the region has been found in dedicatory offerings, burials, and ceramics. In the Huaca Larga pyramid, archaeologists found the lavish burial site of a prominent Inca general. Some archaeologists believe that a fire that razed central Huaca Larga coincided with the beginning of the colonial period in Peru.

The on-site Museo de Sitio Túcume exhibits the work of Heyerdahl and American archaeologist Wendell C. Bennet – the first to scientifically excavate the site in 1936.

of the National Institute of Natural Resources, SERNANP, to enter the park.

Túcume

C3 | 21 miles (33 km) N of Chiclayo on the Old Pan-American Hwy to Piura | From Chiclayo and Lambayeque | 10am-4:30pm Tue-Sun | tucume.com

Also known as the Valley of the Pyramids, this site is located in the plains of the Lambayeque Valley and was the capital of the Lambayeque culture. The settlement was occupied by the Chimú from 1375 to 1450, until the Incas conquered the Chimú kingdom and inhabited the city until 1532.

↑ Artifacts and pottery on display at Túcume's archaeological museum

EAT

Fiesta Chiclayo Gourmet
Acclaimed chef Hector Solís adds contemporary flair to the traditional cuisine of Lambayeque, cooked by age-old methods.

C3 | Av Salaverry 1820, Chiclayo | restaurantfiestagourmet.com

$/$/$

Big Ben
Sip a pisco sour and sample scallops or tasty *parihuela* (seafood soup) overlooking the ocean.

C4 | Av Larco 1184, Huanchaco | bigbenhuanchaco.com

$/$/$

Café con Mar
This breezy beachside spot is the perfect place to enjoy a fruit breakfast bowl or afternoon cake while watching the waves.

B2 | Del Wawa, Jr Piura 139, Máncora | bigbenhuanchaco.com

$/$/$

La Sirena d'Juan
Savor tuna sashimi or ceviche, lobster, freshly made pastas, and excellent desserts made by Cordon Bleu-trained chef Juan Seminario. There's a good wine list, too.

B2 | Av Piura 316, Máncora | 073 339 311 | 12:30-4pm & 7-11pm Wed-Mon

$/$/$

Scenic landscape beyond the Kuélap ruins

THE NORTHERN HIGHLANDS

Evidence of human habitation in this area dates back to around 7000 BCE, but it was the Chachapoya culture that first left a lasting impression on the region. From around 800 CE, these expert agriculturalists carved terraces into mountain slopes and covered lowland areas with intricately drained field systems. The spectacular ruins of the imposing citadel of Kuélap (900–1100 CE) are a testimony to Chachapoyan skill. The group's wonderful weavings were much admired by the Inca, who conquered these "warriors of the clouds," as they were known, in the late 15th century, shortly before the arrival of the Spanish. In 1532, only a year after landing in Peru, Pizarro and his troops famously captured the Inca leader Atahualpa in the regional capital of Cajamarca. Atahualpa was ransomed, but Pizarro, upon receiving the payment, did not release him; the Inca leader was executed nine months later, thereby precipitating the end of the Inca Empire. Today, visitors come to Cajamarca to see Atahualpa's El Cuarto del Rescate (Ransom Chamber) and the thermal baths where he was said to be relaxing when surprised by the Spanish, as well as to experience the city's extravagant carnival celebrations.

THE NORTHERN HIGHLANDS

THE NORTHERN DESERT
p222

THE NORTHERN HIGHLANDS

Must Sees
1. Cajamarca
2. Kuélap

Experience More
3. Leymebamba
4. Los Baños del Inca
5. Ventanillas de Otuzco and Combayo
6. Chachapoyas
7. Cumbemayo
8. Cañón del Sonche
9. Karajía
10. Levanto
11. Revash
12. Catarata Gocta

CAJAMARCA

C3 | **532 miles (856 km) N of Lima** | **2 miles (3 km)**
From Lima & Trujillo | **iPerú, Jirón Cruz de Piedra 601; cajamarca.org**

Laid out in a traditional Spanish grid plan, the north Andean capital of Cajamarca has been a favorite haunt of travelers since Inca times. Its colonial- and independence-era architecture rivals that of Cusco and Arequipa for elegance. Cajamarca also makes a great base from which to explore the countryside, which is renowned for its dairy products. The best time to visit is during Peru's most raucous celebration, Carnaval.

① Centro Cultural Municipal Miguel Espinach

Calle Cruz del Piedra 613 | **933 515 663** | **8am-1pm & 3-7pm Mon-Sat**

Formerly home to the local government, this mansion is now a cultural center with several exhibition rooms, a library and, upstairs, the Museo de las Marionetas. Run by a third generation puppeteer, this puppet museum showcases some ghoulish-looking marionettes with painted papier-mâché heads representing characters from Carnaval and other local festivals. There is also a five-minute puppet show.

② Iglesia de San Francisco

Plaza de Armas | **933 515 663** | **10am-noon & 4-6pm daily**

The church and convent of San Francisco rivals Trujillo's cathedral on the Plaza de Armas with its Neo-Classical appearance. It has a fine altar, catacombs, and a religious art museum. To the right of the church is the Capilla de la Virgen de los Dolores, the city's prettiest chapel. It houses a statue of the city's patron saint, La Virgen de los Dolores, which is carried around the streets during religious celebrations.

③ La Catedral

Plaza de Armas | **8-11am & 6-9pm daily**

On the northwest of the Plaza de Armas – with its lawns, benches, and imaginatively trimmed topiary – rises the cathedral. Begun in the 17th century, it was not consecrated until 1762. Its fine carved-stone facade is a beautiful example of the Baroque style championed in colonial Peru. The main altar is in the Churrigueresque style, covered from top to bottom in gold leaf. The walls of the cathedral incorporate a large amount of Inca masonry.

↑ Stunning facade of the Iglesia de San Francisco

← Quintessential colonial architecture near Cajamarca's Plaza de Armas

Did You Know?

Spanish authorities levied a tax on religious buildings here, so many are unfinished to avoid paying this.

④
El Cuarto del Rescate

📍 Amalia Puga 722
🕐 9:30am-2:30pm Tue-Sat
🚫 Public hols

Reopened in 2025 following restoration, this house (the Ransom Chamber) is the only remaining Inca building in the city, displaying its typical trapezoidal niches and doors, and some original masonry. The chamber is 39 ft (12 m) long, 23 ft (7 m) wide, and 10 ft (3 m) high, and has plenty of historical significance. One theory claims that Atahualpa, the last sovereign Inca ruler, was held captive by the Spaniards in this room. Another says that it was the room which the Inca promised to fill with gold and silver for his freedom.

⑤
El Complejo de Belén

📍 Calle Belén 🕐 9am-1pm & 2:30-6pm Tue-Sun
🚫 Public hols

This impressive colonial-era complex spreads across a group of buildings with several patios and institutions. These include the Institute of Culture (INC), a small medical museum, and one of Cajamarca's finest churches, the Iglesia Belén. The church is regarded as one of Peru's best examples of the Baroque style, with its gold-leaf altars and an ornate cupola with oversized cherubs holding a centerpiece made up of flowers.

The interesting Museo Arqueológico y Etnográfico lies across the street (at Junín y Belén) in what once served as the Women's Hospital and morgue. It houses a wide collection of artifacts, ceramics, and weavings from the region.

⑥
Cerro Santa Apolonia

📍 SW of Plaza de Armas

This hill is a great spot for getting a feel of the city and can be explored via a series of splendid walks through gardens with native plants. Located here are the remains of Chavín- and Inca-era stone carvings. One of the rocks, known as the Silla del Inca (the Seat of the Inca), is shaped like a throne.

Must See

STAY

Costa del Sol Wyndham

Overlooking the historic main plaza, this hotel has great service and includes a gym and a pool.

📍 Jr Cruz de Piedra 707
🌐 costadelsolperu.com/en/hotels

S/ S/ S/

El Cabildo Hostal

A block from the city's main square, this restored 300-year-old house has a charming courtyard.

📍 Jirón Junin 1062
📞 976 459 971

S/ S/ S/

Did You Know?

Kuélap is thought to have contained three times more stone than the Great Pyramid at Giza in Egypt.

→ One of hundreds of round stone houses throughout the site

KUÉLAP

C3 ❏ 58 miles (93 km) S of Chachapoyas ☏ 939 392 347 ❏ From Chachapoyas to Tingo, then a four-hour hike ❏ From Nuevo Tingo ⏱ 8am–5pm daily

The imposing fortress of Kuélap is the main attraction of the Chachapoyas region. It ranks among the finest and most impressive ruins in Peru, occupying a perfect vantage point, set on a dramatic ridge high above the Río Utcubamba, amid verdant, rolling countryside.

↑ Beautiful bromeliads and orchids growing on one of the ruined walls

Reclaimed by the surrounding forest for more than 300 years, it wasn't until 1843 that this site was rediscovered by a local judge, and it wasn't truly explored until the late 19th and early 20th centuries. Ceramics unearthed in Kuélap indicate that the area had been inhabited since 500 CE, but the majority of the construction occurred between 900 and 1100 CE. The result was a fortress bigger than any other single structure in Peru. The complex had an outer wall protecting over 400 circular houses, thought to have been home to about 3,500 people. It also had terraces, outlying settlements, and burial areas beyond the main walls. When the Incas arrived in around 1470, they found Kuélap, full of formidable

Must See

Chachapoyan warriors, a difficult place to conquer. They were unable to take control of the fort and only five Inca buildings have been found here.

Exploring Kuélap

The funnel-shaped entrance, one of three main entrances into the fortress, becomes narrower as you go farther in, until eventually it is wide enough for only one person.

El Tintero is the most visited structure within the walls and its name means "inkwell" because of its shape. Early surveys attributed a variety of functions to this building, ranging from a water reservoir to a jail – even a torture chamber and a cemetery. However, studies now suggest that the building had astronomical functions, since the small entrance lines up with the sun at the most favorable times for planting crops.

The 23-ft- (7-m-) high lookout tower, Torreón, at the north end of Pueblo Alto, is one of the main features at the ruins and provide views in every direction. Here, archaeologists found an arsenal of broken stone axe heads and, piled on the floor, 2,500 stones of a perfect size to fit in the slingshots that defenders would have used.

↑ Mysterious inverted-cone-shaped structure, El Tintero, on the southern side of the citadel

THE CHACHAPOYA PEOPLE

The name Chachapoya is commonly believed to come from the conflation of two Quechua words, *sacha* and *puyu*, together translating as forest-cloud. The Chachapoya people were famous for their shamans, and were known as great sorcerers and herbalists. The people were skilled agriculturalists, and renowned for their weaving. The finds displayed at the Museo Leymebamba *(p244)* testify to the range of techniques, such as plain weaves, brocades, and embroidery, used on a single textile.

EXPERIENCE MORE

3
Leymebamba

D3 **50 miles (80 km) SE of Chachapoyas**

The attractive market town of Leymebamba, about a 10-hour drive from Cajamarca, is not covered by most travel itineraries of Peru. However, the surrounding countryside is wonderful for exploring on foot or horseback. Just south of the town, the **Museo Leymebamba** houses the amazing archaeological finds from the nearby Laguna de los Cóndores. Among the 5,000 artifacts on display are some 150 exceptionally well-preserved mummies, plus an ethnographic display on life in the region. The museum also has a colorful orchid garden, planted with more than 100 native species of this plant. Just across the road, a small café serves excellent snacks and has feeders that attract 17 species of hummingbirds. The town has a handful of lodgings or can be visited on a day trip from Chachapoyas.

Museo Leymebamba
Av Austria, San Miguel **10am–4:30pm daily** **museos.cultura.pe/museos/museo-leymebamba**

4
Los Baños del Inca

C3 **3 miles (5 km) E of Cajamarca** **5am–7:30pm daily**

A pleasant way to spend an afternoon is to wallow in the thermal baths at the Baños del Inca, just a short taxi or bus ride from Cajamarca. The baths date back to pre-Inca times. It is believed that the last Inca, Atahualpa, and his army had camped at the baths when Spanish conquistador Pizarro arrived – hence the name.

Today, the baths are part of a vast resort, which gets particularly busy at weekends. The complex features picnic and play areas, several restaurants, a hotel, saunas, and massage stations.

5
Ventanillas de Otuzco and Combayo

C3 **Otuzco: 5 miles (8 km) NE of Cajamarca** **From Cajamarca** **8am–6pm daily**

One of the oldest cemeteries in Peru, the Ventanillas de Otuzco date back about 3,500 years. The necropolis comprises a series of burial niches carved into the volcanic rock of the cliff, some of which are decorated with carvings. The chieftains of Cajamarca were buried in these niches. From a distance, they look like windows, hence the Spanish name *ventanillas* (little windows).

A collection of these niches can be found at Combayo, 18 miles (30 km) southeast of Cajamarca. Both of the sites can be visited on a tour from Cajamarca. Otuzco is a 90-minute walk from Los Baños del Inca.

> **LA LAGUNA DE LOS CÓNDORES**
>
> Hidden away in cloud forest, the spellbinding Laguna de los Cóndores is also known as the Laguna de las Momias (Lake of the Mummies). In 1997, hundreds of mummies, overlooked by the Spanish, were recovered from cliff tombs surrounding the lake. They now reside in Leymebamba's museum. It's a demanding 12-hour trail to the tombs, which climbs to 12,139 ft (3,700 m) before descending to the lake shore. A three-day trip can be organized with agencies in Chachapoyas or Leymebamba.

6 Chachapoyas

C3 | 204 miles (329 km) NE of Cajamarca | From Lima | From Cajamarca

Though it is an unremarkable place in itself, good transportation links make Chachapoyas the gateway to northern Peru's finest archaeological sites. Its pretty central square hosts a bronze bust of independence leader Toribio Rodríguez de Mendoza and is flanked by colonial buildings. One houses the Museo el Reino de las Nubes, which introduces local sights, including a scale model of Kuélap *(p242)*. For a fine overview of the city, the Mirador de Luya Urco in the northwest affords panoramas across the rooftops.

The city is the ideal base from which to visit nearby ruins attributed to the Chachapoya, or "Cloud People," an unusually fair-skinned race that excelled in building mountaintop fortresses and buried their dead in cliffside mausoleums. They were absorbed into the Inca Empire sometime in the 15th century.

---

7 Cumbemayo

C3 | 13 miles (20 km) SW of Cajamarca

The mountainous region of Cumbemayo, southwest of Cajamarca *(p240)*, is famous for a canal and aqueduct carved from rock and pieced together by deft stonemasons with great skill. The structure is thought to be about 2,000 years old and perhaps had ritual as well as practical significance, considering the great effort that went into its construction. It originally carried water from the Atlantic watershed over to the Pacific side through an intricate system of tunnels and canals, some of which are still in use.

To one side of the aqueduct is a rock, shaped like a face, into which an artificial cave has been carved. Inside the cave, with the aid of a torch one can make out 3,000-year-old petroglyphs which have feline features. This is a hallmark of the Chavín *(p69)* style, which dominated this part of Peru at that time.

Don't miss the odd natural rock formation known as the Bosque de Piedras (Stone Forest), clearly visible from the Cajamarca–Cumbemayo road. Here, limestone rock masses have eroded, forming tapered shapes which are reminiscent of the human form, giving them their Spanish name, *los frailones* (the big monks).

← Fascinating "little windows," or *ventanillas*, at Otuzco

↑ Hikers at one of the austere, monk-like rock formations at Cumbemayo

---

EAT

Café Fusiones
Sandwiches, salads, and desserts using regional organic products are on offer in a colorful and cozy setting. Organic local coffee is roasted and ground on site.

C3 | Jirón Ortiz Arriet 779, Chachapoyas | cafefusiones.com

S/ S/ S/

Kentikafé
This outdoor café serves up delicious cakes, but the real attraction is the hummingbirds that come to sip from feeders in the trees.

D3 | Av Austria s/n, Leymebamba | 971 118 273

S/ S/ S/

THE SPATULETAIL

Endemic to this region of Peru, the spatuletail is a rare hummingbird species known for its courtship dance using four tail feathers, two ending in dark blue disks. It has a striking blue cap and a turquoise throat. Illegal hunting for the male's heart, believed to be an aphrodisiac, has led to a dramatic decline in their population. Travelers can spot them at Reserva Huembo (p57).

8
Cañón del Sonche

C3 5 miles (8 km) N of Chachapoyas From Chachapoyas

Around 5 miles (8 km) north of Chachapoyas (p245), a viewing platform (for which there is a small entrance charge) perches on the edge of the 3,156-ft (962-m) Cañón del Sonche. Verdant, folded valley sides plunge into this dramatic canyon, where the Sonche river has carved a 7-mile (11.5-km) route between the mountains.

When the skies are clear, it's possible to see Gocta Falls in the distance north, while turkey vultures glide in the skies above. In the rainy season (December–April) the canyon is transformed, with waterfalls cascading down from the mountains and into the valley. At sunset, the diminishing light brings a delicate, otherworldly hue to the scenery.

9
Karajía

C3 30 miles (48 km) SW of Chachapoyas, near Luya From Chachapoyas

Oversized, colorfully painted vertical sarcophagi made of earth, wood, and straw and decorated with faces, were the final resting places of important members of the famous Chachapoyan culture. Many of these coffins have been discovered and the ones found at Karajía are the easiest to visit from Chachapoyas. The site is reached by minibuses from Chachapoyas to Luya, from where it is a 3-hour hike. Tours from Chachapoyas are also available. Karajía is a 45-minute walk from Cruzpata.

Cavernas Quiocta, near Lamud, a town about an hour and a half's drive from Karajía, can be combined with a visit to Karajía. This series of caves contains Inca remains, pools, and geological formations. Visitors need to ask for a guide in Lamud and should visit between 8am and 5pm.

10
Levanto

C3 14 miles (22 km) S of Chachapoyas

An original and unrestored Inca road joins Chachapoyas with Levanto, which is situated at a height of 9,488 ft (2,892 m).

It was first settled by the Spanish in 1532, and remains a small village with only a few remnants of its colonial past.

A few miles away is the site of Yalape (built 1100–1300) which has classic circular buildings adorned with geometric friezes, and the remains of an irrigation system. This is part of the second-largest known Chachapoyan fortress after Kuélap, with other sites nearby.

Most visitors make it a day trip, arriving by the morning bus uphill from Chachapoyas and returning along the Inca road downhill on foot.

HIDDEN GEM
Huaylla Belén

A few hours' drive from Levanto, a winding river known as the "Silver Serpent," filled with rainbow trout, snakes through verdant meadows in the Huaylla Belén Valley. This picturesque spot is ideal for relaxed picnicking or fly fishing. Several operators offer guided fishing trips.

→ Cliff mausoleums of Revash, looking like miniature clay houses

11 Revash

C3 | 37 miles (60 km) S of Chachapoyas, near Santo Tomás

Named for the Revash culture, contemporary with the Chachapoyans (p242), this site is famed for its *chullpas* (funerary chambers). These small, multihued buildings perch precariously on ledges high up on the limestone cliffs. They are made from mud and stone walls, then plastered over and painted, and topped with peculiar gabled roofs. The *chullpas* have been looted, but a dozen burials and funerary offerings were discovered by archaeologists. A variety of pictographs can be seen on the cliff behind the structures.

There are daily minibuses from Chachapoyas to Santo Tomás, the nearest town to the Revash site. Visitors should disembark at the Santo Tomás turnoff. Allow three hours for the steep climb up to the ruins. Near Santo Tomás is the village of Yerbuena, which has a busy Sunday market.

12 Catarata Gocta

C3 | Near San Pablo

In 2002 it was discovered that this huge waterfall, hidden in the cloud forest and known only to the locals, was one of the highest in the world. Stefan Ziemendorff, a German hydro-engineer, saw the falls on the Río Cocahuayco and his preliminary measurements of its height were an astounding 2,531 ft (771 m). Though this is a two-tiered fall, the tiers are close enough for the World Waterfall Database to consider them to be one. It rates them among the top ten in the world.

Gocta is on the east of the main Chachapoyas–Pedro Ruíz road. Taxis from either town can be taken for San Pablo, where informal guides take visitors on a trail which lasts 1–2 hours to a view of the upper falls. En route, good views of both tiers are available. To see the falls from the bottom, it is necessary to backtrack and take another taxi to the smaller hamlet of Cocachimba, and then to walk about three hours each way through the cloud forest.

STAY

La Casona de Chachapoyas
Built in the late 1800s, this charming two-story house is now an attractive hotel. The cozy, individually decorated rooms have whitewashed walls, folk art, and sturdy antique furniture.

C3 | Jirón Chincha Alta 569, Chachapoyas | lacasonadechachapoyasperu.com

$ $ $

Gocta Natura
Tucked into restored cloud forest, the plush cabins and hot tub of this boutique lodge have dramatic views of the Gocta Falls. Home-cooked meals are included. The owners support local conservation projects.

C3 | Cocachimba | goctanatura.com

$ $ $

Dense jungle of the rainforest

THE AMAZON BASIN

The incredibly ecologically diverse Amazonian rainforest is home to more species of animals and plants than any other area on earth. While little is known about the history of its original human inhabitants, recent laser-technology research has started to uncover evidence of early civilizations that grew here. At the height of the Inca Empire, the upper Amazon Basin was incorporated into Antisuyo (the empire's eastern quarter) and scarlet macaw feathers and jungle fruits were traded for metal tools. After the conquest, the Spaniards concentrated on the coastal and highland regions. Their greatest impact was in the unintended introduction of diseases, such as smallpox and influenza, to which citizens had no resistance.

In the 16th century, colonial outposts were established in places such as Moyobamba, but the Amazon was not permanently occupied by the colonizing Europeans until a few missions were built in the 18th century. With the 1880s rubber boom, the migrant population exploded and many Indigenous communities were displaced as a result. Four decades later, the boom collapsed and the once-opulent towns survived by logging, exploitation of jungle crops, and export of animals for zoos.

The discovery of oil in the 1960s fueled another population boom, soon followed by a nascent tourism industry. Slowly, cities such as Iquitos, Pucallpa, and Puerto Maldonado gained renewed importance, and *ribereños* (river-dwellers) began to clear forests for agriculture.

Amazonia covers almost 60 per cent of Peru's territory, yet despite its vastness and beauty, its forests and Indigenous populations are under constant threat. The Indigenous communities here continue to fend off illegal logging, mining, agricultural expansion, and drug-trafficking, with minimal help from the government.

THE AMAZON BASIN

Must Sees
1. Iquitos
2. Reserva Nacional Pacaya-Samiria
3. Reserva de la Biósfera de Manu
4. Ríos Tambopata and Madre de Dios Area

Experience More
5. Pevas
6. Yurimaguas
7. Tarapoto
8. Moyobamba and Alto Mayo
9. Pucallpa
10. Ucayali River Towns
11. Puerto Bermúdez
12. The Chanchamayo Region
13. Villa Rica
14. Oxapampa
15. Pozuzo
16. Parque Nacional Yanachaga-Chemillén

↑ The renowned floating wooden houses in Iquitos

IQUITOS

E2 · 373 miles (600 km) NE of Pucallpa · From Panama only · From Lima · From Pucallpa or Yurimaguas · Plaza de Armas, Napo 161; iquitos-peru.com

Set on the banks of the Río Amazonas, the city of Iquitos is the capital of the Peruvian Amazon. It takes its name from the Iquito people – one of many Indigenous groups exploited by the Jesuits who founded a mission here in 1797. Today, this busy metropolis includes a lovely waterfront, markets, and architectural gems.

① Malecón Tarapacá

One block off the main square, Iquitos' waterfront boulevard is the perfect place to unwind, whether browsing the crafts stalls at the Centro Artesenal Anaconda, or sipping a cocktail in an outdoor bar at sunset.

> **INSIDER TIP**
> **Reaching Iquitos**
>
> This is the largest city in the world that is inaccessible by road; you can fly from Lima or Pucallpa, or take a boat from Pucallpa or Yurimaguas.

② Museo de las Culturas Indígenas Amazónicas

Malecón Tarapacá 332 · 10am–6pm daily · fundamazonia.org

Showcasing the varied traditions and rituals of 40 of the Peruvian Amazon's Indigenous peoples, this fascinating anthropological museum contains a wealth of information and artifacts, from extravagant ceremonial headdresses and jewelry to ancient weaponry and musical instruments.

③ Museo Barco Histórico "Ayapua"

Moored by Plaza Ramón Castilla · 10am–6pm Thu–Tue · fundamazonia.org

Built in Germany in 1906, and lovingly restored, this steam ship turned museum offers insights into

→ Sculpture from the Museo de las Culturas Indígenas Amazónicas

Must See

Iquitos' boom era. It explores the extravagance and brutality of the notorious rubber barons, such as Fitzcarrald, fed by the exploitation of the Amazon's natural resources and populations.

④ Belén

South of the city center, the vast, sprawling market of Belén is the beating heart of Iquitos and is famous for its huge variety of jungle produce. Whether you explore on your own or sign up for a guided tour, Pasaje Paquito, a narrow alleyway filled with stalls selling unique jungle remedies, is not to be missed. Below the market, the famous wooden houses of Belén *barrio* perch on stilts or float on balsa rafts when the river waters are high.

⑤ Centro de Rescate Amazónico

📍 Carretera Iquitos-Nauta, 2.8 miles (4.5 km) SW of Iquitos ☎ 991 476 519
🕘 9am-3pm Tue-Sun

Working with a US aquarium, this Amazonian rescue center predominantly rehabilitates orphaned manatees. The guided tour (usually in Spanish) lasts one hour and tells you all you need to know about the rescue, rehabilitation and release program of these extraordinary-looking and elusive aquatic mammals.

⑥ Reserva Nacional Allpahuayo-Mishana

📍 Carretera Iquitos-Nauta, 16 miles (26 km) S of Iquitos
🚍 From Iquitos ☎ 956 750 555 🕘 8am-5pm daily

Known in particular for its rare white-sand forests, or *varillales*, this relatively diminutive (in Amazonian terms) yet biodiverse reserve lies a short ride outside Iquitos. It offers trails of varying lengths, popular with birdwatchers drawn by over 500 bird species, five of which are endemic to the reserve. Tour guide services can be contracted at the reserve. One possible route is an informative tour of native Amazonian fruit trees and medicinal plants, close to the reserve's scientific research center. During the high-water months (usually Dec–May), local ecotourism operators can take you along the flooded blackwater channels of the Río Nanay, offering opportunities to swim in creeks or stay overnight in rustic lodgings with guided night walks that bring you close to the sights and sounds of the reserve's nocturnal creatures.

> The vast, sprawling market of Belén is the beating heart of Iquitos and is famous for its huge variety of jungle produce.

STAY

Casa Morey
This historic mansion features period furniture and modern comforts. Reserve an upstairs suite with French windows and a spectacular river view.

📍 Plaza Ramón Castilla
🌐 casamorey.com

RESERVA NACIONAL PACAYA-SAMIRIA

◮E3 ⌂190 miles (306 km) SW of Iquitos ⛴ ℹ SERNANP, Calle Jorge Chávez 930, Iquitos; 065 223 555

Sandwiched between the Ucayali and Marañón tributaries to the Amazon, this reserve is Peru's second-largest protected area and its largest expanse of seasonally flooded jungle. Laced with several rivers, countless creeks, and mirror-like lagoons, these blackwater wetlands are extremely picturesque.

To really savor the experience at this reserve, staying several days is a must, with options ranging from a romantic riverboat cruise to a rustic lodge with daily forays into the reserve by motorized dugout. The reserve teems with wildlife, from anacondas and river turtles to 13 species of monkeys. Farther away from human habitation, elusive large mammals such as tapirs, pumas, and jaguars can even make an appearance. When water levels are low, guided night-hikes reveal a world of shy nocturnal creatures, including spiders, frogs, and snakes. Village visits are great opportunities to buy locally made crafts and experience shamanic rituals. For the truly adventurous, the Indigenous Cocama-Cocamilla of Lagunas offer unique jungle tours, paddling tourists in dugout canoes. While sleeping on makeshift beds and washing in the river is not for everyone, the silence of the forest, broken only by squawking macaws, is magical.

← Beautiful Peruvian night monkeys in the treetops

> **STAY**
>
> **The Treehouse Lodge**
> Experience a unique night's sleep in the rainforest canopy. This all-inclusive lodge gives you a personal guide and treehouse, with surround jungle-sound and a raucous dawn chorus to wake you. It's on the Río Yarapa, one of the tributaries of the Río Ucayali.
> 🌐 treehouselodge.com
> ⓈⓈⓈ

← Traveling by boat on the Río Samiria, one of three river basins within the reserve

Must See

Did You Know?

The large Amazon or pink river dolphins *(Inia geoffrensis)* found in the lagoons here, get pinker with age.

↑ The large Río Marañón, which borders the reserve in the north

RESERVA DE LA BIÓSFERA DE MANU

G5 From Cusco From Boca Manu Urb. Santa Martha E-12, San Jerónimo, Cusco; visitmanu.com

This stunning UNESCO World Heritage Site covers an impressive 7,700 sq miles (20,000 sq km) of the Manu Basin. Manu Biosphere Reserve drops from 13,120 ft (4,000 m) above sea level north of Cusco, through remote cloud forests containing some of the most diverse bird populations on earth, to lowland rainforests which are home to a proliferation of jungle flora and fauna.

The reserve has three zones. Over 80 per cent lies in the "intangible zone," which is the abode of Indigenous peoples who have almost no contact with the outside world; travelers are prohibited. The "multiple-use" zone is where the one road from the highlands enters, and has several villages. The "reserved zone" is the relatively flat rainforest of the Río Manu, and traveling into this zone is possible only by boat. It allows tourism, and camping on beaches is permitted with authorized guides. Canopy platforms and towers are also available for visitors. Meandering in huge curves, the river in this zone sometimes leaves behind oxbow lakes known as *cochas*, which are the haunt of the rare giant river otter and some spectacular waterbirds.

The wide-ranging elevations of the cloud forest create ideal environments for birds, and new ornithological species are frequently recorded here. Mixed feeding flocks of dozens of bird species are a highlight, and hikers on steep trails are regularly rewarded with sightings of woolly monkeys and brown capuchins.

Must See

↑ A haven of tropical forest reflected in a beautiful lake at the Reserva de la Biósfera de Manu

TOP 4 WILDLIFE TO SPOT

Toucans
These striking birds live in the forest canopy and are mainly fruit eaters.

Giant Katydids
Resembling a leaf, these are one of the thousands of insect species in the reserve.

Woolly Monkeys
This group inhabit the cloud forest and have a prehensile tail which can be used to hold objects.

Hoatzins and Horned Screamers
Both known for their ornate head plumes, these birds are commonly found around oxbow lakes.

1 The Río Manu flows across the reserve, which is home to a vast variety of flora and fauna. The jungle around the river is home to rare monkeys, birds, and elusive jungle cats.

2 Over a dozen monkey species roam the forests here. Woolly monkeys live in groups.

3 The paradise tanager, found in the reserve's cloud forest, is a beautiful bright bird known for its seven-colored plumage.

RÍOS TAMBOPATA AND MADRE DE DIOS AREA

🅰 G5   📍 37 miles (60 km) SW of Puerto Maldonado   ✈ From Lima   🚌 From Cusco

The beautiful rivers, pristine lakes, and primary rainforests of southeastern Peru are teeming with wildlife, making this the most biodiverse area of Peru's Amazon. Offering the highest concentration of jungle lodges, staffed by naturalist guides and reached only by river, this region is a must for those seeking wildlife adventures.

The stunning Río Madre de Dios flows from the highlands near the Reserva de la Biósfera de Manu into Bolivia. Most of the land south of this river is protected by national parks. The vibrant frontier city of Puerto Maldonado sits at the confluence of the Madre de Dios and Tambopata rivers, and is the best base for visiting the area. After the rubber boom, this city turned to logging, rainforest agriculture, and gold panning. Reserva Nacional de Tambopata provides excellent access to the rainforest. It attracts over 630 species of birds and 1,200 species of butterflies.

Panoramic view above the Madre de Dios region; Lago Sandoval *(inset)*

Must See

1. Views of the ubiquitous corrugated-metal roofed buildings can be seen from a 98-ft- (30-m-) high tower in Puerto Maldonado.

2. Riverside mud cliffs with abnormally high salt content attract hundreds of parrots and macaws, who nibble on the clay to obtain minerals.

3. Lago Sandoval, just off the Río Madre de Dios, is home to the endangered giant river otter.

Did You Know?

The banks of the Río Tambopata are home to capybaras, the world's largest rodents.

THE SHIPIBO-CONIBO

One of Peru's 40 Indigenous peoples of the Amazon, the Shipibo-Conibo are renowned for their shamanic knowledge of medicinal plants and use of ayahuasca (p260). This knowledge is reflected in the geometric designs (known as *kené*) on their ceramics, textiles, and bodies. Many Shipibo live in the Ucayalí Valley, where they are under threat from illegal logging, drug trafficking, and agricultural expansion.

→ Ceramic jug

EXPERIENCE MORE

5
Pevas

F2 ⏵ 90 miles (145 km) downriver from Iquitos ⏵ From Iquitos

The oldest town on the Peruvian Amazon, Pevas is made up of wooden structures, many with thatched roofs. Founded by missionaries in 1735, the town, sadly, has no buildings left from that era. It is known for not having cars, banks, or a post office. Most of the friendly inhabitants belong to the Indigenous Bora, Huitoto, Yagua, or Ocainas peoples, or are mestizo.

The town's most famous resident was artist Francisco Grippa, who died in 2024. The fate of his towering hilltop studio and gallery – where he used to welcome guests with beer and bananas – is yet to be decided.

6
Yurimaguas

D3 ⏵ 240 miles (390 km) SW of Iquitos ⏵ From Iquitos ⏵ From Tarapoto

Founded by a Jesuit priest in 1710, this town derives its name from two Indigenous groups, the Yoras and the Omaguas, who predate the arrival of the missionaries. These groups no longer exist, though there are reports that some Yoras still live in the more remote jungle regions.

Yurimaguas remained a tiny outpost until the rubber boom, with tilework from its early days visible along the east end of Avenida Arica. It became the main port on the Río Huallaga, known as the Pearl of Huallaga, and today, life centers around the river port – the gateway for excursions to Pacaya-Samiria and Iquitos. However, the rapid 20th-century growth seen in Iquitos and Pucallpa has bypassed Yurimaguas. Despite being closer to Iquitos, it has been the forgotten option, while Pucallpa has long been considered the best route from Lima to the Amazon. Highways now connect Yurimaguas with Tarapoto and locals hope that the town will develop.

> **Did You Know?**
>
> Yurimaguas is the last town on the Rio Huallaga that can be reached by road; after that, it's boat or plane.

AYAHUASCA

Ceremonies involving drinking ayahuasca tea - a vine used in spiritual medicine and a powerful hallucinogen - have become big tourist business, offered by some lodges, who bring in a local shaman, or in specialist retreats. Most participants report positive experiences but unpleasant purging (usually vomiting) is common as the plant rids the body of chemicals such as salt; details about the shaman, venue, and ceremony need careful research.

↑ Busy day-to-day life of an Amazonian river port at Yurimaguas

7

Tarapoto

D3 ⌂ 72 miles (116 km) SE of Moyobamba ✈🚌 From Moyobamba or Chiclayo ℹ Jirón Ramírez Hurtado; 042 526 188; 8–11am daily

The bustling town of Tarapoto is the largest and fastest-growing city in San Martín. At a height of 1,181 ft (360 m), it is a place for fishing, swimming, and relaxing, with some of the finest waterfalls in Peru. The Río Mayo, 19 miles (30 km) away, offers white-water rafting from June to October.

Tarapoteños enjoy a good party, and their festivals feature street dances, folk music, costumed processions, and plenty of food. Among their many sought-after local drinks is *uvachado*, which is a potent brew made by soaking grapes in a cocktail of sugar-cane alcohol, cinnamon, and honey for a month.

The famous Quechua-speaking hillside town of Lamas is 18 miles (28 km) northwest of Tarapoto. The self-proclaimed "capital folklórica de la Amazonia" welcomes travelers interested in traditional dance, music, and folklore, thatch and mud-wall architecture, or arts and crafts. Guided tours are available from Tarapoto.

Of the many lakes in this area, the Laguna Sauce (also known as Laguna Azul) is the most popular, with hotels and camping facilities, swimming, boating, and angling. Avoid weekends and holiday periods to escape the crowds.

↑ Crossing a footbridge above the Alto Mayo at Moyobamba

Getting there is half the fun as taxis and minibuses cross the Río Huallaga on a balsa raft on the 32-mile (52-km) drive.

8

Moyobamba and Alto Mayo

D3 ⌂ 99 miles (160 km) E of Chachapoyas 🚌 From Chachapoyas 🌐 moyobamba.com

Located on the edge of the Amazon Basin, this area was likely first inhabited by the Chachapoyas people, before the Spaniards established the small town of Moyobamba in the 1540s. Despite destructive earthquakes in the 1990s and 2000s, it has recovered well and provides access to the high subtropical jungle. Locals call it the City of Orchids due to the abundance of these flowers in the city's botanical gardens.

Moyobamba is the oldest city in this region and, according to some, Túpac Yupanqui (*p195*) made this area a base from which the Incas made incursions into the surrounding areas. The name Moyobamba derives from the Quechua word *muyupampa*, which means a "circular plain."

Located on the upper Río Mayo basin, Moyobamba's main visitor attractions are essentially water-related. The Baños Termales San Mateo, fed by natural hot springs, are popular with the locals. Located just to the south of town, they can be reached by *motocarro* (a motorcycle rickshaw). Just an hour's drive from Moyobamba are the Cataratas del Gera, the most popular among the many falls in the region.

← Intricate carving from one of Tarapoto's colorful crafts centers

---

STAY

Ulcumano Ecolodge
A handful of idyllic, simple cabins set in fabulous cloud forest.

D5 ⌂ Sector La Suiza Chontabamba, 6 miles (10 km) SW of Oxapampa 🌐 ulcumanoecolodge.com.

$ $ $

Carolina Egg Gasthaus
Relaxing B&B in a flower-filled garden.

D5 ⌂ Av San Martín 1085, Oxapampa 🌐 carolinaegg.com

$ $ $

Albergue Frau María Egg
Wooden chalets surrounded by lush greenery. Expect superb breakfasts.

D4 ⌂ Av Los Colonos, Pozuzo 🌐 pozuzo.com

$ $ $

↑ Colorful boats moored along the river bank in Pucallpa

9
Pucallpa

E4 **178 miles (288 km) NE of Lima** **From Lima & Iquitos** **From Lima** **From Iquitos**

A late-blooming city in the Peruvian Amazon, Pucallpa is now among its fastest growing; in 1900, it had a population of just 200. The highway from Lima came in 1930, changing Pucallpa into a major logging center. Exploration for oil, gas, and gold has further boosted the city's economy, making Pucallpa the most important port on the Río Ucayali. More recently, land has been cleared for palm oil cultivation at the expense of Indigenous territory.

Not attractive in the traditional sense, Pucallpa's modern city center still has a certain charm. Funds have been invested in revamping the main plaza and the attractive pedestrianized street that leads down to the bustling, leafy waterfront. Most travelers use the city as a base or pitstop. For artistically inclined visitors, however, an essential destination here is the **"Usko-Ayar" Escuela de Pintura Amazónica**, where shaman and painter Pablo Amaringo teaches, works, and exhibits his esoteric pieces inspired by ayahuasca (p260) visions in the rainforest.

Just 3 miles (5 km) northeast of downtown Pucallpa is Yarinacocha, a lake which offers some pleasant recreational opportunities, including boat trips to look for dolphins or to visit the Chullachaqui botanical garden, where sloths and green iguanas may be seen. There are Shipibo villages to visit, too, such as San Francisco and Santa Clara, both reachable by transport from the lakeside village of Puerto Callao.

"Usko-Ayar" Escuela de Pintura Amazónica
Sánchez Cerro 465
9am–5pm Mon–Fri

10
Ucayali River Towns

E4–E2 **Btwn Pucallpa & Iquitos** **From Iquitos or Pucallpa**

For decades, the main waterway linking Iquitos (p252) with the rest of Peru has been along the Río Ucayali from Pucallpa. Two- and three-decked riverboats ply the river between Pucallpa and Iquitos, delivering everything from motorcycles to medical equipment to the villages and small towns in between. The riverboats also provide passenger transportation to locals, most of whom hang their own hammocks on the second or third deck, while stuffy cabins with bunk

---

> **HIDDEN GEM**
> **Maroti Shobo Craft Center**
>
> This women's crafts cooperative in the main square of Yarinacocha, 3 miles (5 km) north of Pucallpa, sells pieces made by Shipibo women from around 40 villages. Items are primarily patterned textiles but beautiful ceramics and jewelry are also sold. Open 8am–5pm daily.

beds are also available for extra charge. Basic on-board meals are also provided on these boats. The boats stop frequently at the many small villages along the river. The trip from Pucallpa to Iquitos, with the current, takes around four days, while the return, against the current, can take as long as six (faster *expreso* boats take one or two days).

The main towns on the route are Contamana and Requena, both of which have basic hotel and restaurant facilities. Contamana, located 267 miles (430 km) from Iquitos, is known for its hot springs and a macaw clay lick that can be reached by car via a 14-mile (22-km) dirt road.

Requena, a growing town, lies about 100 miles (160 km) from Iquitos. It has a small cathedral and is close to Laguna Avispa, which is 5 miles (8 km) by boat. This is a popular spot with the locals for fishing, both with lines and nets, and swimming in the calm, warm lake waters. Birdwatchers enjoy the small lake, not for any rare species, but for chances to observe some of the best-known Amazonian birds in their natural surroundings. Watching long-toed jacanas running speedily over the tops of the water lilies and other aquatic vegetation is a beautiful sight for any bird-lover. Female jacanas mate with several partners, moving on after each laying and leaving the males to take on the majority of hatching duties, a rare behavior among birds.

⑪
Puerto Bermúdez

🅔E4 📍160 miles (255 km) S of Pucallpa 🚌From La Merced or from Pucallpa via Constitución ℹ️Mincetur, Av Capitán Larry; 065 792 558

Well off the beaten track, and inaccessible after heavy rains, this quiet jungle town's claim to fame is that it lies in the geographical center of Peru. Much of the surrounding forest has been cleared for cacao, plantain, and yucca plantations, but the scenic Río Pichis affords opportunities for relaxing boat trips, and visits to picturesque local waterfalls. Tourism is in its infancy here, and lodgings and other visitor facilities are basic. Even so, rewarding day trips can be organized to the scenic forested Reserva Nacional del Sira, home to Asháninka and Yanesha communities, and brimming with spectacular orchids and stunning birdlife.

↑ Hammocks strung on a Ucayali riverboat deck, a cooler and cheaper option than a cabin

EAT & DRINK

Vater Otto
Cozy drinking den with a wide range of craft and imported German beers, spirits galore, and a lively vibe. The drinks are inexpensive and the bartenders are friendly. There's also a sibling bar by the main plaza.

🅓D5 📍Jr Bolívar 514, Oxapampa 📞986 995 841

S/ S/ S/

Restaurante Típico Prusia
Pozuzo's Austro-German heritage has permeated the cuisine here. This restaurant is famous for its wurst and smoked pork, accompanied by fried plantain. Occasional Tyrolean dancing performances are put on here throughout the year.

🅓D4 📍Av Cristóbal Johann 110, Prusia, Pozuzo 🌐tipicoprusia.com

S/ S/ S/

Parrillada Orlando's
Expect sizzling meat from the grill accompanied by piles of *patacones* (deep fried squashed plantain) and hearty salads at this no-nonsense local favorite. Its pitchers of Camu Camu are equally popular.

🅔E4 📍Jirón Aguaytia s/n, Pucallpa 📞937 657 573

S/ S/ S/

12

The Chanchamayo Region

🅰 D5 📍 193 miles (310 km) NE of Lima

As the road crests a barren Andean pass some 193 miles (310 km) northeast of Lima, it swoops down into the warm, lush Chanchamayo Valley, filled with fruit orchards and coffee plantations. The delicious coffee and fruit juices slip down nicely in the restaurants and cafés of La Merced – the valley's main town and center – and nearby San Ramón.

La Merced, with its good transportation links, is the gateway to adventure. About 34 miles (55 km) south of the town is one of Peru's most-visited waterfalls, the Catarata Bayoz. The spectacular falls form tiers of swimming holes, perfect for cooling off in the lush, humid jungle. Farther along this road is the frontier-town Satipo, in the ancestral heartland of the beleaguered Asháninka people *(p74)*. Visitors are welcome in several of their remote communities.

North of La Merced, on the high road, are the idiosyncratic Peruvian-Tyrolean communities of Oxapampa and Pozuzo; along the low unpaved road is the town of Villa Rica.

13

Villa Rica

🅰 E5 📍 33 miles (53 km) N of La Merced 🚌 From La Merced or Oxapampa

A giant coffeepot in the Plaza de Armas greets arrivals in Villa Rica. Last of the Austro-German settlements in this region, established in 1928, this is coffee central – the country's best beans are produced in fincas in the neighboring Pichis and Palcazu valleys. Some, such as Finca Santa Rosa, can be visited on a tour. The annual Feria de Café (July/August) is heaven for coffee connoisseurs, with a full program of gastronomic, artisanal, and cultural entertainment.

14

Oxapampa

🅰 D5 📍 49 miles (78 km) N of La Merced 🚌 From La Merced or Lima 🛈 turismo oxapampa.com

This provincial capital owes much of its clean, ordered streets to its Tyrolean roots. The same goes for the interesting architecture, as the town is dotted with wooden gabled houses, with wide eaves and decorative, carved balconies. The Iglesia Santa Rosa, on the main square, is also an impressive wooden structure.

Tropical warmth tempered by fresh mountain air makes the climate here extremely pleasant. Surrounded by the cloud-forested hills of the *selva alta* – the "high jungle" – this town makes a great base for forays into the Parque Nacional Yanachaga-Chemillén, while thrill-seekers should consider the roller-coaster mountain bike ride to Pozuzo. For music-lovers, Oxapampa is synonymous with Selvámonos (p67), a feel-good, family-friendly festival of cultural activities, street partying, and alternative music.

15
Pozuzo

D4 50 miles (80 km) N of Oxapampa From Oxapampa

A serpentine descent down an unmade road from Oxapampa leads you to tiny Pozuzo, set in a lush, steep-sided valley streaked with waterfalls. Pozuzo's Austro-German roots make a visit to this tidy jungle community distinctly surreal. Founded in 1857 by Tyrolean settlers at the invitation of the Peruvian government, Pozuzo has evolved a hybrid Peruvian-Tyrolean culture, where yucca and plantain accompany schnitzel and wurst; German-style beer is served in tankards at the local microbrewery; and dancers clad in lederhosen and dirndls dance the polka. More of this history is on display in the museum. For nature lovers, riverside walks and the chance to see the outlandish courtship displays of the cock-of-the-rock *(Rupicola peruviensis)*, the national bird of Peru, are additional attractions.

16
Parque Nacional Yanachaga-Chemillén

D4 19 miles (30 km) N of Oxapampa SERNANP, Prolongación Pozuzo 156, Oxapampa; sernanp.gob.pe

This little-known national park is one of the country's most varied, bordered by Yanesha and Asháninka communities. Extending over 470 sq miles (1,220 sq km), the reserve protects a fabulous species-rich landscape, ranging from cloud-forest-clad mountains cleft by deep canyons, to scrubland and low-lying tropical forest. Four separate entrances get you close to different habitats and abundant wildlife. Three of these areas are within easy reach of Oxapampa and have lovely, simple camping spots or bunkhouses. The Huampal sector, near Pozuzo, offers a view of the impressive Cañón de Hunacabamba and bountiful birdlife, including the exhibitionist cock-of-the-rock and the torrent duck, a white-water diving specialist. An enjoyable hiking trail features in the San Alberto area, while the San Daniel zone has beautiful orchids fringing a reed-lined lake. However, the more inaccessible eastern Paujil sector is the biggest gem: steamy rainforest surrounding a biological station, laced with lovely rivers, and a lake harboring giant river otters. Getting here requires many hours by road and boat and an adventurous spirit but the ample rewards include possible sightings of tapir at a nearby clay lick, monkeys swinging nimbly through the treetops, and caiman sunning themselves on sandbanks.

> **Did You Know?**
>
> Elementary school uniform in Pozuzo is based on traditional Tyrolean dress.

← Enjoying the cooling spray at the Catarata Bayoz, Chanchamayo

> **INSIDER TIP**
> **Asháninka Village Visits**
>
> Be wary of the brief, often exploitative and voyeuristic visits to Asháninka communities included in many tours from La Merced. If you want to spend time in a community (some offer homestays), contact the Asociación Regional de Pueblos Indígenas de Selva Central (ARPISC; aidesep.org.pe/node/12) in Satipo.

265

NEED TO KNOW

Train stationed at Aguas Calientes

Before You Go 268

Getting Around 270

Practical Information 274

BEFORE YOU GO

Things change, so plan ahead to make the most of your trip. Be prepared for all eventualities by considering the following points before you travel.

AT A GLANCE

CURRENCY
Nuevo Sol (PEN)

AVERAGE DAILY SPEND

SAVE	SPEND	SPLURGE
S/100	S/300	S/500+

BOTTLED WATER	COFFEE	BEER	DINNER FOR TWO
S/1.50	S/6	S/9	S/90

ESSENTIAL PHRASES

Hello	Hola
Please	Por favor
Thank you	Gracias
Excuse me	Con permiso
I don't understand	No entiendo

ELECTRICITY SUPPLY
Standard voltage is 220v. Power sockets are mainly type C, fitting two-pin, round, pronged plugs, or type A, flat-pronged plugs. Some fit both types.

Passports and Visas

For entry requirements, including visas, consult your nearest Peruvian embassy or check the country's official tourism website, **iPerù**. Citizens of the UK, US, Canada, Australia, New Zealand, and the EU are generally granted a 90-day stay upon arrival. A passport valid for at least six months from the date of departure is required.
iPerù
w peru.travel/en

Government Advice

Now more than ever, it is important to consult both your and the Peruvian government's advice before traveling. The **UK Foreign, Commonwealth, & Development Office**, **US State Department**, **Australian Department of Foreign Affairs and Trade**, and **iPerù** websites provide up-to-date travel safety information.
Australian Department of Foreign Affairs and Trade
w smartraveller.gov.au
UK Foreign, Commonwealth, & Development Office
w gov.uk/foreign-travel-advice
US State Department
w travel.state.gov

Customs Information

You can find information on the laws relating to goods and currency taken in or out of Peru on either the **iPerù** or **LimaEasy** websites.
LimaEasy
w limaeasy.com/peru-guide/legal-stuff/what-you-can-and-can-t-bring-into-peru

Insurance

We recommend taking out a comprehensive insurance policy covering theft, loss of belongings, medical care, cancellations and delays, and dangerous activities like mountain climbing, and read the small print carefully. For medical emergencies, be ready to pay upfront and claim on insurance after, as most hospitals adopt a pay-first policy.

Vaccinations

No vaccinations are officially required but travelers planning on visiting the Amazon jungle are advised to get a yellow fever vaccination. Malaria is prevalent in the eastern sections of the jungle; discuss necessary prophylactics with your doctor before traveling.

Money

The unit of currency in Peru is the Nuevo Sol, although US dollars are widely accepted at high-end hotels, travel agencies, and restaurants. Banks are the safest places to exchange money, but rates are better at *casas de cambio* (foreign currency exchanges) or street money changers; never change large sums of money at the last two. Credit cards and contactless payments are widely accepted in cities, and ATMs are found in major towns and cities. Carry small change for bus and taxi fares.

Tip wait staff 10 per cent, hotel porters S/3-5 per bag, and tour guides S/15–S/20 per day if the service is good.

Booking Accommodations

Most lodgings across Peru are available to reserve online. In many parts of the jungle and remoter sections of the Andes, however, accomodations need to be reserved via telephone or upon arrival. The 18 per cent IGV tax (which doesn't apply to those staying fewer than 59 days) shouldn't be included in rates but confirm this before paying.

Peak season (July to August) sees prices rise, particularly in Cusco, where advance reservations are recommended. The coast is popular during summer (December to February); rates increase and prior reservations are essential. Rates and demand for lodgings also rise in all cities and towns during festival periods.

Travelers with Specific Requirements

While facilities for travelers with specific requirements are improving, they are still inadequate. Wheelchair ramps and disabled restrooms are rare and bus travel can be complicated. Only high-end hotels have more accessible rooms. The following tour agencies make arrangements:

Accessible Journeys
w disabilitytravel.com
Apumayo
w apumayo.com
Latinamerica for All
w latinamericaforall.com

Language

Spanish and Quechua are Peru's official languages, with Spanish the most widely used. Aymara is also recognized, along with 48 other Indigenous languages. English is used and understood by workers in tourism. Outside large cities, expect only a basic (if any) knowledge of English – a basic grasp of Spanish will go a long way.

Opening Hours

> Situations can change quickly and unexpectedly. Always check before visiting attractions and hospitality venues for up-to-date opening hours and booking requirements.

Lunchtime Some museums close for lunch.
Sunday Banks and some museums are closed, with shops open for limited hours.
Public holidays All banks, information offices, and some tourist attractions close.

PUBLIC HOLIDAYS

Jan 1	New Year's Day
Mar/Apr	Maundy Thursday
Mar/Apr	Good Friday
May 1	Labor Day
Jun 29	Feast of Saints Peter and Paul
Jul 28-29	Independence Day
Aug 30	St. Rose of Lima Day
Oct 8	Anniversary of the Battle of Angamos
Nov 1-2	All Saints' Day
Dec 8	Immaculate Conception
Dec 9	Battle of Ayacucho
Dec 25	Christmas Day

GETTING AROUND

Whether you are visiting for a week or a more lengthy adventure, discover how best to reach your destination and travel like a pro.

AT A GLANCE

TRANSPORTATION COSTS

LIMA
S/3.50
Metropolitana bus fare

CUSCO
S/90
10-hour bus from Arequipa

IQUITOS
S/200
15-hour speedboat from Yurimaguas

TOP TIP
Avoid on-the-spot fines – be sure to stamp your ticket to validate your journey.

SPEED LIMIT

HIGHWAY
60 mph (100 km/h)

MAJOR ROAD
50 mph (80 km/h)

URBAN AREAS
37 mph (60 km/h)

SMALL STREETS
25 mph (40 km/h)

Arriving by Air

The main international gateway into Peru is Jorge Chávez International Airport in Lima. It receives direct flights from Panama City in Panama and Miami in the US – the main hubs for Latin America – as well as Houston and Atlanta in the US. Air Canada also offers direct flights from several Canadian cities. From Europe, most flights depart from Madrid, although KLM and Air France run direct flights from Amsterdam and Paris, respectively.

While unofficial taxis charge a cheaper fare from Lima Airport to the city center, it's much safer to take a cab through the airport's official **Taxi Green** service, the **Airport Express Lima** transfer service, or the **Quick Llama** shuttle. The latter two only offer transfers to and from Miraflores.

Airport Express Lima
w airportexpresslima.com
Taxi Green
w taxigreen.com.pe
Quick Llama
w quickllama.com

Arriving by Land

Visitors can enter Peru overland through Ecuador, Bolivia, or Chile. There are several border crossings for vehicles – the main ones are from Huaquillas in Ecuador to Aguas Verdes in Peru, from Arica in Chile to Tacna in Peru, and from Desaguadero in Bolivia to Desaguadero in Peru. From Bolivia, there is also a frequent bus service from La Paz and Copacabana to Puno, and on to Cusco. From Chile, most buses travel from Arica to Tacna, although the reopened railroad line between the two cities is an alternative. From Tacna, connecting buses continue on to Arequipa or Lima. From Ecuador, direct buses run from Guayaquil to Tumbes and Máncora in Peru. All buses should stop on both sides of the border and wait for passengers to complete the necessary passport formalities.

Arriving by Boat

Peru is an important stop on the itineraries of several international cruise lines, which stop off

GETTING TO AND FROM LIMA AIRPORT

Public Transportation	Journey time	Fare
Taxi	40 mins	S/60
Bus or shuttle	1 hr	S/20

in the port of Callao, near Lima. A selection of companies also stop off in the port of Salaverry in Trujillo for visits to the nearby Mochica temples.

For the most adventurous, Peru can be reached by boat along the Amazon River coming from Manaus, Brazil. Vessels are slow boats, with the journey to Iquitos in Peru taking four days; bring a hammock, food, and water, and plenty of insect repellent. The smaller ports of Tabatinga in Brazil and Leticia in Colombia are also connected by speedboat to Santa Rosa in Peru at a tri-border, from where a ferry transports passengers upriver to Iquitos. These ports can be reached by air from Bogotá (Colombia) or Manaus (Brazil).

Transportation Around Peru

With a nation reliant on public transportation, infrastructure between large cities is steadily improving in Peru, although road conditions in remote coastal areas and into the Andes leave a lot to be desired. Long-distance buses and domestic flight routes are the most expedient methods of traversing the country. Within cities and smaller urban areas, organized networks of *colectivo combis* (minibuses), *colectivo* cars (shared taxis), and even *mototaxis* (tuk-tuks) in jungle regions and coastal cities provide transportation. Few train routes remain, although those that do are often taken for the scenery – and have tourist prices to match. Transport around the Amazon region is primarily by boat, with options including motorized dugouts, *lanchas* (larger cargo boats), or quicker *rápidos* (passenger speed boats).

Domestic Air Travel

In a country with such rugged terrain, internal flights offer a convenient alternative to long bus journeys. However, flights can be canceled or delayed at short notice due to unpredictable and extreme weather conditions (especially during the rainy season from December to March) or other unavoidable situations, so always reconfirm flight timings. Air travel is also generally more expensive than the bus, although not excessively so if purchased several weeks in advance.

Lima acts as the central hub for air travel. It is possible to fly directly from Cusco to Arequipa and Puerto Maldonado and from Iquitos to Pucallpa, but for most other places you have to fly via Lima. Flights from the capital to larger destinations run several times a day.

LATAM is the largest and most expensive of the main airlines and operates the most extensive network of regular flights. These include Lima to Arequipa, Cusco, Iquitos, Pucallpa, Ayacucho, Juliaca, Trujillo, and Tumbes. There are also a number of low-cost airlines, including **Star Perú**, **Sky Airline**, **JetSMART**, and **ATSA Airlines**.

ATSA Airlines
w atsaairlines.com
JetSMART
w jetsmart.com
LATAM
w latam.com
Star Perú
w starperu.com
Sky Airline
w skyairline.com

Train Travel

All of Peru's surviving railroad services are in the highland regions south of Lima. Train is the main way most visitors travel from Cusco to Machu Picchu Pueblo (Aguas Calientes), the station for Machu Picchu. You can also take the train from Ollantaytambo in the Sacred Valley. **PeruRail** and **Inca Rail** offer competing services from Cusco to Machu Picchu. Expect to pay S/275 for the cheapest option and over S/2,000 for the most luxurious service. There are also services between Cusco and Puno.

Inca Rail
w incarail.com
PeruRail
w perurail.com

Boats and Ferries

Peru has no coastal ferry services. In the jungle, it is possible to take affordable *lanchas* (cargo boats), which connect cities such as Iquitos with Pucallpa and Yurimaguas. To travel on them, you'll need to bring a hammock or rent a private cabin. You can also find upscale river cruises from Iquitos, which explore the national reserves of Allpahuauyo-Mishana and Pacaya Samiria, accessible only by boat. On Lake Titicaca, vessels shuttle passengers between Puno's port and the islands, but there is no regular service to Bolivia.

Long-Distance Buses

Intercity luxury bus services are often the way to go for covering long distances, with the majority operating overnight services. Companies such as **CIVA**, **Cruz del Sur**, **Movil Tours**, and **Oltursa** are more comfortable, much safer, and more reliable than other services. These deluxe buses offer fully reclining bed-like seats, direct non-stop travel, air conditioning, movies, reading lamps, and on-board restrooms.

Always check departures carefully; buses tend to leave from the central terminal of the city, although this isn't the case in Lima, where most companies have their own depots. While most arterial routes through Peru are paved, roads in rural, mountainous, and jungle areas can be jarringly poorly maintained – and the buses are in a similar state.

On all journeys, be sure to bring all valuable items on board with you and keep them attached to your person, as theft can be an issue. Traveling overnight was once considered too dangerous for foreign visitors; although this is no longer the case along the coast, overnight journeys can be more risky in the more remote and mountainous regions, where the chances of accidents are increased, especially during the rainy season.

The larger, more modern companies sell tickets and publish bus timetables online. You can always reserve in person at their office, or directly at the bus terminal, but it is often easiest to book online. Reservations should be made well in advance during peak travel periods, such as May to November, Easter (Semana Santa), Christmas, and the national Fiestas Patrias (July 28 and 29). Fare prices are significantly higher during these times.

CIVA
w civa.com.pe
Cruz del Sur
w cruzdelsur.com.pe
Movil Tours
w moviltours.com.pe
Oltursa
w oltursa.pe

JOURNEY PLANNER

Indicating the main journey times between the key cities in Peru, this map includes both long-distance bus journeys and, where the journey would be longer than 12 hours by bus, flight times.

··· Direct bus routes
-- Direct flight routes

Arequipa to Cusco	10 hrs
Arequipa to Puno	6 hrs
Chiclayo to Máncora	6 hrs
Ica to Arequipa	12 hrs
Lima to Arequipa	1 hr 30 mins
Lima to Chachapoyas	1 hr 20 mins
Lima to Cusco	1 hr 20 mins
Lima to Ica	4 hrs
Lima to Trujillo	8 hrs
Trujillo to Chiclayo	3 hrs
Lima to Iquitos	2 hr 40 mins

Colectivos

The cheapest way to get around major Peruvian cities is via *colectivo* minibuses (also known as *combis*) and *colectivo* cars (shared taxis). Both also run rural routes between cities and towns, offering an often faster means of getting between the two than by bus. Fixed routes are indicated by signs on the windscreens of the *colectivo* minibuses. Conductors call out street names as the minibus hurtles along the road, cramming in as many passengers as possible. *Colectivo* cars usually take four passengers and *colectivo* minibuses anywhere from 12 upward. However, these vehicles have an appalling safety record and you're often better off with a taxi.

Taxis

While taxis can be flagged down in the streets, it is far safer to reserve one by phone. **Easytaxi** and **Taxi Real** are friendly and safe services to use. Taxi hailing apps are not recommended in Peru, as drivers are known to game the system and scam passengers – with little chance of redress.

Short journeys within cities outside Lima rarely cost more than S/10. Since taxis do not have meters, be sure to agree a price in advance. Prices increase by about 35 per cent after midnight.

Easytaxi
w easytaxi.com/pe
Taxi Real
w taxireal.com

Mototaxis

In provincial towns, motorcycle rickshaws, known as *mototaxis* or *motocarros*, are common. While they are not the safest means of transport, nor the most comfortable, they are cheaper than regular taxis. A more convenient alternative is to contact your hotel or tour agency to hire a car and driver, or a taxi by the hour or day.

Traveling by Car

Traveling at your own pace in a car is one of the most flexible ways to explore Peru. However, poor road conditions and aggressive drivers are just a few of the hazards. Car theft is also an issue.

Car rental is available with international companies in Lima, while in more rural areas, you'll likely find more informal local companies. Make sure you understand the rental agreement and all costs involved before signing. Four-wheel drive vehicles are best for remote rural areas, with motorcycle rental usually limited to jungle towns. An International Driving Permit is not legally required, but can be helpful in proving the authenticity of your driver's license.

Outside of cities, *grifos* (fuel stations) can be scarce, so fill up at every possible opportunity. Fuel is expensive, with costs rising according to the grade, diesel being the cheapest.

Rules of the Road

When driving in Lima on its multiline highways, jam-packed with aggressive, honking traffic, it can often feel like road rules don't exist, and it's very wise to avoid driving in the capital where possible. On narrow rural roads, be aware of other drivers attempting risky overtaking maneuvers and always be ready to drop back out of harm's way. Use your horn when driving around blind bends on mountainous or other rural roads.

It's best to avoid driving at night, where possible, due to the increased likelihood of an accident or robbery, particularly on highland roads. Police checkpoints along highways usually present no problems, and it's sensible to carry a photograph of your passport and an original driver's license to present if requested. Keep drinking water, food, warm clothes, and a spare tire inside your vehicle in case of emergency.

Cycling

Cycling is increasingly popular in Peru, especially mountain biking and bikepacking, with bike rental and repair shops ubiquitous in major towns and cities as a result. Good spots for mountain biking include the Colca Canyon, while a popular route for bikepackers is Peru's Great Divide, an off-road trail through the Cordillera mountains. Alternatively, tour operators in places such as Cusco, Arequipa, and Huaraz offer some great day or multiday guided biking adventures through spectacular scenery. The independent cyclist should consult **Bikemap**, which offers dozens of routes across Peru.

Lima's best places to cycle include the route along the Miraflores clifftops and along Avenida Arequipa, from Miraflores to the city center, on Sunday mornings, when it is closed to traffic.

Bikemap
w bikemap.net

Walking

In most towns and cities the main sights are concentrated in the historic centers, which are easy and safe to explore on foot. Lima is not as pedestrian-friendly as other places, but it does have several walkable areas, including the historic center, Barranco, and Miraflores; transport is necessary between different areas.

Outside of the urban centers – and especially in the Andes – longer walks or hikes are guaranteed to be trip highlights. The best-known areas for trekking are around Cusco, including the Inca Trail, the Cañón del Colca (reachable from Arequipa), and in the Cordillera Blanca (accessible from Huaraz). Rainforest walks in the Amazon are usually shorter affairs, focused on wildlife viewing and learning about tropical ecosystems.

PRACTICAL INFORMATION

A little local know-how goes a long way in Peru. Here you will find all the essential advice and information you will need during your stay.

AT A GLANCE

EMERGENCY NUMBERS

AMBULANCE
106

POLICE
105

FIRE SERVICE
116

TIME ZONE
GMT-5; no daylight saving.

TAP WATER
Tap water is not safe to drink. Instead, use water purification tablets, a water filter or sterilization device, or buy bottled water.

WEBSITES AND APPS

iPerù
This website has information about destinations, is receptive to emails *(peru.travel)*, and has a 24-hour WhatsApp message service: (51) 944 492 314.

SpanishDict Translator
This handy app includes a Spanish-English dictionary (with audio pronunciations for dictionary entries) and a translator function.

Personal Security

Crime like theft and pickpocketing does exist so be alert to your surroundings. Only use ATMs during the day and avoid walking alone in deserted areas at night. Carry copies of important documents, such as your passport, and be aware of scams involving fake police officers – never accompany one into a car. If something does get stolen, English-speaking tourist police offices exist in a number of cities, where you can register for a *denuncia* (a document required by your insurance company).

As a strictly Catholic society with a macho culture, the country's attitudes toward homosexuality remain hostile, despite a number of laws protecting LGBTQ+ rights: homosexuality itself was legalized in 1924; laws prohibiting discrimination based on sexual orientation were introduced in 2017; and trans people were permitted a national identity card in accordance with their chosen gender identity in 2021. Same-sex couples should refrain from sharing affection in public. There is, however, an established gay scene in the Miraflores and Barranco districts of Lima. It is safe for women to travel alone but Peruvian men can be persistent in their attention. Wearing a wedding ring or traveling in a group can be a disincentive.

Health

Peru's health-care system is fairly good, with several public hospitals in Lima, and top-notch, English-speaking private clinics such as **Clínica Anglo Americana**. There are English-speaking private hospitals and clinics in Arequipa and Cusco, including **Clínica Arequipa** and **Clínica Peruano-Suiza** (Cusco) . Elsewhere, health-care facilities are more variable and often nonexistent in rural areas. A list of recommended hospitals can be found on the iPerù tourism website *(p268)*.

Malaria is common in jungle regions; cover up and use repellent in the evenings. Zika, mainly transmitted by mosquito bite, is also a risk, and pregnant women are advised against traveling to Peru. There is no vaccination, so follow measures for avoiding mosquito bites.

Stomach upsets caused by unfamiliarity with the food or contaminated water are common. Pharmacies are well-stocked and open long hours in all major towns and cities, but communicating can be a trial without Spanish, so remember to bring basic medicines from home.

Altitude sickness, with symptoms including shortness of breath, fatigue, headaches, and nausea, may affect visitors to highland areas. Rest, drinking lots of water, and avoiding intense exercise can help alleviate symptoms, as can drinking coca-leaf tea. If any symptoms develop, descend to a lower altitude and seek medical advice. At altitude, the sun can also be very strong and so a high SPF sunscreen is definitely recommended.

Clínica Anglo Americana
w clinicaangloamericana.pe
Clínica Arequipa
w clinicarequipa.com.pe
Clínica Peruano-Suiza
w cps.com.pe

Smoking, Alcohol, and Drugs

Smoking is banned in public places, including on all public transportation.

Peru has a strict limit of 0.05 per cent BAC (blood alcohol content) for drivers. This is roughly equivalent to a small beer.

Possession of, or trafficking in, illegal drugs is considered an extremely serious offense, with lengthy prison terms; there is no bail for drug-trafficking offenses.

ID

There is no legal requirement to carry a copy of your ID, though it is recommended to keep a photocopy of your passport on you at all times. You may be required to show ID when making credit card payments. For entrance to Machu Picchu, you must show your original passport.

Local Customs

Peruvians are polite and fairly conservative. A handshake is exchanged at the start and end of a meeting. People who know each other greet with a single kiss. Personal space is not a respected commodity – buses and streets are crowded.

Modest clothing, including below-the-knee shorts and t-shirts that cover the shoulders, is advised. Wearing revealing clothes or shorts in a church is considered disrespectful; both men and women should cover their shoulders and legs. Be respectful when taking photographs at religious sites, too.

Responsible Tourism

Machu Picchu and Rainbow Mountain are two of Peru's most popular attractions, with crowds surging during the peak season (July to August). Consider visiting these sites in the off-season to lessen the impact on their fragile environments.

There are other ways visitors can travel more responsibly around Peru: eat at locally owned restaurants, purchase souvenirs directly from artisans, and book tour operators and lodges belonging to the sustainably focused **APTAE** organization.

APTAE
w aptae.pe

Cell Phones and Wi-Fi

Travelers with GSM cell phones usually have reception in all cities and large towns. It is also possible to buy a local sim card cheaply from vendors around the country. Most hotels, hostels, and cafés offer free Wi-Fi to customers.

Post

The Peruvian mail service is run by the privately owned Serpost, with branches in all major cities and towns. International letters and postcards usually take a few weeks to reach their destination.

Taxes and Refunds

An 18 per cent sales tax (IGV) is often added to hotel stays. However, foreigners spending less than 59 days in Peru are not required to pay this charge; producing your passport is enough to get it removed. Tax refunds for departing visitors exist, but they are hard to acquire.

Discount Cards

It's worth bringing a student ID card, as these can lead to discounts of up to 50 per cent in museums and historical sites across the country.

INDEX

Page numbers in **bold** refer to main entries.

A

Abra de Warmiwañusca 180, **181**
Accommodations
  reservations 269
  see also Homestays; Hotels
Achiote 75
Adoration of the Magi (Cusco School) 179
Adventure sports **46-7**
Afro-Peruvian music 53
Aguas Calientes 39, **183**, 184
Aguilar, Maria Luisa 72
Air travel 270, 271
Alcohol 51, 275
Almagro, Diego de 70
Altitude sickness 51, **213**, 275
Alto Mayo **261**
Amazonas River 252
Amazon Basin 21, 43, **248-65**
  hotels 253, 254, 261
  map 250-51
  restaurants and bars 59, 263
  river adventures **64-5**
Amazonian people **74**
Amazon rainforest **43**, 56
Amazon River 43
  adventures **47**
  boat trips 10, 47, 64-5, 271
Amphitheater (Caral) **217**
Ancient monuments **60-61**
  Batán Grande **234**
  Cahuachi **146-7**
  Caral **216-17**
  Cementerio de Chauchilla **147**
  Chan Chan 11, 223, **232**
  Chavín de Huántar **214-15**
  Chinchero **194-5**
  Choquequirao **39**
  Combayo **244**
  Complejo Arqueológico El Brujo **233**
  Complejo Wari **205**
  Cumbemayo canal and aqueduct **245**
  El Cuarto del Rescate (Cajamarca) **241**
  Huaca del Sol y de la Luna 61, **232**
  Huaca Huallamarca (Lima) **112-13**
  Huaca Pucllana (Lima) **108-9**
  Intipunku **183**
  Karajía **246**
  Koricancha (Cusco) **176**
  Kuélap 60, **242-3**

Ancient monuments (cont.)
  Machu Picchu 10, 36-7, 39, 171, 180, **184-9**
  Miculla Petroglyphs **148-9**
  Moray 190-91, **194**
  Nazca Lines 11, 60, 61, **140-41**
  Ollantaytambo **195**
  Pachacámac (Lima) **133**
  Palpa Lines 61, **140**
  Paracas Necropolis 142
  Patallacta **180**
  Phuyupatamarca 37, **182**
  Pikillacta **192**
  Pisac Ruins 194
  Raqchi **193**
  Revash **247**
  Rumicola **192**
  Runkurakay **181**
  Sacsayhuamán (Cusco) **175**
  Sayacmarka **182**
  Sechín **221**
  Sillustani Burial Towers **168-9**
  Tambo Colorado 61, **145**
  Temple of Kotosh (Huánuco) 203
  Tipón 37, **193**
  Túcume **235**
  Ventanillas de Otuzco **244**
  Wiñay Wayna **182-3**
  see also Castles and fortifications; Museums and galleries; Pyramids; Temples
Andean people **74**
Apps 274
Archeology **60-61**
  archeological digs **217**
Architecture, Lima's colonial **86-7**
Arequipa 151, **154-61**
  hotels 156
  map 155
  restaurants 155
Arequipa, Canyons, and Lake Titicaca 17, **150-69**
  hotels 156, 163, 167, 168
  itinerary 28-9
  map 152-3
  restaurants 155, 164
Art
  Cusco School **179**
  Lima for Art Lovers **82-3**
Asháninka people 74, 263, 264, **265**
Atahualpa 69, 70, 190, 237, 241
Austro-German settlers 264-5
Avenida Sáenz Peña (Lima) 124
Ayacucho 41, 197, **200-201**
  map 201

Ayacucho, Battle of 204
Ayahuasca 75, 191, **260**
Aymara people 74, 165
Azulejos 95

B

Bahia de Paracas 143
Bajada de los Baños (Lima) **121**, 124
Baños Termales de Monterrey **221**
Baños Termales de Putina **148**
Barranco (Lima) 85, **116-25**
Bars and clubs
  Amazon Basin 263
  Arequipa and Puno 169
  Cordillera Blanca 220
  Cusco 177
  Lima 53, 84, 85, 121
  peñas 13, **84**
Batán Grande 223, **234**
Beaches **42**, **54-5**
  Lima 120, 121, 132
  Northern Desert 233, 234
  Southern Coast 147
Beer 50
Belaúnde, Fernando 72
Belén (Iquitos) **253**
Bingham, Hiram 171, 182
Bird-watching 10, **56-7**
Boat travel 270-71, 272
  Amazon Basin 10, 47
  Islas Ballestras 142, 144
  Reserva de la Biosfera de Manu 256
  Reserva Nacional Pacaya Samiria 254
  Tambopata and Madre de Dios rivers 258-9
  Ucayali river 262-3
Bolívar, Simon 71, 131
Bolivia 72, 270
Boluarte, Dina 73
Border crossings 270
Bosque El Olivar (Lima) **113**
Bungee jumping 46
Bus travel 270, 272-3
Butterflies 63

C

Cahuachi **146-7**
Cajamarca 237, **240-41**
  Carnaval 40
  hotels 241
  map 241
Calca **194**
Callao Islands (Lima) **131**

Calle Córdoba (Monasterio de Santa Catalina, Arequipa) 160
Calle Hatunrumiyoc (Cusco) 177
Callejón de Huaylas 207, 218, 219, 220, 221
Camino Sagrado de los Incas 180
Campo Santo, Yungay 219
Cañón de Cotahuasi 13, 47, 168
Cañón del Colca 13, 57, 166-7
Cañón del Pato 218
Cañón del Sonche 246
Canopy walkways 56
Cápac Ñan (Royal Road) 69, 180
Caral 68, 216-17
Caraz 218
Caretaker's Hut (Machu Picchu) 186
Carhuaz 218-19
Carnaval (Cajamarca) 40
Car rental 273
Casa Andina Observatory 39
Casa Boza y Solís-Prefecture (Ayacucho) 201
Casa de Aliaga (Lima) 86, 97, 102
Casa del Moral (Arequipa) 154
Casa-Museo Mario Vargas Llosa (Arequipa) 156-7
Casa Ricardo Palma (Lima) 111
Casa Tristán del Pozo (Arequipa) 156
Casa Urquiaga (Trujillo) 226-7, 228
Casona Iriberry (Arequipa) 154
Castles and fortifications
 Fortaleza del Real Felipe (Lima) 130
 Kuélap 242-3
 Yalape fortress 246
Catarata de Yumbilla (Chachapoyas) 42
Catarata Gocta 246, 247
Cathedrals *see* Churches and cathedrals
Caves
 Cavernas Quiocta (near Lamud) 246
 Cueva de Pikimachay 68, 205
 Gruta de Huagapo (Palcamayo) 205
Cell phones 275
Cementerio de Chauchilla 60, 147
Central Sierra 19, 196-205
 hotels 205
 map 198-9
 shopping 201
Centro Cultural Municipal Miguel Espinach (Cajamarca) 240

Centro de Rescate Amazónico (Iquitos) 253
Centro de Textiles Tradicionales (Cusco) 44, 176
Ceramics 45, 204
 Mochica 128
Cerro Blanco sand dune 146
Cerro Santa Apolonia (Cajamarca) 241
Cerros de Amotape, Parque Nacional de 234-5
Ceviche 49
Chacas 220-21
Chachapoyan civilization 237, 243, 245, 246
Chachapoyas 42, 245
Chacraraju 210, 211
Chala 147
Chanchamayo Region 264
Chan Chan 11, 223, 232
Charles I, Emperor 94
Charles IV of Spain 71
Chavín, Cult of 68, 69, 214
Chavín de Huántar 207, 214-15
Chicama 42, 55
Chicha 50
Chiclayo 233
Chile 72, 270
 visiting 149
Chimú Kingdom 69, 128, 223, 232, 235
Chinatown (Lima) 100
Chinchero 194-5
Choco Museo (Cusco) 176-7
Choquequirao 39
Chucuito 58, 165
Churches and cathedrals
 Catedral de Puno 164, 165
 Compañía de Jesús (Ayacucho) 201
 Iglesia de la Compañía (Arequipa) 156
 Iglesia de la Compañía (Cusco) 175
 Iglesia de la Merced (Lima) 103
 Iglesia de San Augustin (Trujillo) 229
 Iglesia de San Francisco (Cajamarca) 240
 Iglesia de San Francisco (Trujillo) 228
 Iglesia de San Juan Batista (Puno) 164, 165
 Iglesia de Santa Catalina (Monasterio de Santa Catalina, Arequipa) 160-61
 Iglesia de Santo Domingo (Ayacucho) 200

Churches and cathedrals (cont.)
 Iglesia La Merced (Arequipa) 157
 Iglesia la Merced (Trujillo) 227
 Iglesia San Francisco (Arequipa) 155
 Iglesia San Francisco de Paula (Ayacucho) 201
 Iglesia Santiago Apóstol de Pomata (Lake Titicaca) 162
 Iglesia Santisima Cruz (Lima) 125
 Iglesia y Monasterio del Carmen (Trujillo) 229
 La Catedral (Arequipa) 154
 La Catedral (Cajamarca) 240
 La Catedral (Cusco) 178-9
 La Catedral (Lima) 96, 103
 La Catedral (Trujillo) 226, 228
 La Cathedral (Ayacucho) 201
 La Ermita (Lima) 120-21, 124, 125
 Las Nazarenas (Lima) 100-101
 San Francisco (Lima) 87, 92-5
 San Pedro de Andahuaylillas 192
 San Pedro (Lima) 87, 98
 Santo Domingo (Cusco) 176
 Santo Domingo (Lima) 99
Circuito Mágico del Agua (Lima) 84, 95
Claustro los Naranjos (Monasterio de Santa Catalina, Arequipa) 159
Claustro Mayor (Monasterio de Santa Catalina, Arequipa) 159, 160
Climate 42
Cloud forest 59
Coca 51, 75, 165
Cocina (Monasterio de Santa Catalina, Arequipa) 160
Coffee 51, 264
Colectivos 273
Collagua people 151, 166
Collas 168
Colonial architecture (Lima) 86-7
Combayo 244
Common District (Machu Picchu) 189
Compañía de Jesús (Ayacucho) 201
Complejo Arqueológico El Brujo 233
Complejo Wari 205
Concepción 203
Condors 166
Conquering Kingdoms 69
Conquistadores 70

Contamena 263
Convento *see* Monasteries and convents
Cordillera Blanca 19, 46, **206-221**
  bars and cafés 220
  hotels 219
  map 208-9
  restaurants 220
Cordillera Huayhuash **221**
Cordillera Vilcabamba 38
Corruption 73
COVID-19 pandemic 73
Craft beer 50
Crafts **44-5**
  Maroti Shobo Craft Center (Puerto Callao) **262**
  see also Shopping
Crime 274
Criolla 53
Cruises 64, 270-71
Cruz del Cóndor 57
Cult of the Sun **191**
Culture
  Inca **190-91**
  indigenous people 12
Cumbemayo **245**
Currency 268
Cusco 69, 70, 171, **174-9**
  hotels 175
  map 175
  restaurants and bars 177
Cusco and the Sacred Valley 18, **170-95**
  hotels 47, 175, 187
  itinerary 30-31
  restaurants 177, 193
  shopping 195
Cusco School **179**
Customs information 268
Cycling 46, 142, 218, 273

D

Dance **52-3**, 84, 85
Delfín, Victor
  El Beso 82-3, 115
  house and studio (Lima) **123**
Disabled travelers 269
Discount cards 275
Dress code 275
Drugs 275
Dugout canoes 65

E

Early Horizon period 69
Earthquakes
  Cordillera Blanca 207, 219
  Lima **101**
Easter 41
Ecuador 234, 270
El Beso (Delfín) 82-3, 115
El Candelabro geoglyph 142, 143

El Chaco (Paracas) **144**, 145
El Complejo de Belén (Cajamarca) **241**
El Cuarto del Rescate (Cajamarca) 237, **241**
El Dorado 70
Electricity supply 268
Emergency numbers 274
Entertainment
  Arequipa 156
  Lima 84-5, 113
Estadio Nacional (Lima) **95**
Etiquette 275

F

Farming, Inca 190
Fejos, Paul 182, 183
Ferries 272
Festivals and events 11, **40-41**, **66-7**
  Inca 191
Fiesta de la Virgen de la Candelaría **41**, 165
Fishing 47, 246
Flights, sightseeing 141
Folklore (Puno) **165**
Food and drink 11
  ceviche **49**
  festivals 41, 49
  fruits **49**
  Peru for Foodies **48-9**
  Peru for Home Brews **50-51**
  pisco 12, **50**
  walking food tours 97
Fortaleza del Real Felipe (Lima) 130
Fountains (Machu Picchu) **186**
Fruits **49**
Fujimori, Alberto 73
Funerary Rock (Machu Picchu) **187**

G

Geoglyphs 137, 140-41, 142, 143
Gourds, painted 45
Government advice 268
Graffiti (Lima) 120
Granda, Chabuca 123, 125
Gran Teatro Nacional del Perú (Lima) 85
Guano 137, 144
Guerrilla war 73
Guinea pigs **94**
Guzmán, Abimael 73

H

Health 274-5
  insurance 268
  vaccinations 269
Heyerdahl, Thor 235
Hidden gems **60-61**

Hiking and trekking 46
  Andes 12
  Cañón del Colca **167**
  Carhuaz 218-19
  Choquequirao **39**
  Cordillera Blanca 46, 207
  Cordillera Huayhuash 58, 221
  Inca Trail **180-83**, 184
  Inca treks **38-9**
  Jungle Trek **39**
  Lares Trek **38**
  Montaña Machu Picchu **189**
  Parque Nacional Huascarán 210-213
  Salkantay Trek **38**
  Vinicunca (Rainbow Mountain) 43, **192**
Historic buildings
  Biblioteca Municipal (Lima) 125
  Casa Boza y Solís-Prefecture (Ayacucho) **201**
  Casa de Aliaga (Lima) 86, **97**, 102
  Casa de la Identidad Regional (Trujillo) 228
  Casa de la Emancipación (Trujillo) 229
  Casa del Moral (Arequipa) **154**
  Casa de los Leones (Trujillo) 229
  Casa de Osambela (Lima) 86-7
  Casa de Pilatos (Lima) 86
  Casa Garci Holguin (Trujillo) 228
  Casa Orbegoso (Trujillo) 229
  Casa Riva-Agüero (Lima) 102
  Casa Tristán del Pozo (Arequipa) **156**
  Casa Urquiaga (Trujillo) **226-7**, 228
  Casona Iriberry (Arequipa) **154**
  El Complejo de Belén (Cajamarca) **241**
  El Cuarto del Rescate (Cajamarca) 237, **241**
  Quinta del Virrey Pezuela (Lima) 131
History **68-73**
Hogar de un Suspiro (Rivera) 83
Homestays (Lake Titicaca) 58, 74, 163
Hospitals 274
Hotels
  Amazon Basin 253, 254, 261
  Arequipa, Canyons, and Lake Titicaca 156, 163, 167, 168
  Central Sierra 205
  Cordillera Blanca 219
  Cusco and the Sacred Valley 47, 175, 187
  jungle lodges 13

Hotels (cont.)
 Lima 113
 Northern Highlands 241, 247
 remote retreats 59
 Southern Coast 145
Huaca del Sol y de la Luna 61, **232**
Huaca Huallamarca (Lima) **112–13**
Huaca Pucllana (Lima) **108–9**
Huancavelica **204**
Huancayo **202**
Huanchaco **233**
Huánuco 197, **202–3**
Huaraz 207, **220**
Huáscar 69, 70
Huascarán, Parque Nacional 43, **210–213**
Huayllabamba **180–81**
Huaylla Belén Valley **246**
Huayna Cápac 69, 70
Huayna Picchu **189**
Huayno 52

I

Ica **144–5**, 146
ID 275
Iglesia *see* Churches and cathedrals
Inca **69**
 Cápac Ñan (Royal Road) **69**, 180
 culture and religion **190–91**
 experience Inca Peru **36–7**
 Inca Trail 37, **180–83**, 184
 Inca treks **38–9**
 Museo Inka (Cusco) 37, **174**
 Museo Nacional de Arqueologia, Antropologia e Historia del Perú (Lima) 131
 Spanish conquest and rule 70–71
 see also Ancient monuments; Museums and galleries
Inca Trail 37, **180–83**, 184
Indigenous people **74–5**
 homestays 58, 163
Insurance 268
Internet access 275
Intihuatana (Machu Picchu) **187**
Intipunku **183**
Inti Raymi 41, 191
Inti (Sun God) 190
Iquitos 47, **252–3**, 262, 263
 hotels 253
 map 253
Isla Amantaní (Lake Titicaca) 58, 163, **164**
Isla Ballestas 57, 142, **144**
Isla de la Luna (Lake Titicaca) **162**
Isla del Sol (Lake Titicaca) **162**
Isla El Frontón (Lima) 131
Isla San Lorenzo (Lima) 131
Isla Suasi **163**
Islas Uros (Lake Titicaca) 74, **162–3**
Isla Taquile (Lake Titicaca) 58, 163, **164**
Itineraries **22–35**
 2 Weeks Across Peru 22–5
 3 Days in Lima 80–81
 4 Days on the Southern Coast 26–7
 5 Days in Canyon Country 28–9
 5 Days in Cusco and the Sacred Valley 30–31
 10 Days in Northern Peru 32–5

J

Jaguars 62
Jesuits 71
Jewelry 45
Juli **164**
Jungle Trek **39**

K

Karajía **246**
Kayaking 47
Koricancha (Cusco) **176**
Kuélap 60, 237, **242–3**

L

La Ermita (Lima) **120–21**, 124, 125
Laguna 69 210, 211, 212
Laguna Avispa 263
Laguna de los Cóndores **244**
Laguna Parón 218, 219
Lagunas Llanganuco 212, **213**
Laguna Wilcacocha 212
Lagunillas 143
Lake Titicaca 47, 151, **162–5**
 homestays 58, 74, 163
 map 163
La Marina Lighthouse (Lima) 114
Lamas 261
Lambayeque culture 61, 223, 233, 235
La Merced 264, 265
Lampa **169**
Lanchas (cargo boats) 65
Landscape **42–3**
Language 269
 essential phrases 268
 indigenous people 74
 phrase book 284–6
Larco Hoyle, Rafael **129**
Larcomar (Lima) 85, **110**, 115
Lares Trek **38**
Las Nazarenas (Lima) **100–101**
Las Pocitas 54, 55, **234**
Last Supper (de la Puente) 94
Last Supper (Zapata) 178, 179
Lavandería (Monasterio de Santa Catalina, Arequipa) **160**
Leguía, Augusto 72
Levanto **246**
Leymebamba **244**
Ley Seca (Dry Law) 51
LGBTQ+ safety 274
Lima 16, 70, **76–133**
 airport 270, 271
 Barranco 116–25
 bars 84, 85, 121
 beaches 120, 121, 132
 Beyond the Center 126–33
 Central Lima 88–103
 colonial architecture 86–7
 earthquakes 101
 food scene 48
 hotels 113
 itinerary 80–81
 map 78–9
 map: Barranco 118–19
 map: Beyond the Center 127
 map: Central Lima 90–91
 map: Miraflores and San Isidro 106–7
 Miraflores and San Isidro 104–115
 nightlife 13, 84–5
 restaurants 100, 111, 122, 129
 walks 102–3, 114–15, 124–5
Llachón 58
Llamas 63
Local customs 275
López Antay, Joaquin 200–201
Los Baños del Inca **244**
Lugar de la Memoria (LUM) (Lima) **113**

M

Machu Picchu 10, 36–7, 39, 171, 180, **184–9**
 ID at 275
Machu Pichu Pueblo (Aguas Calientes) **183**, 184
Madre de Dios River 56, 65, **258–9**
Mail services 275
Malaria 274
Malecón de Miraflores (Lima) **114–15**
Malecón Tarapacá (Iquitos) **252**
Manco Cápac 69
Máncora 42, 54, 55, 223, **234**
Mantaro Valley **203**
Manu Basin 43, 56, **256–7**

Maps
  Amazon Basin 250–51
  Arequipa 155
  Arequipa, Canyons, and Lake Titicaca 152–3
  Ayacucho 201
  Cajamarca 241
  Central Sierra 198–9
  Cordillera Blanca 208–9
  Cusco 175
  Iquitos 253
  journey planner 272
  Lake Titicaca 163
  Lima 78–9
  Lima: Barranco 118–19
  Lima: Beyond the Center 127
  Lima: Central Lima 90–91
  Lima: Miraflores and San Isidro 106–7
  Northern Desert 224–5
  Northern Highlands 238–9
  Peru 14–15
  Southern Coast 138–9
  Trujillo 227
Marañon river 254
Marinera 52
Markets
  Andean food markets 36
  Belén (Iquitos) **253**
  for crafts 45
  Mercado Central (Lima) **97**
  Pisac 36, 194
Maroti Shobo Craft Center (Puerto Callao) **262**
Maté de coca 51
MATE - Museo Mario Testino (Lima) **122**
Miculla, Petroglifos de **148–9**
Middle Horizon period 69
Military dictatorship 72
Miraflores and San Isidro (Lima) 85, **104–115**
Miraflores Clifftops (Lima) **110–111**
Moche culture 69, 223, 233, 234
  Museo de las Tumbas Reales de Sipán 230–31
  Museo Larco (Lima) 128
Monasteries and convents
  Convento de la Recoleta (Arequipa) **155**
  Convento de los Descalzos (Lima) **99**
  Convento de Santa Catalina (Cusco) **177**
  Convent of Santa Rosa de Ocopa (Concepción) 203
  Convent of Santa Teresa and San Jose (Arequipa) 157
  Iglesia y Monasterio del Carmen (Trujillo) 229
  Monasterio de Santa Catalina (Arequipa) **158–61**
  San Francisco (Lima) **92–5**

Monasteries and convents (cont.)
Money 269
Monkeys 63
Montaña Machu Picchu **189**
Monumento a la Libertad (Trujillo) 228
Moray 190–91, **194**
Mototaxis 273
Mountain-biking 46, 218, 273
Mount Alpamayo 211, 218
Mount Artesonraju 211
Mount Huascarán 211
Mount Pirámide 218, 219
Mount Salkantay 38
Movimiento Revolucionario Túpac Amaru (MRTA) 73
Moyobamba 249, **261**
Mummies 146, 157, 233, 244
  Cementerio de Chuachilla 60, **147**
  Huaca Pucllana (Lima) 109
  Inca culture and religion 191
Mundo Alpaca (Arequipa) 45, **156**
Mural de la Humanidad (Trujillo) 227
Murals 83, 227
Museums and galleries 124
  80m2 Livia Benavides (Lima) 124
  Casa-Museo Joaquín López Antay (Ayacucho) **200–201**
  Casa-Museo Mario Vargas Llosa (Arequipa) **156–7**
  Casa Ricardo Palma (Lima) 111
  Centro Cultural Municipal Miguel Espinach (Cajamarca) **240**
  Choco Museo (Cusco) **176–7**
  Lugar de la Memoria (LUM) (Lima) **122**
  MATE - Museo Mario Testino (Lima) **122**
  Mundo Alpaca (Arequipa) 45, **156**
  Museo Amano (Lima) **112**
  Museo Andrés del Castillo (Limas) **97**
  Museo Antonini (Nazca) 146
  Museo Arqueológico de Ancash (Huaraz) 220
  Museo Arqueológico Nacional Brüning (Chiclayo) 61, 233
  Museo Barco Histórico "Ayapua" (Iquitos) **252–3**
  Museo Carlos Dreyer (Puno) 165
  Museo de Arte Contemporáneo (Lima) 83, **122**
  Museo de Arte de Lima 37, 82, **98–9**

Museums and galleries (cont.)
  Museo de Arte Italiano (Lima) **101**
  Museo de Arte Precolombino (Cusco) 61, **174**
  Museo de Arte Religioso (Cusco) **177**
  Museo de Arte Religioso de la Catedral (Lima) 103
  Museo de Arte Virreinal de Santa Teresa (Arequipa) **157**
  Museo de la Coca y Costumbres (Puno) 165
  Museo de la Electricidad (Lima) **120**
  Museo de la Memoria (Ayacucho) **200**
  Museo de las Culturas Indígenas Amazónicas (Iquitos) **252**
  Museo de las Tumbas Reales de Sipán 60, **230–31**, 233
  Museo del Automóvil Colección Nicolini (Lima) **133**
  Museo del Banco Central de la Reserva (Lima) 103
  Museo del Juguete (Trujillo) **227**, 229
  Museo de Oro del Perú (Lima) **132**
  Museo de Sitio Bodega y Quadra (Lima) **96–7**
  Museo de Sitio Julio C. Tello (Reserva Nacional de Paracas) 142, 143
  Museo de Sitio Submarino Abtao (Lima) **130–31**
  Museo Ferroviario (Tacna) 149
  Museo Histórico Municipal (Arequipa) 155
  Museo Inka (Cusco) 37, **174**
  Museo Jade Rivera (Lima) 124
  Museo Larco (Lima) 37, 61, **128–9**
  Museo Leymebamba 244
  Museo Machu Picchu (Cusco) **177**
  Museo Nacional de Arqueología, Antropología e Historia del Perú (Lima) **131**
  Museo Nacional de la Cultura Peruana (Lima) **101**
  Museo Nacional de Sicán (Chiclayo) 233
  Museo Naval de Perú (Lima) **130**
  Museo Pedro de Osma (Lima) **123**
  Museo Regional Adolfo Bermúdez Jenkins (Ica) 60, 145

Museums and galleries (cont.)
  Museo Santuarios Andinos de la Universidad Católica de Santa María (Arequipa) **157**
  Museo y Convento de Santa Catalina (Cusco) **177**
  Palacio de las Artes Miraflores (Lima) 83
  Pinacoteca (Monasterio de Santa Catalina, Arequipa) **161**
  "Usko Aya" Escuela de Pintura Amazónica (Pucallpa) 262
  Wu Galeria (Lima) 83
  Yavari (Puno) 165
Music **52-3**
  festivals 41
  nightlife 84

N

National parks and nature reserves
  Chaparrí Conservation Reserve 56
  Owlet Lodge reserve 57
  Pantanos de Villa (Lima) **132-3**
  Parque Nacional Cerros de Amotape 234-5
  Parque Nacional Huascarán 43, **210-213**
  Parque Nacional Yanachaga-Chemillén **265**
  Reserva Abra Patricia 57
  Reserva de la Biosfera de Manu 43, 56, **256-7**
  Reserva Nacional Allpahuayo-Mishana **253**
  Reserva Nacional del Sira 263
  Reserva Nacional de Paracas 42, 46, **142-3**
  Reserva Nacional de Tambopata 258
  Reserva Nacional Pacaya Samiria **254-5**
  Reserva Paisajística Nor Yauyos Cochas **203**
Natural wonders **42-3**
Nature reserves *see* National parks and nature reserves
Nazca 140, 141, 145, **146**
Nazca Lines 11, 60, 61, **140-41**
Nazca people 69, 128, 131, 137, 146
Nightlife
  Arequipa 156
  Lima 13, **84-5**
Northern Desert 20, **222-35**
  itinerary 32-5
  map 224-5
  restaurants 235

Northern Highlands 20, **236-47**
  hotels 241, 247
  itinerary 32-5
  map 238-9
  restaurants 245

O

Odebrecht scandal 73
Off the beaten track **58-9**
Oil industry 249, 262
Ollantaytambo **195**
Opening hours 269
Oxapampa 41, 59, **264-5**

P

Pachacámac (Lima) **133**
Pachacútec 69, 184
Paddington Bear statue (Lima) 114, 115
Palaces
  Palacio Arzobispal (Lima) 103
  Palacio de Gobierno (Lima) **97**, 102
  Palacio de Torre Tagle (Lima) 86, 103
  Palacio Iturregui (Trujillo) 229
Palcamayo **205**
Palomino Islets 131
Palpa Lines 61, **140**
Pantanos de Villa (Lima) **132-3**
Paracas civilization 61, 128, 137, 140
Paracas, Reserva Nacional de 42, 46, **142-3**
Paragliding 46
Parks and gardens
  Bosque El Olivar (Lima) **113**
  Parque Antonio Raimondi (Lima) 115
  Parque del Amor (Lima) 82-3, 111, 115
  Parque de la Muralla (Lima) **98**
  Parque El Libro (Lima) 114
  Parque Grau Miraflores (Lima) 114
  Parque Kennedy (Lima) **110**
  Parque Municipal (Lima) **122-3**
  Parque San Marcelino Champagnat (Lima) 115
  see also National parks and nature reserves
Parque Nacional *see* National parks and nature reserves
Passports 268
Patallacta **180**
Paucartambo 41
Peñas 13, **84**
Personal security 274
Perú Mucho Gusto 41, 49

Peruvian War of Independence 71
Petroglifos de Miculla **148-9**
Pevas **260**
Pharmacies 275
Photography
  etiquette 275
  wildlife 65
Phrase book 284-6
Phuyupatamarca 37, **182**
Picanterías 49
Pikillacta **192**
Pikimachay, Cueva de 68, **205**
Pinacoteca (Monasterio de Santa Catalina, Arequipa) **161**
Pisac **194**
Pisco (drink) 12, **50**
Pisco river valley 145
Piskacucho 180
Pizarro, Francisco 70, 89, 96, 97, 171, 237
Plants **75**
Plaza de Armas (Cusco) **174**
Plaza de Armas (Trujillo) **226**, 228
Plaza Mayor (Lima) **102-3**
Plaza San Martín (Lima) **100**
Politics 73
Postal services 275
Pozuzo 59, **265**
Prices
  average daily spend 268
  transportation 270
Public holidays 269
Public transportation 271, 272-3
  prices 270
Pucallpa 47, 65, 249, **262**
Pucusana 132
Puente de los Suspiros (Lima) **121**, 124, 125
Puente, Diego de, *Last Supper* 94
Puerto Bermúdez **263**
Puerto Inca 147
Puerto Maldonado 249, 258, 259
Puka Wamani (de Szyslzo) 82
Puno 41, 162, **164-5**
Punta Arquillo 143
Punta Hermosa 132
Punta Olimpica 212, 220
Punta Rocas 132
Punta Sal 54
Punta San Fernando 147
Punta San Juan de Marcona 147
Puya raimondii **211**
Pyramids
  Batán Grande **234**
  Cahuachi **146-7**
  Chavín de Huántar 214
  Great Pyramid (Caral) **217**
  Huaca del Sol y de la Luna 61, **232**
  Huaca Huallamarca (Lima) **112-13**

Pyramids (cont.)
  Huaca Pucllana (Lima) **108-9**
  Pachacámac **133**
  Pyramid of the Circular Altar (Caral) **217**
  Pyramid of the Gallery (Caral) **217**
  Pyramid of the Huanca (Caral) **217**
  Túcume **235**
  see also Ancient monuments

Q

Q'eswachaka Rope Bridge **37**
Quebrada Rajucolta 212
Quechua 12, 74, 165
Quinta del Virrey Pezuela (Lima) 131
Quinua **204**
Quipus 191, 216

R

Rail travel 271
  Tren Macho (Huancayo to Huancavelica) **202**
Rainforest, Amazon **43**, 56
Raqchi **193**
Reasons to Love Peru **10-13**
Refunds, IGV 275
Reiche, Maria 140
Religion, Inca **190-91**
Requena 263
Reserva de la Biosfera de Manu **256-7**, 258
Reserva Nacional Allpahuayo-Mishana **253**
Reserva Nacional del Sira 263
Reserva Nacional de Paracas **142-3**
Reserva Nacional de Tambopata 258
Reserva Nacional Pacaya Samiria **254-5**
Reserva Paisajística Nor Yauyos Cochas **203**
Responsible tourism 275
Restaurants
  Amazon Basin 59, 263
  Arequipa, Canyons, and Lake Titicaca 155, 164
  Cordillera Blanca 220
  Cusco and the Sacred Valley 177, 193
  Lima 100, 111, 122, 129
  Northern Desert 235
  Northern Highlands 245
  picanterías 49
  Southern Coast 146
Revash **247**
Ríos Tambopata and Madre de Dios Area 43, **258-9**
Ritual ceremonies **109**

Rivera, Jade
  Hogar de un Suspiro 83
  Museo Jade Rivera (Lima) 124
Riverboat cruises 64
Road travel 270, 273
Royal Sector (Machu Picchu) **186**
Rubber 249, 259, 260
Rules of the road 270, 273
Rumicolca **192**
Runkurakay **181**

S

Sacred Plaza (Machu Picchu) **187**
Sacred Rock (Machu Picchu) **188**
Sacred Valley *see* Cusco and the Sacred Valley
Sacrifices 109, 191
Sacsayhuamán (Cusco) **175**
Safety
  government advice 268
  LGBTQ+ 274
  personal security 274
  women 274
Saint *see* San; Santa; Santo
Salinas de Maras 194
Salkantay Trek **38**
San Bartolo 132
San Blas District (Cusco) **176**
San Francisco (Lima) 87, **92-5**
San Isidro (Lima) *see* Miraflores and San Isidro
San Martín de Porras 98
San Martín, José de 71, 100, 131, 143, 144
San Pedro de Andahuaylillas **192**
San Pedro (Lima) 87, **98**
Santa Cruz Trek 210, **212**, 218
Santa Rosa de Lima **99**
Santo Domingo (Cusco) **176**
Santo Domingo (Lima) **99**
Sapa Inca 190
Sayakmarca **182**
Scuba diving 55
Sea-kayaking 54
Seasons 42
Sea travel 270-71
Sechín **221**
Selvámonos (Oxapampa) 41
Semana Santa **41**
Sendero Luminoso *see* Shining Path
Señor de Wari **61**
Shady, Ruth 216, 217
Shamans 75, 260
Shining Path 72, 73, 131, 197, **200**
Shipibo-Conibo people **259**, 262

Shopping
  Amazon Basin 262
  Ayacucho 201
  Cusco and the Sacred Valley 176, 195
  for crafts 45, 262
  Lima 125
  see also Crafts
Sicán Kingdom 223
Sillustani Burial Towers **168-9**
Sipán, Lord of 230-31, 233
Smoking 275
Sor Ana de los Angeles Monteagudo **160**, 161
Southern Coast, The 17, **136-49**
  beaches 147
  hotels 145
  itinerary 26-7
  map 138-9
  restaurants 146
Spanish conquest and rule 70-71
Spatuletails **246**
Specific requirements, travelers with 269
Spectacled bears 62
Speed limits 270
Stand-up paddle-boarding 54
Street art 82, 83
Sucre, Antonio José de 204
Sun protection 275
Supay pa Wasin Tusuq (Scissors Dance) 53
Surfing 42, 55, 121, 233, 234
Szyslzo, Fernando de 82, 115, 122

T

Tacna **149**
Tahuantinsuyu 69
Tambo Colorado 61, **145**
Tambopata River **258-9**
Tap water 274
Tarapoto **261**
Tarata **148**
Taxes 275
Taxis 273
Teatro Municipal (Lima) 85
Telephones 275
Tello, Julio C. 121, 183
Temples
  Huaca del Sol y de la Luna 61, **232**
  Koricancha (Cusco) **176**
  Raqchi **193**
  Temple of Kotosh (Huánuco) 203
  Temple of the Condor (Machu Picchu) **188**
  Temple of the Sun (Machu Picchu) **188-9**
  Temple of the Sun (Ollantaytambo) 195

Temples (cont.)
   Temple of the Three
      Windows (Machu Picchu)
      188
   see also Ancient monuments;
      Pyramids
Testino, Mario 122
Textiles 44, 45, 176
Theater 85
Thermal springs
   Aguas Calientes 39, **183**
   Baños de Barro (Máncora)
      234
   Baños de Pariacaca 218
   Baños Termales de
      Monterrey **221**
   Baños Termales de Putina
      148
   Baños Termales San Mateo
      261
   Calca 194
   Llucho 168
   Los Baños del Inca **244**
Tickets, transportation 272
Time zone 274
Tipón 37, **193**
Titicaca, Lake *see* Lake Titicaca
Tiwanaku 69
Toledo, Francisco de 71
Trains *see* Rail travel
Travel
   city transportation 273
   getting around **270-73**
   government advice 268
   journey planner map 272
   responsible tourism 275
   to Machu Picchu 184
Trekking *see* Hiking and trekking
Tres Cruces **42**
Trujillo 223, **226-9**
   map 227
   walk 228-9
Túcume **235**
Tumbes **234**
Túpac Amaru II 71, 171
Túpac Yupanqui 261

U

Ucayali River 254, 259, 262
   Ucayali River Towns **262-3**
Utcubamba River 242

V

Vaccinations 269
Valverde, Vicente de 99
Vargas Llosa, Mario 123, 156-7
Velasco Alvarado, General Juan 72
Ventanillas de Otuzco **244**
Vicuñas 44, 63
Villa Rica **264**
Vinicunca (Rainbow Mountain) 43, **192**
Viracocha 178
Virgen del Carmen (Paucartambo) 41
Visas 268

W

Wakaywilka (Mount Veronika) 180
Walking (pedestrians) 273
   see also Hiking and
      trekking
Walks
   A Short Walk: Barranco (Lima) 124-5
   A Short Walk: Malecón de Miraflores (Lima) 114-15
   A Short Walk: Plaza Mayor (Lima) 102-3
   A Short Walk: Trujillo's Centro Historico 228-9
Wari culture 69, 171, 197
   Huaca Pucllana (Lima) 108-9
   Museo Larco (Lima) 128
   Museo Nacional de Arqueologia, Antropologia e Historia del Perú (Lima) 131
   Pikillacta and Rumicolca **192**
   Señor de Wari **61**
   Wari Ruins (near Ayacucho) **205**
War of the Pacific 72, 131
Waterfalls
   Catarata Bayoz 42, 264
   Catarata de Yumbilla (Chachapoyas) **42**
   Catarata Gocta 42, 246, **247**
Websites 274
White-water rafting 47, 261
Wi-Fi 275
Wildlife **62-3**
   Amazon river dolphins 255
   bird-watching 10, **56-7**
   Centro de Rescate Amazónico (Iquitos) **253**
   condors 57, **166**
   Islas Ballestas 57, 144
   Parque Nacional Huascarán 210
   Peruvian hairless dog **232**
   photography 65
   Reserva de la Biosfera de Manu 256-7
   Reserva Nacional de Paracas 142-3
   Reserva Nacional Pacaya Samiria 254
   spatuletails **246**
   Whale watching 55
   see also National parks and nature reserves
Wiñay Wayna **182-3**
Windsurfing 54
Wine, Ica 145
Women travelers 274
Woodwork 45
Workshops, craft 45

Y

Yanachaga-Chemillén, Parque Nacional **265**
Yanahuara district (Arequipa) 154
Yanesha people 263
Yavari (Puno) 165
Ychsma culture 108
Yurimaguas 65, **260**

Z

Zapata, Marcos, *Last Supper* 94, 178, 179
Ziplines 46
Zorritos 54, **234-5**
Zubarán, Francisco 92

PHRASE BOOK

In Peru, there are three main different forms of pronunciation of Spanish: variations from the Andes, from the coast (Lima being its center), and a combination of the two which has emerged during the last 50 years due to internal migration.

In the variation from the Andes, sometimes the **e** and **o** become **i** and **u**; thus, **ayer** would be pronounced 'a-yeer' and **por** is '**poor**'. There is often a distinction between **ll** and **y**, where the pronunciation would be like the English **y** for **yes** and **j** for **job** respectively. It is also common that **r** and **rr** are pronounced similarly.

In the variation from the coast, there is a clear distinction between **r** and **rr**. Sometimes the **s** becomes **h** before another consonant as in **pescado** "pehkado." In addition, the **ll** and **y** are pronounced the same, such as in the English **j** for job. Finally, the **d** at the end of the word may become **t** or may be omitted; for example, **usted** would be pronounced "oos**teh**."

In the variation which combines Andean and coastal pronunciations, there is also a clear distinction between **r** and **rr**. In this variation, the **ll** and **y** are also pronounced as in the English **j** for **job**. In addition, the sounds **b**, **d**, **g**, and **y** may become silent between vowels; for example, **cansado** would be pronounced 'kansa-o'. Finally, the **s** may become **h** before another consonant, as in **fresco** "frehko."

SOME SPECIAL PERUVIAN WORDS

¡A la firme!	a la feermeh	Sure!
agua de caño	agwa deh kan-yo	tap water
bravazo	brabaso	wonderful
brevete	brebeteh	driver's license
carro	karro	car
chamba	chamba	job; work
chelear	cheleh-ar	to drink beer
chévere	chebaireh	cool, great
chibolo	cheebolo	young person
chorear	choreh-ar	to steal
coco	koko	dollar
del carajo	del karaho	excellent, very good
estar con la bicicleta	estar kon la beeseekleta	to have diarrhea
estar hasta la coronilla	estar asta la koronee-ya	to be fed up
feria	fair-ya	market
hacer cholito a alguien	asair choleeto a algen	to deceive someone
los tombos	los tombos	the police
pan comido	pan komeedo	it is easy
pata	pata	pal, friend
pueblo jóven	pweblo hohven	shanty town
rubia	rroob-ya	beer

EMERGENCIES

Help!	¡Ayuda!	ah-yoo-dah
Stop!	¡Pare!	pareh
Call a doctor	Llamen un médico	yamen oon medeeko
Call an ambulance	Llamen a una ambulancia	yamen a oona amboolans-ya
Police!	¡Policía!	poleesee-a
I've been robbed	Me robaron	meh rrobaron
Call the police	Llamen a la policía	yamen a la poleesee-a
Where is the nearest hospital?	¿Dónde queda el hospital más cercano?	dondeh keda el ospeetal mas sairkano?
Can you help me?	¿Me puede ayudar?	meh pwedeh a-yoodar?
They stole my...	Me robaron mi...	meh rrobaron mee...

COMMUNICATION ESSENTIALS

Yes	Sí	see
No	No	no
Please	Por favor	por fabor
Excuse me	Disculpe	deeskoolpeh
I'm sorry	Lo siento	lo s-yento
Thanks	Gracias	gras-yas
Hello!	¡Hola!	houla
Good day	Buen día	bwen dee-a
Good afternoon	Buenas tardes	bwenas tardes
Good evening	Buenas noches	bwenas noches
Night	Noche	nocheh
Morning	Mañana	man-yana
Tomorrow	Mañana	man-yana
Yesterday	Ayer	a-yair
Here	Acá	aka
How?	¿Cómo?	komo
When?	¿Cuándo?	kwando
Where?	¿Dónde?	dondeh
Why?	¿Por qué?	por keh
How are you?	¿Qué tal?	keh tal
Very well, thank you	Muy bien, gracias	mwee byen gras-yas
Pleased to meet you	Encantado /mucho gusto	enkantado/ moocho goosto
It's a pleasure!	¡Es un placer!	Es oon plahcer
Goodbye, so long	Adiós, hasta luego	ad-yos, asta lwego

USEFUL PHRASES

That's fine	Está bien	esta b-yen
Fine!	¡Qué bien!	keh b-yen
How long?	¿Cuánto falta?	kwanto falta?
Do you speak a little English?	¿Habla un poco de inglés?	abla oon pako deh eengles?
I don't understand	No entiendo	no ent-yendo
Can you speak more slowly?	¿Puede hablar más despacio?	pwedeh ablar mas despas-yo?
I agree/OK	De acuerdo/ bueno	deh akwairdo/ bweno
Certainly!	¡Claro que sí!	klaro keh see
Let's go!	¡Vámonos!	bamonos
How do I get to...?	¿Cómo se llega a...?	komo se yega a...?
Which way to...?	¿Por dónde se va a...?	por dondeh seh ba a...?

USEFUL WORDS

large	grande	grandeh
small	pequeño	peken-yo
hot	caliente	kal-yenteh
cold	frío	free-o
good	bueno	bweno
bad	malo	malo
so-so	más o menos	mas o menos
mediocre	regular	regoolar
sufficient	suficiente	soofees-yenteh
well/fine	bien	b-yen
open	abierto	ab-yairto
closed	cerrado	serrado
entrance	entrada	entrada
exit	salida	saleeda
full	lleno	yeno
empty	vacío	basee-o
right	derecha	dairecha
left	izquierda	eesk-yairda
straight on	(todo) recto	rrekto

under	debajo	debaho
over	arriba	arreeba
quickly	pronto	pronto
early	temprano	temprano
late	tarde	tardeh
now	ahora	a-ora
soon	ahorita	a-oreeta
more	más	mas
less	menos	menos
little	poco	poko
much	mucho	moocho
very	muy	mwee
too much	demasiado	demas-yado
in front of	delante	delanteh
opposite	enfrente	enfrenteh
behind	detrás	detras
first floor	primer piso	preemair peeso
ground floor	sotano piso	soutano peeso
elevator	ascensor	asensor
restroom	baño	ban-yo
women	mujeres	moohaires
men	hombres	ombres
toilet paper	papel higiénico	papel eeh-yeneeko
camera	cámara	kamara
batteries	pilas	peelas
passport	pasaporte	pasaporteh
visa	visa	beesa
tourist card	tarjeta turistica	tarheta tooreesteeka

HEALTH

I don't feel well	Me siento mal	meh s-yento mal
I have a stomach ache/ headache	Me duele el estómago/ la cabeza	meh dweleh el estomago la kabesa
I have altitude sickness	Tengo mal de altura	tengo mal deh altoora
He/she is ill	Está enfermo/a	esta enfairmo/a
I need to rest	Necesito descansar	neseseeto deskansar
drug store	farmacia	farmas-ya

POST OFFICE AND BANK

bank	banco	banko
I'm looking for a bureau de change	Busco una casa de cambio	boosko oona kasa deh kamb-yo
What is the dollar rate?	¿A cómo está el dolar?	a komo esta el dolar?
I want to send a letter	Quiero enviar una carta	k-yairo emb-yar oona karta
postcard	postal	postal
stamp	estampilla	estampee-ya
draw out money	sacar dinero	sakar deenairo

SHOPPING

I would like/ want...	Me gustaría/ quiero...	meh goostaree-a/ k-yairo...
Do you have any...?	¿Tiene...?	t-yeneh...?
expensive	caro	karo
How much is it?	¿Cuánto cuesta?	kwanto kwesta?
What time do you open/close?	¿A qué hora abre/cierra?	a ke ora abreh/ s-yairra?
May I pay with a credit card?	¿Puedo pagar con tarjeta de crédito?	pwedo pagar kon tarheta deh kredeeto?

SIGHTSEEING

avenue	avenida	abeneeda
beach	playa	pla-ya
castle, fortress	castillo	kastee-yo
cathedral	catedral	katedral
church	iglesia	eegles-ya
district	barrio	barr-yo
garden	jardín	hardeen
guide	guía	gee-a
house	casa	kasa
map	mapa	mapa
highway	autopista	owtopeesta
museum	museo	mooseh-o
park	parque	parkeh
road	carretera	karretaira
square	plaza	plasa
street	calle, callejón	ka-yeh, ka-yehon
town hall	municipalidad	mooneeseepaleedad
tourist bureau	oficina de turismo	ofeeseena deh tooreesmo

TRANSPORT

When does it leave?	¿A qué hora sale?	a keh ora saleh?
When does the next train/bus leave for...?	¿A qué hora sale el próximo tren/bus a...?	a keh ora saleh el prokseemo tren/boos a...?
Could you call a taxi for me?	¿Me puede llamar un taxi?	meh pwedeh yamar oon taksee?
airport	aeropuerto	a-airopwairto
railroad station	estación de ferrocarriles	estas-yon deh fairrokarreeles
bus station	terminal de buses	tairmeenal deh booses
customs	aduana	adwana
boarding pass	tarjeta de embarque	tarheta deh embarkeh
car hire	alquiler de carros	alkeelair deh karros
bicycle	bicicleta	beeseekleta
rate	tarifa	tareefa
insurance	seguro	segooro
fuel station	estación de gasolina	estas-yon deh gasoleena
garage	garage	garaheh
I have a flat tire	Se me pinchó una llanta	seh meh peencho oona yanta

STAYING IN A HOTEL

I have a reservation	Tengo una reserva	tengo oona rresairba
Are there any rooms available?	¿Tiene habitaciones disponibles?	t-yeneh abeetas-yones deesponeebles
single/double room	habitación sencilla/doble	abeetas-yon sensee-ya/dobleh
twin room	habitación con camas gemelas	abeetas-yon kon kamas hemelas
shower	ducha	doocha
bath	tina	teena
balcony	balcón	balkon
I want to be woken up at...	Necesito que me despierten a las...	neseseeto keh meh desp-yairten a las...
warm/cold water	agua caliente/fría	agwa kal-yenteh/ free-a
soap	jabón	habon
towel	toalla	to-a-ya
key	llave	yabeh

EATING OUT

I am a vegetarian	Soy vegetariano	soy begetar-yano
Can I see the menu, please?	¿Me deja ver el menú, por favor?	me deha ber el menoo por fabor?
fixed price	precio fijo	pres-yo feeho
What is there to eat?	¿Qué hay para comer?	keh I para komair?
The bill, please	la cuenta, por favor	la kwenta por fabor
glass	vaso	baso

cutlery	**cubiertos**	*koob-yairtos*
I would like some water	**Quisiera un poco de agua**	*kees-yaira oon poko deh agwa*
wine	**vino**	*beeno*
The beer is not cold enough	**La cerveza no está bien fría**	*a sairbesa no esta b-lyen free-a*
breakfast	**desayuno**	*desa-yoono*
lunch	**almuerzo**	*almwairso*
dinner	**comida**	*komeeda*
raw	**crudo**	*kroodo*
cooked	**cocido**	*koseedo*

MENU DECODER

aceite	*asayteh*	oil
agua mineral	*agwa meenairal*	mineral water
ajo	*aho*	garlic
anticucho	*anteekoocho*	kebab
arroz	*arros*	rice
asado	*asado*	roasted
atún	*atoon*	tuna
azúcar	*asookar*	sugar
bacalao	*bakala-o*	cod
betarraga	*betarraga*	beetroot
café	*kafeh*	coffee
camarones	*kamarones*	prawns
carne	*karneh*	meat
carne de chancho	*karneh deh chancho*	pork
causa	*kowsa*	potato salad
cerveza	*sairbesa*	beer
chancada	*chankada*	maize cake
chifa	*cheefa*	Chinese food
choro	*choro*	mussel
dulce	*doolseh*	sweet
ensalada	*ensalada*	salad
fruta	*froota*	fruit
guargüero	*gwargwairo*	sweet fritter filled with fudge
helado	*elado*	ice cream
huevo	*webo*	egg
jugo	*hoogo*	fruit juice
langosta	*langosta*	lobster
leche	*lecheh*	milk
mantequilla	*mantekee-ya*	butter
marisco	*mareesko*	seafood
mazamorra	*masamorra*	pudding made with corn starch, sugar, and honey
pachamanca	*pachamanka*	meat barbecued between two hot stones
pallar	*pa-yar*	butter bean
palta	*palta*	avocado
pan	*pan*	bread
papas	*papas*	potatoes
pescado	*peskado*	fish
picante	*peekanteh*	spicy meat stew
pisco	*peesko*	eau-de-vie made from grapes
plátano	*platano*	banana
pollo	*po-yo*	chicken
postre	*postreh*	dessert
potaje	*potaheh*	soup
puerco	*pwairko*	pork
queque	*kekeh*	cake
queso	*keso*	cheese
refresco	*refresko*	drink
sal	*sal*	salt
salsa	*salsa*	sauce
sopa	*sopa*	soup
té	*teh*	tea
té de yuyos	*teh deh yoo-yos*	herbal tea
tuco	*tooko*	tomato sauce
vinagre	*beenagreh*	vinegar
zapallo	*sapa-yo*	pumpkin

TIME

minute	**minuto**	*meenooto*
hour	**hora**	*ora*
half an hour	**media hora**	*med-ya ora*
quarter of an hour	**un cuarto**	*oon kwarto*
week	**semana**	*simana*
next week	**la próxima semana**	*la prosima simana*
month	**mes**	*mes*
last month	**el mes pasado**	*el mes pasadou*
Monday	**Lunes**	*loones*
Tuesday	**Martes**	*martes*
Wednesday	**Miércoles**	*m-yairkoles*
Thursday	**Jueves**	*hwebes*
Friday	**Viernes**	*b-yairnes*
Saturday	**Sábado**	*sabado*
Sunday	**Domingo**	*domeengo*
January	**Enero**	*enairo*
February	**Febrero**	*febrairo*
March	**Marzo**	*marso*
April	**Abril**	*abreel*
May	**Mayo**	*ma-yo*
June	**Junio**	*hoon-yo*
July	**Julio**	*hool-yo*
August	**Agosto**	*agosto*
September	**Setiembre**	*set-yembreh*
October	**Octubre**	*oktoobreh*
November	**Noviembre**	*nob-yembreh*
December	**Diciembre**	*dees-yembreh*

NUMBERS

0	**cero**	*sairo*
1	**uno**	*oono*
2	**dos**	*dos*
3	**tres**	*tres*
4	**cuatro**	*kwatro*
5	**cinco**	*seenko*
6	**seis**	*says*
7	**siete**	*s-yeteh*
8	**ocho**	*ocho*
9	**nueve**	*nwebeh*
10	**diez**	*d-yes*
11	**once**	*onseh*
12	**doce**	*doseh*
13	**trece**	*treseh*
14	**catorce**	*katorseh*
15	**quince**	*keenseh*
16	**dieciséis**	*d-yeseesays*
17	**diecisiete**	*d-yesees-yeteh*
18	**dieciocho**	*d-yes-yocho*
19	**diecinueve**	*d-yeseenwebeh*
20	**veinte**	*baynteh*
30	**treinta**	*traynta*
40	**cuarenta**	*kwarenta*
50	**cincuenta**	*seenkwenta*
60	**sesenta**	*sesenta*
70	**setenta**	*setenta*
80	**ochenta**	*ochenta*
90	**noventa**	*nobenta*
100	**cien**	*s-yen*
500	**quinientos**	*keen-yentos*
1000	**mil**	*meel*
first	**primero/a**	*preemairo/a*
second	**segundo/a**	*segoondo/a*
third	**tercero/a**	*tairsairo/a*
fourth	**cuarto/a**	*kwarto/a*
fifth	**quinto/a**	*keento/a*
sixth	**sexto/a**	*seksto/a*
seventh	**sétimo/a**	*seteemo/a*
eighth	**octavo/a**	*oktabo/a*
ninth	**noveno/a**	*nobeno/a*
tenth	**décimo/a**	*deseemo/a*

ACKNOWLEDGMENTS

This edition updated by
Contributor Sara Humphreys
Senior Editor Dipika Dasgupta
Senior Art Editor Vinita Venugopal
Project Editors Lucy Sara-Kelly, Anuroop Sanwalia
Proofreader Debra Wolter
Indexer Helen Peters
Assistant Picture Research Administrator Manpreet Kaur
Senior Picture Researcher Nishwan Rasool
Deputy Manager, Picture Research Virien Chopra
Publishing Assistant Simona Velikova
Jacket Picture Researcher Laura O'Brien
Senior Cartographer Mohammed Hassan
Cartography Manager Suresh Kumar
Pre-production Coordinator Tanveer Zaidi
Senior Production Controller Samantha Cross
Deputy Managing Editor Dharini Ganesh
Managing Editor Beverly Smart
Managing Art Editor Gemma Doyle
Senior Managing Art Editor Priyanka Thakur
Editorial Director Hollie Teague
Art Director Maxine Pedliham
Publishing Director Georgina Dee

DK would like to thank the following for their contributions to the previous edition: Maryanne Blacker, Jorge Riveros Cayo, Steph Dyson, Eleanor Griffis, Dominic Hamilton, Rob Rachowiecki, Joby Williams.

The publisher would like to thank the following for their kind permission to reproduce their photographs:

(Key: a-above; b-below/bottom; c-center; f-far; l-left; r-right; t-top)

123RF.com: Maria Luisa Lopez Estevill 210-211bc; Mark Green 202tr; 215tc; 217br; Craig Hastings 24-25ca; Patricio Hidalgo 226tc; saiko3p 212-213tr

Adobe Stock: ELVIZZ 49cl, Beto Santillan 42t

Al Frio y Al Fuego: 59crb

Alamy Stock Photo: 500px 134-135; age fotostock 19tl, 66rc; 66br, 71tr; 112tc, 126-127, 196-197, / Toño Labra 103br; Eyal Aharon 55bl; Alpineguide 67r; Archivart 179br; Archive PL 72cr; Aurora Photos 41cl, 67tr; Matthias Bachmaier 42br; BHammond 45cl; Sabena Jane Blackbird 128cl; Brett Bodkins 218-219bc; Andrew Briggs 181cr; Michele Burgess 169cr, 169b; Charles O. Cecil 52-53bl, 129cra; Jonathan Chancasana 264-265bl; B Christopher 66tl; Rafal Cichawa 148-149bl; Classic Image 69cra; Thornton Cohen 34cra; Ionut David 45tl, 192-193tc; Michael DeFreitas South America 49crb; 128-129bs, 232clb; 233br; 235bl; dpa picture alliance 61crb; Maxime Dube 34-35tc, 246-247br; Education & Exploration 1 122-123tc; Julio Etchart 73bl; FirstShot 92cr; Fotoholica Press Agency 165tr; Oliver Gerhard 245tr; Nicholas Gill 59cl; GL Archive 70tc; Bernard Golden 75cra, 110-111tl, 121t, 240br, 263bl; Granger Historical Picture Archive 191cr; Mark Green 65cl, 133b, 156rc, 203tr, 259br; Hemis 66cl, 92fclb, 161crb, 194tl; Heritage Image Partnership Ltd 70cr; Bob Hilscher 147tl, 182-183bl; History and Art Collection 69br; The History Collection 71br; Image Source 202-203bl; imageBROKER 12tc, 62tl; Nicolett Jakab 21ca, 75cl, 248-249; Jon Arnold Images Ltd 102clb; Judith Katz 220tl; Paul Kennedy 16c, 76-77; Keystone Pictures USA 73tl; Daniel Korzeniewski 163cr; Karol Kozlowski Premium RM Collection 109br, 159tl; Jesse Kraft 34cla; Jason Langley 24tl, 204b; Frans Lemmens 228bc, 231tl; K.D. Leperi 64br; Nika Lerman 184br; Yadid Levy 176tc; Martin Lindsay 156-157br; Inga Locmele 158-159bl; Alex Lowry 67cr; Don Mammoser 132t, 143bl; Mauritius Images Gmbh 144-145b; Melvin Migin 56-57bc; Aivar Mikko 219tr; Minden Pictures 246cla; J.Enrique Molina 100tl, 130bl, 217cla, 217cr; Carlos Mora 40br, 67tl, 252br, 260b, 261bc; National Geographic Image Collection 57crb, 220-221br; Newscom / Juan Francisco Melgar 101b; NortePhoto.com / Luis Gutierrez 149tr; North Wind Picture Archives 190cra; Mirosław Nowaczyk 65br; Frank Nowikowski 129ca; Efrain Padro 38bl, 183tr; Ville Palonen 254bl; Ida Pap 55cr; Andrew Paul Travel 177bl; pawlopicasso 69tr; PERU Landmarks and People by Vision 159ca; peruvianpictures.com 72br; Karin Pezo 37br; PhotoBliss 92fcrb; Photononstop 63cl; PJF Military Collection 217cra; Graham Prentice 86cra; Prisma Archivo 69bc, 70bl, 70br; Jussi Puikkonen 48br, 80cr; Stefano Ravera 148tl, 179tc; Realy Easy Star 60tr, 60cla; Sergi Reboredo 13tc, 74-75br, 167clb, 230cra; Reciprocity Images 160bc; Reda &Co Srl 244b; robertharding 40-41tl, 145tr, / Karol Kozlowski 124bl; Grant Rooney 228clb; Henryk Sadura 160tl; Worawan Simaroj 146-147br; South America 85bl; Stock Connection Blue 257clb; Tetra Images / Henryk Sadura 114bl; The Print Collector / Heritage Images 68t; Mark Towner 20cb, 236-237; Giovanni Mereghetti / UCG / Universal Images Group 266-267; Mireille Vautier 112bl; Greg Vaughn 129tr; Ivan Vdovin 232b; Davor Vukovic 160-161tr; David Wall 80crb; John Warburton-Lee Photography 67br; Yola Watrucka 38-39tc; Xinhua 67bl; Zoonar GmbH 30crb; ZUMA Press; Inc. 53tr; Mariana Bazo / ZUMA Press Wire 73crb.

AWL Images: John Coletti 93; Hemis 74cra; Karol Kozlowski 85cr; Nigel Pavitt 75tl; Alex Robinson 214br; Andrew Watson 233tr.

Bridgeman Images: Native Peruvians gather potatoes from their terraced farms (colour litho); Herget; Herbert M. (1885-1950) / National Geographic Image Collection 68bc; Facsimile of a drawing by Felipe Guaman Poma from his 'El Primer Nueva Coronica y Buen Gobierno' / Werner Forman Archive 191cl.

Centro de Textiles Tradicionales del Cusco: 44tc.

Cervecería del Valle Sagrado: 50tl.

Depositphotos Inc: pxhidalgo 23tr; roussien 35cla; ssviluppo 26br; vitmarkov 28crb.

Dorling Kindersley: Demetrio Carrasco / Museo de Sitio Huaca Pucllana 109tl, 109tr, 109ftl, / San Francisco Monastery, Lima 94br; / Santa Rosa de Ocopa Convent 99tr; Nigel Hicks 261tc, / Museo Tumbas Reales de Sipan 231cr, 231bl; Linda Whitwam 26tc.

Dreamstime.com: A41cats 8cl; Adfoto 66bl; Galyna Andrushko 58-59tc; Rui Baião 25tr; Barbarico 242bl; Manuel Mauricio Huerta Berrocal 82bl; Bhofack2 50-51bc; Larisa Blinova 11tc, 51cr; Byelikova 166bl; Chrishowey 11br; Rafał Cichawa 215bc; Coconutdreams 165bc; Sorin Colac 43br; Steven Cukrov 123br; Danflcreativo 189tr; Danilovets 8cla; Ionut David 36-37t, 174tc, 188tc; Neil Denize 39cr; Donyanedomam 11cr; Drmonochrome 193bl; Duncanandison 211tl; Dvrcan 24-25tc, 115tr, 125tl; Joan Egert 257crb; Emicristea 185; Aurora Esperanza Ángeles Flores 36br; Lider Garcia 116-117; Gkadams92 87cra; Albert Gonzalez 32cr; Diego Grandi 30tc, 32bl, 61cla, 113br; Juan José Napán Guevara 53cl, 82-83bs; Pablo Hidalgo 104-105; Patricio Hidalgo 26crb, 230-231bl; Ildipapp 51tl; Imagezebra 141tr (all); Jarcosa 71bl; Vladislav Jirousek 6tl; Mariusz Jurgielewicz 258cra; Karol Kozlowski 109ftr; Jesse Kraft 80bl, 92crb, 190-191bc, 200tc, 243cr; Debra Law 189c; Libux77

58-59bc; Lindrik 22tl, 80tc; Makasanaphoto 68br, 211cra; Markpittimages 28tc; Sergey Mayorov 60-61bc; Giulio Mignani 17bl, 150-151; Pixattitude 62-63bl, 63tc, 258-259bl, 259tr, 259cra; Ondřej Prosický 10clb; Pytyczech 10cla; Kseniya Ragozina 18ca, 170-171; Riopatuca 191ca; Luis Antonio Rosendo 262t; Roussien 242-243tc; Saiko3p 28cr; Salparadis 257bl; Suebmtl 22tr; Petr Švec 23tl; Takepicsforfun 30cr; Roman Tiraspolsky 187tc; Viennetta 12-13bc; Vitmark 57cl, 166cr; Thomas Wyness 30bl; Michael Zysman 212crb.

Getty Images: Cris Bouroncle 231cra; David Curtis 64-65tl; Danita Delimont 32crb; Fotoholica Press 53bc; Glowimages 140-141bl; hemis.fr 92cb, / Hughes Herve 98-99bl, 120br; Imágenes del Perú 217cb; Ipsumpix 71tl; Jesse Kraft / EyeEm 143br; Michael Langford 259tl; Lonely Planet Images 95br, / Brent Winebrenner 72bl; Manuel Medir 41br; John & Lisa Merrill 47br; Domingo Leiva Nicolas 96-97br; DEA / G. Dagli Orti 132bl; Bruno Perousse 182cl; Jaime Razuri 73cla; Erika Skogg 188-189br; Anibal Solimano 73tr; suraark 87tl; Universal History Archive 72tc; WIN-Initiative 2-3.

Getty Images / iStock: alessandro_pinto 240tc; Peter Bocklandt 54-55tc; Myriam Borzee 226bc; Agustina Camilion 8-9br; DC_Colombia 154tc, 252tc; dimarik 46-47bc; elisalocci 54bl; Fabiolm 187bl; flavijus 87cla; hadynynh 12clb, 52tr; holgs 34tl; JohnnyLye 43cl; Juliandoporai 194-195br; marktucan 35tr; Mauro_Scarone 10-11bc; OscarEspinosa 63crb; OSTILL 141br; PatricioHidalgoP 149cl; paulobaqueta 184crb; piginka 67cl; poweroffforever 57tr; raisbeckfoto 96t; rchphoto 168tl; RMDobson 255; RPBMedia 256-257tl; RStelmach 205tr; saiko3p 74bl 166-67t; Iuliia Serova 143crb; Starcevic 164tl; stbaus7 48-49tl; Stockphoto24 19cb, 206-207; tbradford 46tl, 108-109bl; Carrie Thompson 94tr; torukojin 191tl; travelview 22-23ca; xeni4ka 26clb.

Mundo Alpaca - Arequipa; Peru: 28bl, 44-45bl.

Picfair.com: Rui Baiao 43tc; Mariano Diaz Gargiulo; Argentina 17cc, 136-137; Paul Neuman 4.
Don Porfirio's; Lima: 13br, 84bl.

Jade Rivera: *Hogar de un Suspiro* by Jade Rivera 83cb.

Robert Harding Picture Library: Heiko Beyer 92cra; Michael DeFreitas 32tc, 88-89; Robert Frerck 20tl, 222-223; Laura Grier 162-163tl; Karol Kozlowski 13cr, 66tr; Tono Labra 95tl; Gerard Lacz 56tc; Jose Enrique Molina 8clb; Alex Robinson 38-39bc; Matthew Williams-Ellis 24cla, 47tr, 142-143tl.

Shutterstock.com: Ernesto Arias / EPA-EFE 84-85tl; Milton Rodriguez 130-131t, 234-235t; Beto Santillan 37cla; Jerome Stubbs 184cl; Christian Vinces 86-87, 216-217bl.

SuperStock: Album / J.Enrique Molina 179cra; Cultura Limited 180-181tl; Minden Pictures / Cyril Ruoso 254cl.

Front flap:
Alamy Stock Photo: Alpineguide tc; National Geographic Image Collection cra; Brett Bodkins cb; **Dreamstime.com:** Larisa Blinova br; Ondřej Prosický cla; **Picfair.com:** Paul Neuman bl.

Cover images:
Front and spine: **Dreamstime.com:** Emicristea.
Back: **Alamy Stock Photo:** Eyal Aharon c, Inga Locmele tr; **Dreamstime.com:** Emicristea b, Giulio Mignani cla.

Mapping:
Base Mapping for Lima and Peru derived from Netmaps.

Illustrators: Chapel Design & Marketing Ltd., Chinglemba Chingbham, Surat Kumar Mantoo, Arun Pottirayil, T. Gautam Trivedi, Mark Arjun Warner

---

DK | Penguin Random House

First edition 2008

Published in Great Britain by Dorling Kindersley Limited,
20 Vauxhall Bridge Road,
London SW1V 2SA

The authorised representative in the EEA is
Dorling Kindersley Verlag GmbH. Arnulfstr.
124, 80636 Munich, Germany

Published in the United States by DK Publishing,
1745 Broadway, 20th Floor, New York, NY 10019

Copyright © 2008, 2025 Dorling Kindersley Limited
A Penguin Random House Company
25 26 27 28 10 9 8 7 6 5 4 3 2 1

All rights reserved.

No part of this publication may be reproduced, stored in or introduced into a retrieval system, or transmitted, in any form, or by any means (electronic, mechanical, photocopying, recording, or otherwise), without the prior written permission of the copyright owner.

DK values and supports copyright. Thank you for respecting intellectual property laws by not reproducing, scanning or distributing any part of this publication by any means without permission. By purchasing an authorised edition, you are supporting writers and artists and enabling DK to continue to publish books that inform and inspire readers.
No part of this publication may be used or reproduced in any manner for the purpose of training artificial intelligence technologies or systems. In accordance with Article 4(3) of the DSM Directive 2019/790, DK expressly reserves this work from the text and data mining exception.

The publishers cannot accept responsibility for any consequences arising from the use of this book, nor for any material on third party websites, and cannot guarantee that any website address in this book will be a suitable source of travel information.

A CIP catalog record for this book
is available from the British Library.

A catalog record for this book is available
from the Library of Congress.

ISSN: 1542 1554
ISBN: 978 0 2417 5620 1

Printed and bound in China.

www.dk.com

MIX
Paper | Supporting responsible forestry
FSC™ C018179

This book was made with Forest Stewardship Council™ certified paper – one small step in DK's commitment to a sustainable future.
Learn more at **www.dk.com/uk/information/sustainability**

A NOTE FROM DK
The rate at which the world is changing is constantly keeping the DK travel team on our toes. While we've worked hard to ensure that this edition of Peru is accurate and up-to-date, we know that opening hours alter, standards shift, prices fluctuate, places close and new ones pop up in their stead. So, if you notice we've got something wrong or left something out, we want to hear about it. Please get in touch at travelguides@dk.com.